Gods & Spacemen
Throughout History

By the same author

Gods or Spacemen?
Gods and Spacemen in the Ancient East
Gods and Spacemen in the Ancient West
Gods and Spacemen in Greece and Rome
Gods and Spacemen in Ancient Israel

W. RAYMOND DRAKE

Gods & Spacemen Throughout History

'Sky was the first,
who ruled over the whole world.'

Apollodorus

Henry Regnery Company
Chicago

Library of Congress Cataloging in Publication Data

Drake, Walter Raymond.
    Gods and spacemen throughout history.

    Bibliography: p.
    1. Interplanetary voyages.   2. Civilization—
History.   3. Religion and astronautics.   4. Flying
saucers.   I. Title.
CB156.D73   001.9'42   74-27802
ISBN 0-8092-8283-6

© W. Raymond Drake, 1975. All rights reserved.
First published in Great Britain in 1975
by Neville Spearman Limited, London
Published in the United States in 1975 by Henry Regnery Company
180 North Michigan Avenue, Chicago, Illinois 60601
Manufactured in the United States of America
Library of Congress Catalog Card Number: 74-27802
International Standard Book Number: 0-8092-8283-6

To My Wife
Marjorie

ACKNOWLEDGEMENT

Sincere gratitude is due to Neville Armstrong, the devoted patron of the New Age, for his inspiring encouragement and cosmic understanding.

CONTENTS

CHAPTER ONE

Spacemen

The splendour of the skies thrills men with wonder, our eyes now seek spacemen from the stars. As our cosmonauts land on the Moon, soon on Mars, we sense ancient memories, as if all this has happened before. Perhaps the future lies in the past? New, exciting knowledge confirms ancient lore telling of those days when Earth was young and Celestials descended from the stars. People believed all the planets were inhabited by humans wise or foolish like themselves, ruled by beings on our Sun who were inspired by the spirits on that bright star, Sirius, forming with the myriad worlds of our Milky Way a Galactic Federation linked with neighbouring Andromeda and the distant galaxies beyond. Worlds upon worlds of supermen who sometimes appeared on Earth.

Perfection eventually brings decay. Good becomes eclipsed by evil, then a resurgence of spirit turns darkness to light, raising Man to a higher spiral of evolution fulfilling his cosmic destiny. The Giants rebelled against their overlords to storm the skies, war was waged with titanic bombs, cataclysms split continents down to the sea, their cities smashed, men plunged back to barbarism. Solitary survivors remembered their space teachers and prayed to the stars; some wondrous beings came down again to be worshipped as Gods.

Most records of the remote past perished in fire and flood, engulfed in earthquakes, lost in wars, many were wilfully destroyed by megalomaniac Kings, fanatical priests and ignorant mobs. All that remains of those ages of wonder are vague myths and strange stones standing forlorn far and wide, immutable testimonies to mysteries long forgotten. In our allegedly enlightened days most people date civilisation for only about seven thousand years believing that for countless millennia savages lived in a prolonged Stone Age. Perhaps the greatest rewards from the space programme are not those rocks from the Moon or pictures of Mars and Jupiter but the most tremendous revolution in human thought since the Renaissance. Already men marvel at the vastness of Space, the mystery of Time, the question of inhabited worlds; they imagine Extraterrestrials then wonder again at themselves.

Science is expanding available knowledge so rapidly that now no single mind can fully comprehend the world-scene, or like Aristotle synthesise a universal philosophy; modern research by startling paradox increases potential ignorance. In these closing decades of the twentieth-century the pillars of culture threaten to crash, torrents of new facts and novel ideas swamp our decadent Society; the old religions and philosophies seem to have failed, all political doctrines degenerate to disillusion. The return of the Extraterrestrials fulfils the prophecies, salvation comes from the skies amid signs and wonders.

Earth enters the Aquarian Age. Before the crescendo of cataclysmic events men seek guidance from those vanished civilisations of the past to learn their fateful lesson. The fascinating presence of Unidentified Flying Objects haunting our skies, the enigma of Extraterrestrials alleged to land here, the resurgence of occult and paranormal phenomena transcending our Science, baffle our present generation as beyond rational solution. This mystery links our twentieth-century with the Middle Ages and Antiquity, we wonder whether these secret, silent Witnesses have influenced world-history.

Accumulated traditions among all races in all ages hint at mystery-men not born of woman prompting Man's evolution. Space Intelligences are reported to have communicated spiritual and scientific truths revealing a cosmic culture whose splendour dazzles us. The suggestion that Spacemen have landed throughout history confounds most people today; their conditioned minds are ill-prepared for such startling revelations; for despite the wonders of Science Man knows so little about his own world, almost nothing about himself.

What is Man? We live on a small planet revolving around a dying Sun, a dwarf Star, on one of the spiral arms near the edge of the Milky Way, one of the myriad galaxies of Space. What do we mean in this vast Universe? Why are we here? From the dawn of Time these mysteries have puzzled the spiritual leaders. Today the realisation of Extraterrestrials makes us aware that Man too is a Space Being on the spaceship of Earth whirling from the dark unknown to meet his cosmic destiny.

Plato likened Man to a prisoner in a cave watching the shadows of men and objects on the wall. He fancies the shadows to be the only reality. Should he loose his chains and turn his head to look outside he would become perplexed and believe the shadows more real than the actual things shown to him.[156] With all its wonderful instruments Science perceives only a narrow slit of the Universe.

In the last decade new techniques in astronomy have discovered quasars, pulsars, invisible planets, galaxies transcending the speed of light. Already before the American Sky-Lab telescopes in Space find more exciting phenomena our ideas of the universe are being radically changed. Research into the microscopic field of the atom and cosmic radiation suggests the existence of a twin-universe complementary to our own made of anti-matter,[78] where time is reversed. Physicists now say that just as there is light we cannot see, sounds we cannot hear, so there exists matter we cannot touch, thus confirming the teachings of the Ancients claiming parallel realms co-existing within our own, possibly peopled by beings like ourselves normally invisible to us, as we are to them. To an Extraterrestrial mastering an advanced psycho-science, soaring to transcendent consciousness, our present ideas, profound though they be to us, may seem as primitive as the superstitions of a savage.

The seers of ancient India, Egypt and Babylon knew all Creation emanated from Primal Light, this belief was manifested as Sun worship. The Yogis believed in a chain of worlds, life passing from planet to planet in cosmic evolution, they thought the Universe lived and died to be born again in eternal recurrence. The Christian Church preached the Bible Creation of a three-storey Universe comprising the heavens above, the Earth beneath and the waters under the Earth. There were several heavens, the highest being the habitation of God. Angels moved the Sun, Moon and planets across the firmament which rested upon the world, round, flat, surrounded by a rim of water and supported on pillars from the Great Deep. The biblical cosmology sublimely expressed in the Middle Ages by Dante in 'La Divina Commedia' was challenged in the 16th century by Copernicus whose theories inspired Giordano Bruno to conceive the Universe as boundless empty space with stars as suns, infinite inhabited worlds, a rotating Earth revolving around the Sun. The Inquisition charged Bruno with heresy and after eight years imprisonment he was burned at the stake in AD 1600 on the Campo dei Fiori in Rome.

Astronomers now believe the Universe may be an expanding sphere with the fantastic diameter of sixty thousand million light-years containing more than a thousand million galaxies separated by immense distances, each shining with a hundred billion stars. Dr Zdenek Kopal,[116] Professor of Astronomy at Manchester University, states that there must be one hundred million, million, million planets beyond human comprehension. Dr S.S. Huang[200] suggests as many as eight thousand million inhabited star-systems in our own Milky Way with at least a million planets having advanced civilisations. Extraterrestrials from any world of this vast number could have visited Earth in ages past.

Adepts of the Secret Wisdom believe that Man was created on the spiritual plane and after vast ages descended through grosser vibrations to the seventh plane of our physical Universe; each of us has spiritual, mental, astral, etheric and physical bodies.[1] This difficult conception seems strange to our conditioned minds but is really of fundamental importance, since many experts have reason to think that Spacemen actually do appear from other states of existence beyond our perception.

Scientists now believe that life must exist throughout the immense Universe. Following the discovery of abundant quantities of formaldehyde throughout Space, David Buhler of the radio-astronomy observatory at Green Bank in Virginia presumes that the methane, water-vapour and ammonia could form complex molecules to constitute living cells and descend on our Earth in clouds of gas, similar clouds could bring life to all the planets, the Milky Way and other galaxies. Analysis of organic compounds found in meteorites reveals hydrocarbons, complicated chains of fatty substances, analogous but not completely identical to those of terrestrial metabolism, suggesting that though life-forms evidently exist elsewhere, they may differ somewhat from life on Earth. In December 1970 the National American Space Administration stated that for the first time Man possessed irrefutable proof of extraterrestrial life. A research-team directed by Dr Cyril Ponnamperuma analysed substance from a meteorite which fell on September 28th 1969 at Murchison in Australia and found amino-acids and hydrocarbons, constituents of complex organic cells. The meteorite may have originated from the shattered planet Maldek between Mars and Jupiter exploded into the asteroids ages ago. Some biologists believe in pan-spermia, the propagation of seeds of life on the solar-wind throughout the entire Universe, many insist it is the destiny of Cosmic Man to populate all Creation.

All over the world astronomers are now listening with powerful radio-telescopes attuned to the hydrogen-frequency of 1420 megacycles for intelligent signals from the stars. Famous American and Russian scientists in many fields held their first conference from the 5th to 11th September 1971 at the Astrophysics Observatory in Byurakan in Armenia U.S.S.R.; they discussed the possibility of extraterrestrial life, decided on future investigation and formed a permanent Committee to co-ordinate world-wide research.[151]

Dr Zdenek Kopal states that vast numbers of planets have life much more advanced than ours and warns against the dangers of encounters with Extraterrestrials of a superior culture.

'We might find ourselves in their test-tubes, or other contraptions set up to investigate us as we do insects or guinea-pigs. Should we ever hear that Space-phone ringing for God's sake let us not answer, but rather make ourselves as inconspicuous as one can to avoid attracting attention.'

Could Extraterrestrials from the stars have landed on Earth centuries ago?

'No one indeed believes anything unless he previously knows it to be believable.'[175]

St. Augustine, former Pagan philosopher, then first Archbishop of Canterbury, knew sixteen hundred years ago that faith is not enough, the belief must appear possible, therefore probable. Most people agree that since life exists on Earth, it is likely to exist elsewhere. Watching our own difficult journeys to the Moon the average Man naturally doubts whether even Super-Spacemen can travel from distant planets to visit Earth. We can perhaps offer persuasive, if not conclusive, reasons supporting the contention of St. Augustine ' that the belief itself should be believable, possibly true.

Our ancestors thought the world was flat, any mariner sailing too far from shore would fall off the edge into the Abyss of Hell; today our scientists say the limiting speed of light, the fantastic gravities, the expanding Universe, make prolonged space-travel impossible. But aircraft, nuclear-bombs, electricity and many other modern techniques were used thousands of years ago then suddenly forgotten after those great civilisations of the past were destroyed. People on other planets with thousands, perhaps millions, of years of technology may have developed wonders beyond our dreams.

It is admittedly difficult for the ordinary Man to understand Einstein's Special Theory of Relativity, especially when many distinguished scientists have growing doubts; since travel across vast distances is a fundamental requirement for any Spaceman some simple reference must be made to the latest discoveries challenging Einstein's ideas.

The Special Theory of Relativity limits the velocity of light to 300,000 kilometres per second, then Time stops, Mass becomes infinite. Mathematicians allege that cosmonauts speeding at 290,000 kilometres per second would benefit from Einstein's Time-Dilation paradox. At immense speeds Time for the traveller slows down; he himself would age only twenty five years while crossing the vast Milky Way, though 100,000 years had elapsed on Earth, making travel across our own galaxy possible in theory if doubtful in fact. Suppose next week a Spaceship from early Atlantis returns after a trip to Andromeda to find their lost land at the bottom of the sea? Super-Intelligences from distant stars may have actually achieved those dreams of our Science-Fiction Writers and taken short-cuts through hyper-space or teleported themselves with the speed of thought. Indeed it is alleged that some visitants to our Earth do materialise in this way. Fortunately for terrestrial travellers new theories now suggest that the light-barrier may be broken like the sound-barrier a generation ago.

Gerald Feinberg,[177] Professor of Physics at Columbia University, theorises that beyond the light-barrier there exists a universe with particles called 'tachyons' capable of motion faster than light. As their energy diminishes their velocity accelerates to millions of light-years per second until at infinite velocity the particles have neither Mass nor Energy. A Spaceship modulating to the tachyon-drive could cross our Milky Way in one minute, attain the furthest galaxy in a week and soon traverse the vast Universe. Such fantasy baffles our understanding yet to an Extraterrestrial with immense Science the problem may be relatively no more difficult than our landing a Man on the Moon.

The foundation of modern Physics, Einstein's Theory of Relativity, is still not wholly proved, some experiments confirm it, others do not. In April 1971 the American Academy of Science announced that two components of the radio-star, quasar 3C-279, were speeding away at ten times the velocity of light, supporting the thesis of Professor Marco Todeschini[141] of Bergamo, Founder of the Cosmic-Science of Bio-Physics, who with brilliant logic has refuted the fundamental conceptions of Einstein, not only concerning the speed of light but also gravity. Giuseppe Zungri[226] after profound research has apparently surpassed Einstein and produced a startling theory unifying all the energy in the Universe and explaining the propulsion of the UFOs. A fascinating article by Adrian Berry in the *Daily Telegraph* Colour Magazine. 7th May 1971, describes the work of Dr John A. Wheeler, Professor of Physics at Princeton University, who states that to reach the stars a Spaceship could traverse the Superspace inside the curved Universe where, in the hollow interior, Space and Time do not exist, attaining the most distant stars almost instantaneously. These scientific theories transcend our comprehension but we must remember that television, space-flight and atomic-bombs, so familiar to us, would have seemed wild fantasies to our grandfathers.

In astronomical terms inhabited worlds may not be far distant. Fourteen stars within twenty-two light-years from Earth probably have life-forms similar to ourselves, possibly with civilisations much more advanced. For three months in 1960 Dr Frank Drake for 'Project Ozma' directed the antennae of the radio-telescope at Green Bank, Virginia, towards Epsilon Eridani and Tau Ceti only eleven light-years away; the results were disappointing. Josef Schklovski said the experiment might have been better focussed on the tens of thousands of stars about a hundred light-years away with a reasonable certainty of Extraterrestrials. On April 13th 1965, Nicholas Kardaschev of Moscow's Sternberg Observatory startled the world with his announcement of the discovery of two cosmic radio-sources, CTA-21 and CTA-102 whose regular electrical emissions apparently denoted intelligent beings with high technology. Astronomers have since discovered more and regard them as Quasars, billions of light-years distant. These experts could be wrong. In 1967 Cambridge radio-astronomers detected Pulsars with regular beats and talked of 'L.G.M.', 'Little Green Men'. Scientists now consider these sources to be extremely small neutron-stars, though they could be celestial radio-beacons to guide inter-stellar spaceships, not so outrageously fantastic for a possible galactic civilisation!

The most startling revolution in thought of our twentieth-century is surely the realisation by official Science that we are not alone. Earth is surrounded by countless inhabited worlds, some of which must be eager for contact. Perhaps for centuries Extraterrestrials were trying to signal us by radio not knowing that we had not yet invented it, may be people on a planet around Alpha Centauri, the nearest star, are beaming signals we cannot recognise? Russian astronomers seriously suggest that Extraterrestrials on distant planets could communicate by telepathy, perhaps in our dreams. We may be totally unaware of an immense communications-system linking planets and galaxies. Is there some great cosmic Wisdom we have lost? Why did the Ancients believe in astrology, the stars ruling men's lives? Where do our thoughts come from? Do we really know?

For decades Aliens on other worlds may have been attempting communication by laser-beams with our Earth. On the night of December 7th 1900 a fountain of light played for seventy minutes on the planet Mars, analysed by Dr Percy Lowell as a possible code of long and short flashes. About the same time that strange genius, Nikola Tesla, announced he had received on his wireless apparatus vibrations in triplets which he attributed to the Martians.[75] In September 1921 Guglielmo Marconi on his yacht 'Electra' in the Mediterranean received incomprehensible signals in code on the unusual wavelength of 150,000 metres although terrestrial transmitters were then limited to 14,000 metres.[182] Strange radio-echoes were received in 1927, 1928 and 1934. In 1928 Van der Pol and other scientists recorded mysterious echoes arriving from 3 to 30 seconds after transmission. For a three-day period from September 14th-17th 1953 many American viewers were surprised to see on their TV screens the identification-card and call-letters of Station KLEE, signal strong enough to obliterate the local transmission. KLEE was a Station in Houston, Texas. KLEE went out of existence three years before![66] In 1960 the American astronomer, Ronald Bracewell, suggested that the echoes could signify their reflection by a Space-sonde sent by another planet. Using the 1928 data Duncan Lunan, a Scottish University graduate, translated the signals into a graph and by mathematical deduction, found that they apparently emanated from the star, Izar, Epsilon Bootes, about 103 light-years from Earth. This unmanned Spacecraft now in the region of our Moon is believed to have been launched about 13,000 years ago by the inhabitants of a dying planet around Izar into our Solar System with the hope of contacting another world which might help them.

Charles Fort in *The Book of the Damned* draws attention to the phenomena of 'cup marks', strings of cup-like impressions in rocks in Great Britain, America, France, Algeria, Palestine, China, Italy, Spain, India, everywhere. In diverting style he suggests that beings from Space have marked the rocks with electric force. 'The Lost Explorers from Somewhere, and an attempt, from Somewhere, to communicate with them; so a frenzy of showering of messages towards this earth, in the hope that some of them would mark rocks near the lost explorers.'

Some sensitives make startling claims of contact with beings from beyond our solar system, their revelations confound our terrestrial commonsense. Arthur Shuttlewood in Warminster alleges phone-calls from Aliens on Aenstria, a planet still undiscovered. Eugenio Siragusa of Catania, Sicily, a Customs Officer with professional esteem for truth, meets on Mt Etna Extraterrestrials from the Pleiades and Alpha Centauri whom he presumably searches for contraband. Bob Renaud converses with Intelligences on unknown Korendor; many other allegations are made by eccentrics who baffle us. Our egocentric minds not conditioned to the co-existence of humans elsewhere ridicule stories of Spacemen forgetting that inspiration from Celestials forms the very substance of our Bible.

Though scientists still deny the reality of Flying Saucers more than six hundred books, countless magazines published in many countries, television-shows, radio-talks, newspaper articles, eye-witness letters, all tell classic tales of handsome young men, alluring damsels, fearsome humanoids, giants, dwarfs, robots often armed with ray-guns, surprising people today as in the past. A few stories do seem fanciful, open to doubt, but there are serious studies by distinguished researchers describing phenomena which even the sceptic cannot explain.

Spacemen are said to be living among us, most folk would smile that they have never seen a blonde from Venus or met a man from Mars? How do they know? A few weird characters haunt our streets, we can hardly divine whether they are men or women. Many strange things appear to be happening today, even stranger are prophesied for tomorrow. If we care to consider the claims that Extraterrestrials have landed can we suggest from whence they might come?

Our astronomers number brilliant men, we rightly pay tribute to their genius which can measure temperatures in the centre of the Sun and calculate the distance of unseen stars, yet we become somewhat disconcerted when now they tell us that instead of nine planets in our Solar System there may be ten, perhaps eleven, even twelve. Henry J. Courteen, the

American astronomer, has lately discovered an intra-mercurial planet less than 500 miles across and only 9 million miles from the Sun, which he calls Zoe; this may be the phantom planet, Vulcan, observed by Dr Lescarboult in 1859 and a year later by the famous Leverrier, apparently not seen since. Dr Joseph Brady of California calculates that perturbations in the orbit of the outermost, Pluto, are caused by the gravitational attraction of a trans-plutonian planet, Proserpine, three hundred times bigger than Earth, about 6000 million miles distant circling our Sun in 512 years. Leon Lesson with more precise calculations estimates the eccentricities of Pluto are due to two small planets relatively close. Little is known of Mercury, said to be too hot, although the Ancients worshipped its wondrous beings as Gods. Venus, Earth's nearest neighbour, is veiled in mystery. The Russian space-probes telemeter boiling temperatures; this data is contradicted, some astronomers daringly suppose that the well-known ashen-glow may actually be electrical illumination from populous cities.[94] The closer space-probes approach Mars the more exasperating their revelations become. Mariners 6 and 7 opposed the findings of Mariner 4. Thousands of pictures were taken by Mariner 9 in 1971 and 1972, they suggest a tenuous atmosphere, mainly carbon-dioxide, above an arid surface split by canyons and apparent water-courses swept by sand-storms. The two Martian Moons, Deimos and Phobos, once thought to be artificial satellites, are now photographed as huge rocks. There is a growing suspicion that the surprising lack of publicity hints at official censorship. Do some Mars pictures show signs of intelligent life? What if the Martians live in a wonderful civilisation underground with an artificial atmosphere beyond our detection?

Thousands of asteroids are said to be fragments of the exploded planet Maldek, they follow eccentric orbits between Mars and Jupiter, more are still discovered. Some sceptics wonder why they were not found earlier and daringly speculate that they may be immense Spaceships come to surveil Earth. Life on Jupiter with its primeval atmosphere of hydrogen, ammonia and methane around a layer of deep ice seems most remote, though periodic bursts of radio-noise and infra-red emissions may suggest people with high technology broadcasting radio-beams to attract Earth's attention. Ganymede, the largest Jovian Moon, is believed to have an atmosphere, even canals, suggesting civilisation. Surface conditions on frozen Saturn apparently deny any form of life. George Adamski claimed to have flown to the ringed planet in a Spaceship in only nine hours. He described a brilliant culture basking in a sub-tropical paradise. Thomas Donahue, a NASA scientist, is quoted as stating that traces of life exist on Titan, a satellite of Saturn.[119]

Astronomers insist that life cannot possibly exist in the icy wastes and poisonous atmospheres of the remote outer planets, Uranus, Neptune and Pluto, forgetting that these worlds may have internal heat and light of their own from volcanic or radio-active sources with surface layers of oxygen. G.H. Williamson[223] alleges radio-contact with beings on these three outer planets. While we cannot confirm the conversations with such Celestials, we are sadly aware that the same wonderful instruments of the astronomers on satellites only a few hundred miles away show no signs of life here on our own Earth.

Though theory might favour the possibility of Extraterrestrials from planets around neighbouring stars, serious research suggests that many Aliens do not originate from our visible Universe but materialise from Inner Realms, long taught by visionaries of all religions. Physicists without occult influence theorise the existence of subtle states of matter beyond normal perception, scientists now accept that Earth may interpenetrate other worlds, invisible, inaudible to us, inhabited by warm, passionate beings who sometimes manifest to our senses as apparitions or teleport themselves here with or without Spaceships.

'Be not forgetful to entertain Strangers for thereby some have entertained Angels unawares.'[93]

The Christian Fathers debated the existence of Angels mentioned in the Old and New Testaments, the Talmud, Koran and magic texts from Babylon, giving them a shrewder insight into Extraterrestrials than our baffled scientists today. The early Church adopted and adapted the pagan beliefs and symbolism of ancient peoples all over the world, anticipating the conclusions of mediaeval theologians and our modern UFO students, acknowledging that parallel to our own Earth exist realms invisible but real inhabited by beings of finer substance who sometimes materialise among us. Dionysius stated 'There are many blessed armies of the heavenly intelligence surpassing the weak and limited reckoning of our material numbers.'[59] For thousands of years primitive peoples all over the world have believed in a universal animism where stars and stones, trees and rivers, are ruled by Guardian Spirits dwelling beyond our normal vision, who sometimes appeared to mortals; fairy-tales often echo remnants of some psychic wisdom long ago. The Gnani Yogis have long taught that the astral universe is immensely greater than the physical Cosmos, which hangs below like a little solid basket under the huge astral plane.

Emperor Charlemagne passed savage laws against demons and all who held converse with them; in AD 840 Agobard, Archbishop of Lyons, saw wizards from a magic land in the sky called 'Magonia' lynched by a mob. About AD 1260 St. Thomas Aquinas wrote his 'Summa Theologiae' expounding Angelology in terms oddly familiar to modern students of Spacemen. For hundreds of years the Church and the Inquisition fought a terrible crusade against witchcraft, torturing and burning thousands of people all over Europe with a fanaticism we find incredible.

In the 17th century Montfaucon de Villars in 'Le Comte de Gabalis'[140] wrote that 'the air is full of an innumerable multitude of peoples in human shape, a tribe proud in appearance but indeed docile, great lovers of science'; he added that nymphs and salamanders often materialised and consorted with mortals giving birth to heroes like Zoroaster, Hercules, Plato, Alexander, Apollonius of Tyana. We instinctively smile at such superstition until we recall those intriguing sexual experiments with Antonio Villas Boas[21] in 1957, and Barney and Betty Hill in 1961,[77] performed by Spacemen.

Throughout the ages Adepts have hinted at great souls living in secret retreats in the Andes[22] and Tibet preserving the Ancient Mysteries. These Illumined are led by the great occult Master, Koot Hoomi, who is inspired by beings on higher planets obeying the spiritual Hierarchy of the Galaxy. The presence of spaceships and the landing of spacemen is reported all over South America,[170] and it seems that there have been close links between Extraterrestrials and the Masters in the Andes throughout history.

The sudden appearances and disappearances of UFOs, their incredible accelerations and startling manoeuvres prompted Dr Meade Layne and his Borderland Research Associates to theorise the materialisation or dematerialisation of Ether-ships from Etherian Realms. The 'Power and Glory' of the 'Lord' mentioned in the Bible, the flying-cars of the Sylphs described by Montfaucon de Villars, now expounded in scientific terms curiously akin to the ideas of the ancient magicians. George Van Tassell reveals that the Etherians ionize a portion of etheric Space, attune their thoughts to their destination and their ship instantly arrives. They decrease their vibratory frequency until their ship materialises into our Earth's atmosphere, while the reverse process of transcendence returns them at once to their own plane. The etheric ships one moment are on etheric Venus and virtually the next moment manifest above Earth.

The notorious Condon Committee scorned the idea of Spaceships, since these would flout the laws of Science, the scientists closed their eyes to much important evidence and forgot that Extraterrestrials with advanced technology might utilise cosmic forces beyond our dreams. The real truth is that no man knows. It is hardly surprising therefore that some writers dismiss all suggestions of Spacemen from other planets or other dimensions and insist without any solid proof that the visitants may come from the Moon, or more astonishing still from our own Earth.

With daring if doubtful logic Mikhail Vessine and Alexandra Chterbakov explained in 'Komsomolskaya Pravda' on January 10th 1970 that our Moon's low density compared with Earth's suggests it is an artificial satellite launched on a geocentric orbit by unknown beings endowed with intelligence, possibly a giant Spaceship, abode of a civilisation. The Russians allege that the lunar rocks cover two inner shells of extremely hard metal still containing atmosphere; admittedly the ship is becoming a wreck, the stabilizers no longer function, it wobbles badly and the dark patches show parts of the metallic inner sphere stripped of its protective sheath. Caught in Earth's powerful gravitational field the Moon can no longer escape. Dante, Swedenborg and Herschel thought the Moon inhabited. For centuries strange lights in some craters have mystified our astronomers, perhaps they are bases for Spaceships? No Moonmen greeted Neil Armstrong and Buzz Aldrin in July 1969 when they planted the Stars and Stripes in the Sea of Tranquility.

There are suggestions our Earth is hollow and that a wonderful civilisation exists beneath our feet. This seeming Science-Fiction is taken most seriously by many brilliant students who advance arguments difficult to answer. Pictures taken on January 6 1967 by ESSA-3 satellite and on November 23 1968 by ESSA-7[146] seem clearly to show the existence of a hole at the North Pole said to lead to the amazing metropolis of Agharta deep inside our allegedly hollow Earth.[13] The Cyclops are believed to have founded cities underground. Psychics say the Atlanteans built long tunnels from the Pyramids, Tibet and the Andes to sacred centres down below to which fled Initiates when Atlantis was destroyed 12,000 years ago. The Spaceships from the interior appear through vents at the Poles and surveil our Earth, sometimes the Subterraneans surface to live among men. Most of us must admit that we may not know very much, and we suspect that the little we do know may be wrong. Suppose men a million years ago fled miles underground to avoid those nuclear-bombs mentioned in the ancient books? Before the end of this century should war break out between East and West we would be digging down to join them.

As our concept of Space changes, so varies our comprehension of Time. Some gifted scholars resurrect the ancient teachings of the seven-dimensional Universe and believe the future co-exists with past and present in eternal Now; well-authenticated prophecies and precognition apparently prove that the future is already mapped out waiting for our conscious selves to come there.

Today popular opinion seems rightly impressed by the brilliant researches of John A. Keel,[110] who bluntly rejects our own suggestions and alleges that the intruders throughout history are Ultraterrestrials existing in our environment on a Space-Time continuum different from ours. He gravely warns that these Elementals are following a careful plan designed to conquer our human world from within and make all men their slaves.

The problem of Gods and Spacemen is most profound. All we can do is to study the apparent influence of Extraterrestrials throughout history and hope for some enlightenment from the past for our sadly troubled times today.

CHAPTER TWO
The Golden Age

Dare we imagine what titanic events our world has seen and suffered in those vast ages before recorded history began? Spacemen could have landed and lived here for thousands of years beyond all human memory.

Much of the old wisdom means nothing to us, its secret is lost, though for centuries such ideas dominated men's minds as firmly as our transient philosophies today. The Ancients taught that the Earth itself is a living Being infested by millions of humans, whose accumulated thoughts constitute the World-Mind, repository of all knowledge throughout the ages to which sensitives may attune.

Students of the Occult believe our planet is dominated by the Silent Watcher aided by Four Dyan Chohans, Great Souls, who establish telepathic rapport with Spiritual Masters in secluded retreats to plan human destiny. The great German poet, Johann Wolfgang von Goethe, well-versed in the Ancient Wisdom, imagined the Earth inhaled and exhaled once a day causing atmospheric phenomena. Such beliefs seem bizarre to us until we recall that ultra-modern investigators, notably Trevor James[198] and Dr Meade-Layne,[120] think our atmosphere may be actually inhabited by strange, extraterrestrial creatures, an amoeba-family of heat-beings, gaseous vertebrates swimming in the upper air like fish in the sea, sometimes mistaken for UFOs. Spacemen are said to be monitoring the Earth's magnetic-field whose variations may trigger earthquakes; they may record our television and radio; it certainly seems likely that such advanced Beings will study our individual and national thought-waves, and possibly other subtle radiations we have not yet discovered. On the countless occasions mentioned in the Bible, in legends, throughout history and even today, whenever mortals have spoken to Gods or Spacemen, there seems to have been a communication-gap as great as a simple Hottentot talking to a nuclear-scientist.

Astronomers who lecture with assurance on every star in sight are suddenly puzzled by the origin of our own Earth. 'Just as on the microcosmic scale electrons radiate in millionths of a second, so there may be correspondence in the macrocosm where the Sun radiates its planets in a vastly different dimension of Time in millions of years almost beyond human perception.'[62] This theory would account for the belief that ages ago the year contained only 360 days suggesting our Earth orbited nearer the Sun and also for erratic Pluto apparently drifting further into Space to follow its undiscovered companion, Proserpine. Dr C.J. Hyman and C. William Kinsman speculate that 'Earth once pursued the orbit now occupied by Venus, while Mars was in the present Earth orbit.'[109] Immanuel Velikovsky with fabulous erudition proves to his own satisfaction that in historical times the planet Jupiter ejected a comet which scourged our Earth about 1500 BC before orbiting the Sun as the planet Venus; about seven hundred and fifty years later Venus brushed with Mars, their celestial encounter caused devastation all over our own world displacing the Poles.[208] These theories are challenged by the Italian, Quixé Cardinal,[30] who, quoting 'The Book of Enoch', claims that in the original Solar System Venus rotated between Mars and Saturn, Jupiter between Mercury and Earth. Satan rebelled against God and in the cosmic conflict Venus and Jupiter exchanged orbits. The planet Phaeton, better known as Maldek, became shattered into the asteroids. Some cataclysm evidently occurred.

Scientists are surprised by the startling difference between Earth and the other solar planets. On Earth the elements carbon, oxygen and hydrogen predominate, its neighbours have predominance of methane, nitrogen and silica, some possess clouds of sulphur or helium. Studies by radar show that Venus despite its dense protective clouds is pitted with immense craters apparently caused by huge meteors; space-probes show Mars dotted with great volcanoes like our Moon. Our own comparatively flat world seems a stranger, an intruder from another Solar System, like an electron radiated from one unstable atom to form a new isotope with another atom. The displacement of Earth from its parent-star and its wandering through Space until attracted by our own Sun may appear fantastic but not impossible; some experts seriously suggest that our present Moon ages ago drifted from outer Space and became caught by our planet's gravity causing tremendous devastation and could not escape. This thesis of an alien Earth advanced by the Italian scholar, Dino Orlandi,[145] is brilliant and cosmically credible. Psychiatrists admit we use less than 10% of our potential powers. Of the vast number of cells in the human brain surprisingly few seem to be needed now; this suggests that Man has degenerated and through lack of use a large part of his brain is atrophied. Where the First Men originated cannot be known; perhaps from another galaxy or by materialisation from other dimensions; such beings using all their potential brain-power would shine like Gods. The lost science of antiquity was based on natural electricity and radiant energy, particularly psychic-force, known to all the ancient adepts. This knowledge was the remnant of a most wonderful wisdom, when men by the power of united thought could literally move mountains and raise pyramids using psychokinesis, movement by thought, which our own students of extrasensory perceptions are rediscovering today.

Millions of years ago when our Earth was rotating in its original Solar System the First Men, their brain-powers fully developed, attuned their minds to the vast psychic energy latent in the Universe; they could direct beams of psychic force summoned by groups of highly gifted sensitives to create thought-forms, solidified into matter, or in reverse, disintegrate matter into pure thought.

The Stanzas of Dzyan, a quintessence of ancient wisdom, state that the First Race were Ethereans, Androgynes, uni-sexed men-women from the Sun. The Second, the mindless monsters from Jupiter. The Third Race, the Lemurians, were the Fallen Angels from Venus and Mars, Androgynes who ages later split into male and female, lamented by Plato; the

Fourth Race, the Atlanteans, descended from the Moon and Saturn, our present Fifth Race descended from Mercury.[30] Such recondite knowledge is supported in 'Pimandro' by Hermes Trismegistus.

Historians trace civilisation to about 8000 BC and ridicule Edgar Cayce, the renowned American seer, whose psychic recording 5748-1, May 28, 1925, revealed that ten and a half million years ago on an Earth vastly different in geography from today, its population numbered one hundred and thirty-three million. New discoveries by palaeontologists are swiftly extending the age of Man. In 1958 Dr Johannes Huerzeler found a humanoid skeleton six hundred feet down in an Italian coal-mine, possibly ten million years old. Dr Louis Leakey in 1967 at Rusinga and Songer in Kenya discovered fragments of Kenyapithecus Africanus, a man-like creature distinct from ape dated twenty million years ago; on 27 August 1972, his son, Dr Richard Leakey, beside Lake Rudolf in Kenya, unearthed parts of a skull 2,600,000 years old; this '1470' Man was capable of walking erect and was probably not unlike ourselves. Metal objects sometimes found in coal suggest that Man lived on Earth vast ages ago.

The Greeks like most ancient peoples believed in a Golden Age when Earth was ruled by the Gods, then Heroes and Superhuman Kings, followed by wars and cataclysms degenerating to the Ages of Silver, Bronze and Iron.

Apollodorus, an Athenian historian, wrote

'Sky was the first who ruled over the whole world.'

Since the Greek word 'Ouranos' meant 'Sky', Uranus could generalise Spacemen from any stellar system although it could still refer to the planet, Uranus, known to the Ancients. 'Ouranos' known world-wide was identified with 'Varuna', he controlled the Sun, Moon and stars, riding on the Leviathan, a fearsome Sky-monster which the Lord in our Bible described to Job[124] in terms suggesting a Spaceship. The Uranids may represent Galactic explorers from an advanced planet who penetrated our Solar System and installed a transit-station on Earth a million years ago, as our own cosmonauts will establish bases on other planets in centuries to come.

The Greek legends describing world-cataclysms now find

some support from modern Science, with each new advance in astronomy and physics those ancient myths shed their fantasy to shine in truth, not primitive superstition, but as the earliest history of our Earth. In the late 18th century J.D. Titius, a German mathematician, observed a remarkable numerical relationship between the distances of the planets from the Sun, later formulated by Johannes Bode as Bode's Law, which theorised the existence of an unknown planet between Mars and Jupiter. A search was made. In 1801 Piazzi located a tiny planetoid, which he called Ceres, and since then about 5,000 more have been found. Astronomers believe these rocky fragments to be the debris of a planet known to the Ancients as Phaeton or Maldek, destroyed by its own mad scientists ages ago. In these days of hydrogen-bombs the suicide of a planet seems logical, even inevitable, the possible fate of our own sad world. Maldek, further from the Sun would cool down sooner than its inner neighbours, Mars and Earth; its peoples could have attained an advanced civilisation when Earthmen, if we believe the anthropologists, were still swinging like Tarzan in the tree-tops. Human destiny everywhere apparently follows the same fatal pattern. In the fullness of time scientists invent Spaceships and nuclear-bombs, in mad lust for power evil men wage wars, civilisation is destroyed by cataclysms and the sorry survivors have to start again spiralling to new heights until self-destruction drags Man down once more. This tragedy probably happens throughout the whole Universe as legends suggest. Foreseeing eventual disaster Maldek's cosmonauts would by-pass Mars, already civilised, and land on the high mountains of Earth where the rarified air would approximate the thin atmosphere of their own planet. The scarcity of oxygen in the Maldek atmosphere would give its inhabitants that bluish tinge noted in cardiac patients, the Celestials would appear characteristically bluish to the primitive peoples of Earth, today we associate blue blood with Royalty, blue and purple signified the earliest Kings of Antiquity, surely suggesting their origin from Space.[210]

The explosion of Maldek would cause grave destruction to Mars and Jupiter, bombardment by colossal rocks devastating their surface. Above all the distortion of gravitational and electrical fields would convulse both planets. Anticipating disaster refugees from Mars, even Jupiter, would probably flee to Earth and war with colonists from Maldek already there. Today dire warnings prophesy sorry· pollution of our own planet, in a few centuries the air may be poisoned, the rivers filthy, the land parched and over-populated. Fleets of Spaceships may blast off to another planet where they have to fight against earlier invaders.

Invasions of Earth from Space seem confirmed by the Greek Classics which in puzzling confusion relate how Uranus was castrated and dethroned by his son, Cronus (Saturn), who in turn was usurped by his own son, Zeus (Jupiter). The Titans, giant sons of Uranus, refused to submit to Zeus, for whom the Cyclops forged wondrous weapons, after ten years war Zeus overcame the Titans and hurled them down below Tartarus. Hesiod in his 'Theogony' states that Eumelus of Corinth or Arctinus, the poet of the 'War of the Titans', described 'dumb fish afloat with golden faces swimming and sporting through the heavenly water',[96] supporting world-wide legends of war in Space. 'Sons of Uranus' may be symbolism for the succeeding race. Perhaps the Cyclops were called one-eyed because the transparent face of their Space-helmets looked like a huge eye; these Giants may be identified with the Els,[222] a stellar race who built labyrinthine cities underground utilising cosmic energies to delve those long tunnels leading to the subterranean civilisation of Agharta alleged to exist today.

Though little is known of the Uranids, the Golden Age of Cronus is praised by all the poets of Antiquity. Men lived in wondrous peace for all the philosophers agree that in this age of perfection Man was not distracted by Woman. Earth was a Garden of Eden before Eve.

After titanic war convulsing Heaven and Earth Zeus banished Cronus to the mysterious island of Britain guarded by Briareus, a monster with a hundred hands. To punish Man he created Woman. The world's climate changed, lands glowed with heat in summer and froze in winter, in this Silver Age men sought refuge in caves, committed sins, quarrelled and forgot the immortal Gods. The outraged Zeus destroyed them all in a great flood leaving Deucalian and Pyrrha to bring forth those mighty warriors of the Bronze Age who plunged mankind to barbarism. All died from plague, so Zeus created a fourth race of God-like heroes and finally in his questionable wisdom began this Age of Iron which still afflicts our sad world today.

The 'Popol Vuh', the sacred book of the Quiché Mayas, in Guatemala, tells of a most ancient civilisation which knew about the nebulae and the whole solar system, stating that the First Race of Men were capable of all knowledge. They examined the four corners of the horizon, the four cardinal points of the firmament and the round surface of the Earth. Awareness of its sphericity suggests that gifted beings had observed our globe from Space. The Gods could not permit men to be their equals, so obscured their vision causing their fall to decadence; these Mayan traditions evoke the expulsion of Adam and Eve from the Garden of Eden supporting similar legends of the Hindus, Egyptians and Greeks.

Most ancient peoples believed in four World-Ages possibly referring to the lost civilisations of Gondwanaland, Hyperborea, Lemuria and Atlantis, whose existence is seriously debated by scholars today. Scientists generally agree that in our Earth's immensely long history changes in cosmic radiation, fluctuations in its magnetic-field, the crash of previous Moons or collisions by comets, must have caused fantastic cataclysms destroying a succession of cultures in the far past. Egyptian Priests told Herodotus that eleven thousand years earlier the axis of the Earth became displaced. 'The Sun had removed from his proper course four times and had risen where he now setteth and set where he now riseth.'[95] Geologists confirm that many times lands have become seas and seas become lands. The wars in Ancient India suggest that the ice ages may have been caused by immense nuclear-bombs.

CHAPTER THREE
Sons Of The Gods

'In the begining God created numerous worlds destroying one after
the other as they failed to satisfy Him. All were inhabited by Man, a
thousand of whom he cut off leaving no record of Man.'[88]

Today talk of numerous populated worlds existing before
our own Earth is considered science-fiction, though condoned
by some astronomers. We are startled to learn that this
Genesis Rabbra was actually written in the 5th century BC by
bigoted Jewish priests who knew little science and still less
fiction.

If this revelation of inhabited worlds had begun the Book of
Genesis, as indeed it should, the religion and culture of Jews
and Christians must have radically changed. Even the most
orthodox Jews must have seriously doubted whether God,
Creator of the Vast Universe, for reasons still obscure, would
descend to our tiny Earth to patronise a small Semitic tribe.
The 'Lord' in his 'Power and Glory' surely seemed to the
Israelites like Horus, Marduk or Zeus, Gods of neighbouring
Egypt, Babylon and Greece, a Celestial manifesting from the
stars to aid mortals on Earth. The Bible, sublime though it be,
was written solely to indoctrinate the Jews with their
uniqueness in the sight of God. This belief in numerous worlds
must have impressed the Rabbis strongly for them to preserve
their midrash commenting on Genesis for so many centuries,
had they actually published such wisdom, now preached by
our modern Science, the Bible would have inspired all men
with a cosmic religion seeking our Brothers from Space.

'In the beginning God created the heaven and the earth.'[80]

The opening chapters of Genesis contain two separate

accounts of Creation chronicling two distinct epochs, a memory of World-Ages mentioned in ancient myths. The first refers to the creation of the Earth with animals, birds and plants, the creation of Man in God's own image, male and female. God worked six days, on the seventh He rested. The second Creation[80] story states there was neither shrub nor plant growing wild upon the Earth because the Lord God had sent no rain on the Earth nor was there any Man to till the ground. A flood rose from the Earth and watered all the surface. From the dust God created Adam and breathed into his nostrils the breath of life.

Today our latest Science suggests that Genesis 1 refers to Galactic Man,[197] perhaps while Earth rotated around its original Sun, and Genesis 2 concerns Animal Man, possibly the re-creation after cosmic cataclysm whirled Earth into Space to be captured by our present Sun. Scientists now generally agree with Students of the Occult that Earth was inhabited long before the Biblical Adam. Moses, assumed Author of Genesis, and the later prophets who revised the texts, obviously borrowed from the Babylonian creation poem, *Enumah Elish* 'When on High' written about 2500 BC describing Earth emerging from the deep like the plain of Mesopotamia from the floods, peopled by Gods and monsters.

'And God said Let there be light and there was light.'

The early Hebrews, like many ancient peoples, believed the Universe emanates from Light symbolising the Divine Spirit, a most subtle mystery supported by our modern Science. This advanced knowledge is beyond the comprehension of most people without profound study. Did the Writer of Genesis inherit such wisdom from the Initiates of some great civilisation or from Spacemen? In Genesis 1 the word for God was Elohim, the plural of the Ugaritic El meaning several Gods, the Elohim are associated with Galactic man.

Science can say little about the First Creation except to suggest that the Universe is still expanding from a single atom, the secret teachings of antiquity.

Asiatic traditions state that long before Adam there was a vast inland sea north of the Himalayas inhabited by a race of supermen who could live in water, air or fire for they controlled the elements. These were probably the real Elohim, beings of sublime wisdom. Eventually their descendants would become decadent and misuse their wonderful powers to cause some cataclysm. Occult sources tell of the Sanat Kumara, Logos of Venus, descending to this White Island amid the Gobi Sea in a flaming Spaceship.

The first creation of Genesis may have lasted as long as three thousand million years. If the first men were Ethereans as occultists allege they would leave no bones to baffle our palaeontologists.

The second creation, a re-Creation, may have occurred after that colossal catastrophe when Earth wandered alone through Space towards our Solar System; geologists agree that some primeval cataclysm did devastate our Earth making prehistoric species extinct and leaving the few survivors to rebuild civilisation.

Strange as it may seem this titanic disaster blasting Earth long ago may soon be suffered by Pluto. Sensitives allege that the brilliant, decadent, doomed civilisation there languishes in despair. Not surprising, as astronomers predict from the planet's erratic orbit that one day it will probably break away from the Sun's gravitational-field and whirl out into Space until it is attracted by another star. Then the solitary survivors must start again.

Geneticists now believe the ancient teachings that Earth's first humans were uni-sex, reproducing themselves by parthenogenesis, virgin birth; the Goddess Cybele like Aphrodite was often depicted with a phallus and a vulva. Biologically woman's body was physically created before man's, she still has male organs atrophied. In a woman there are twenty-two pairs of chromosomes plus two sexual chromosomes, both X, a man has the same number but one of his sexual chromosomes is a Y. Perhaps by mischance cosmic radiation modified in some women one of their X sexual chromosomes into a Y chromosome producing a mutant, man. Fluctuation in the intensity of cosmic rays caused subtle changes in body-chemistry synthesising male hormones, varying mental-fields affecting human electricity. The power of thought developed the clitoris of woman to the penis of man. The primitive worship of the Earth Mother appears correct, biologically-speaking the Bible errs, Adam was created from Eve.

The Garden of Eden sited in many places, even on Mars, is usually associated with fertile Mesopotamia between the Euphrates and the Tigris. Comyns Beaumont [10] interprets The Book of Enoch as proving that the Garden of Eden was in an antediluvian sub-tropical Scotland; the expulsion of Adam and Eve, his name in Hebrew meant red, is said to be ancient symbolism for the red-skinned Lemurians driven from their wondrous lost continent to roam the world.

The Talmud states that Adam's first wife was Lilith, a fascinating demoness with long wavy hair. Her name derived from the Babylonian *lilitu* meant a female demon or wind spirit, implying a seductress from other realms, a Lamia or Succuba who delighted in seducing sleeping men or a nymph like Egeria, wife of the early Roman King, Numa Pompilius, to whom she imparted great wisdom. Solomon suspected the Queen of Sheba of being Lilith because she had hairy legs, though he managed to father Menelik, first Emperor of Abyssinia; he enjoyed sex more than Adam who was frustrated by Lilith's refusal to lie on her back during sexual intercourse. Witches favoured the superior posture. She arose in the air and left him; three Angels (Extraterrestrials?) brought Lilith back to Adam. The Ancients sometimes referred to Spacemen as Spirits; the alluring Lilith may have been a Spacewoman like the glamorous Aura Rhanes who appeared to Truman Bethuram, or that voluptuous red-head seducing Antonio Villas Boas in Brazil. This suggestion is not startling since if the Sons of the Gods consorted with the Daughters of Men, the Daughters of the Gods would surely flaunt their celestial charms at Men themselves.

Rabbinical traditions allege that since Adam's first marriage to a demoness failed, God then fashioned a woman from bones, flesh and blood; He endowed her with life while Adam watched. On his last attempt the Lord caused Adam to fall into a trance and from a rib in his side he formed woman; esoteric doctrines agree with Plato that the Androgyne was separated into Man and Woman, the reason why the sexes yearn to unite.

The Lord who walked in the Garden of Eden amid the cool

of the evening was possibly the Commander of a space fleet perhaps from Venus, since Cherubim apparently signified Winged Creatures. Psalm 18 verse 10 vividly describes the Lord riding on a cherub on the wings of the wind, his Power and Glory symbolising a Spaceship. Eve, seduced by the serpent signifying wisdom, ate the forbidden fruit, thereby acquiring illicit knowledge. The Rabbis alleged the fruit did not grow on trees but on Eve herself, from this secret part she conceived Cain by the Demon. The Lord evidently used some powerful laser-beam, perhaps a flame-thrower or ray-gun, remembered as a whirling and flashing sword.

'The Life of Adam and Eve', a Book in the Apocrypha written in Aramaic states that the Lord ordered Archangel Michael to conduct Adam in a chariot of fire to the Paradise of Justice, soon Adam entreated to be returned to Earth. The Lord descended in a chariot of cherubims amid the hymns of Angels to pass judgement on Adam and Eve. Gazing up at the sky Eve beheld approaching a chariot of light with four shining eagles preceded by Angels which alighted in the place where Adam was.

Genesis may be interpreted in many ways. Occult traditions suggest that Adam possibly symbolised the red-skinned Lemurians, living on that doomed continent in the Pacific, said to have developed a wondrous Science challenging their Space Teachers who cast them forth from their fabled Garden as the Lord expelled Adam and Eve from Eden.

Startling evidence of Extraterrestrials now appears in the New English Bible, Genesis, Chapter 6, verses 1 and 2

> 'When mankind began to increase and to spread all over the earth and daughters were born to them, the Sons of the Gods saw that the daughters of men were beautiful so they took for themselves such women as they chose.'

This wonderful revelation is repeated in verse 4,

> 'In those days when the Sons of the Gods had intercourse with the daughters of men and got children by them, the Nephilim were on Earth. They were heroes of old, men of renown.'

Sons of the Gods! A footnote to the New English Bible text states that the probable Hebrew reading is 'In those days and also afterwards', suggesting that the Sons of the Gods consorted with Earthwomen probably for centuries all over the world.

The overwhelming importance of this translation with its pregnant implications for our UFO-haunted Earth today shines like a beacon illuming world-history compared with the conventional interpretation in the Authorised Version of James 1. Here the sons of God are spoken of.

The difference between Sons of God and Sons of the Gods is cataclysmic. Our long-conditioned minds cannot grasp its outstanding significance. Sons of God denoted divine Fatherhood, symbolising God's paternal care for the people He created. This concept was cherished by Judaism and specially favoured by Jesus. The Sons of God was a popular term for Holy Men applied to Priests, only later was Son of God made a divine attribute of Jesus by St. Paul. For many centuries 'Sons of God' in Genesis has confounded learned commentators and misled Jews and Christians alike. Only today have scholars with modern learning faithfully, perhaps uncomprehendingly, resurrected the original Sons of the Gods.

The compilers of Genesis well knew the difference between God and Gods. In Chapter 3, verse 4, the Serpent tempting Eve used both words in contrast, saying

'Of course, you will not die. God knows that as soon as you eat it, your eyes will be opened and you will be like Gods knowing both good and evil.'

The Gods who mated with the daughters of men were beings of flesh and blood siring giants, confirmed by traditions all over the world. Surely they were Spacemen.

The Doctrine of Original Sin is usually interpreted as referring to the Fall of Adam and Eve for disobeying God's command. However some theologians believe that Original Sin was not due to Adam and Eve but to the Fallen Angels consorting with the Daughters of Men.

Civilisation on Earth may be much older than we think. Genesis, Chapter 5, records the generations following Adam as Set, Enosh, Kenon, Mahalaleel, Jared, Enoch, Methusaleh, Lamech and Noah. Each is said to have lived for hundreds of years begetting many children. These antediluvian Patriarchs possibly represented distinct races in a succession of ten cycles, each less spiritual than its predecessor.

Berossus in his 'Babyloniaca', a history based on Chaldean temple-records preserved with the greatest care, wrote 'Before the Deluge there were ten Kings reigning 120 Saris, 432,000 years.

The Sumerian King-List found on cuneiform tablets in the Library of Assurbanipal of Nineveh states

> 'When kingship was lowered from heaven the kingship was in Eridu. In Eridu Abulim became King and reigned 28,800 years. Abolge reigned 36,000 years. Two kings reigned 64,800 years. Five cities were they. Eight kings reigned 241,000 years. The Flood swept thereover.'[174]

Celestial Kings came down from the skies to Eridu 370,600 years before the Flood!

Persian myths claim that demons had corrupted the Earth before the coming of Zoroaster, whose first incarnation as Zarathustra is conjectured as about 8,000 BC; traditions from ancient literatures East and West all agree that Earth was once ruled by the Gods who consorted with the daughters of men.

Fifty years ago in an old synagogue in Cairo priests discovered 'The Zadokite Document' which confirmed Genesis and mentioned the landing of Extraterrestrials, their giant offspring and immorality.

> 'Because they walked in the stubborness of their hearts the Watchers of Heaven fell, yea, they were caught thereby because they kept not the Commandments of God.
>
> So too their Sons, whose height was like the lofty cedars and whose bodies were as mountains. They also fell.'[79]

One of the Dead Sea Scrolls discovered by an Arab boy in a cave at Qumram in 1947 describes the Armageddon destined to be fought against the evil giants, Gog and Magog, which would last for forty years and usher in the Era of Divine Favour. The Sons of Light mobilise to give battle against multitudes of Kittians, Egyptians or Assyrians, the Sons of Belial. The Lord will send down Angels and Holy Beings in tens of thousands led by the King of Glory to scatter the

Children of Darkness. Today any visionary prophesying apocalyptic War to end all wars would envision nuclear-missiles, super-tanks, laser-beams, flame-throwers, air-fleets dropping hydrogen-bombs, then dramatic intervention by Spaceships with annihilating blasts.

God himself said the Fallen Angels brought Earth corruption, hence the Flood. Will the next descent of Angels prove different?

> 'Enoch was the first among the children of men among those born on Earth, who learned writing, science, wisdom, who interpreted the signs of heaven according to the order of the months and wrote them in a book because the sons of men knew the time of the year, sub-divided according to the order of months.'

Enoch, a giant, seventh in descent from Adam, has been identified with Thoth, Hermes Thrice-Greatest, Mercury, and Orpheus, all venerated throughout the Ancient World as great astronomers, inventors of arts and sciences, teachers from the stars. He may have represented the Atlanteans. His name Enoch, related to the Hebrew Hanoch meaning Initiator, evokes 'Enki', the Babylonian God of Wisdom, sent down from the skies to promote the civilisation of the whole world, particularly of Sumeria, ancient Mesopotamia. There he resembled Oannes, the being with the body of a fish, probably a celestial in a space-suit, who taught the early Babylonians. The Rabbis believed Enoch, son of Jared, father of Methusaleh and great-grandfather of Noah, to be a sorcerer or magician, in modern terms a great scientist.

In his famous Book Enoch mentions the round shape of the Earth and the inclination of its axis. How could he acquire this knowledge? Genesis states that Enoch lived on Earth for three hundred and sixty-five years, significantly the number of days in the year, which might suggest some astronomical or extraterrestrial wisdom. It astounds us all today to learn that Enoch thousands of years ago apparently anticipated our cosmonauts and gave the first description of flight through Space. The Book of Enoch, Chapter XVIII states

> 'I saw the treasures of all the winds. I saw how God had furnished with them the whole Creation and the firm foundation of the Earth. And I saw the corner-stone of the Earth. I saw the four winds which bear the Earth and the firmament of the heaven. And I saw how the winds stretch

out the vaults of heaven and have their stations between heaven and Earth, these are the pillars of the heavens. I saw the winds of heaven which turn and bring the circumference of the Sun and all the stars to their settings. I saw the winds on the Earth carrying the clouds. I saw the paths of the Angels. I saw at the end of the Earth the firmament of the Earth alone.'[37]

This somewhat naive account evokes the revelations of George Adamski after his alleged trip in a Spaceship and suggests those more scientific commentaries from our own astronauts.

The so-called Slavonic Book of Enoch comprises fragments found in Russia. The main sources are rare manuscripts brought from Abyssinia by the explorer James Bruce in 1772, and known as the Ethiopic Book of Enoch, brilliantly translated by Canon R.H. Charles. Some writings once attributed to Enoch are now believed to be a Testament by Noah. The Slavonic Book of Enoch, Chapter XXXIII states that God had written Books of Wisdom and handed them to Enoch accompanied by the Angels Samuil and Razuil to deliver to his children on Earth.

It relates how Enoch in the first month of his 365th year was alone at home in bed when suddenly anguish tormented his heart. He then perceived by his side two Beings of immense stature surpassing Earth's Giants. Their faces shone like the Sun, their eyes glowed like burning coals and their mouths emitted jets of fire, descriptions evoking the Lord in the Bible, those luminous Apparitions in the Middle Ages and alleged spacemen today. The Celestials wore purple suits interwoven with plumes making a rustling sound, their arms shone with wings of gold as in the classical description of Quetzalcoatl of old Mexico. They told him that the Lord had sent them to conduct Enoch to Him in heaven.

From a huge mothership Enoch looked down on the first heaven, the planet Saturn, with its rings of ice-covered rocks; the planet was the lowest in the scale of evolution with mindless monsters. The second heaven, Jupiter, shrouded in gloom imprisoned those Angels who had rebelled against God; near the planet Enoch saw comets and two groups of asteroids. In the third heaven, Mars, Enoch beheld the Garden of Paradise, and in the centre the Tree of Life,

perhaps the Tree of Knowledge, whence Adam and Eve tasted
the fruit which caused their exile to Earth. Only a few
hundred miles away in the Polar regions Enoch was surprised
and saddened to see the damned freezing amid thick ice.

Enoch now began to call the Angels men, for so they
appeared. They brought him to the fourth heaven, our own
Earth, which Enoch was surprised to see was round, a fact
denied by theologians for thousands of years. He beheld
legions of spirits, dragons and the fabled Phoenix flying
around the Earth suggesting Spaceships, perhaps the aerial
Sylphs so graphically described in Le Comte de Gabalis by
Montfaucon de Villars. In the fifth heaven, Venus, Enoch met
many soldiers, the Egregori, with the appearance of men,
taller than the giants of Earth. Enoch was then transported to
the sixth heaven, Mercury, whose luminous Angels with
radiant faces taught him the motions of the stars, the phases of
the Moon, the revolution of the Sun and the good government
of the world.

His two companions brought Enoch to the seventh heaven,
the Sun, where he beheld Cherubim, Serafim, Thrones,
(possible Spaceships). Enoch was scared to behold so much
glory but his guides re-assured him by showing him the Lord
in the distant tenth heaven seated on a lofty throne among the
Angels who one by one constantly approached Him to receive
orders. The 'Lord's' bodyguard consisted of Cherubim, and
Serafim, with six wings and many eyes who may have been
Spacemen. The Lord sent Gabriel for Enoch, trembling on the
edge of the seventh heaven; he raised him aloft like a leaf in the
wind and whisked him through the eighth heaven, Muzaloth,
place of the changing of the Season, and in the ninth heaven,
Kuvachim, the Houses of the Signs of the Zodiac.

In the tenth heaven called Aravoth, Enoch recognised the
constellation whence came our first ancestors, the star, Altair.
Here he beheld the countenance of the Lord like molten iron
emitting sparks of light. The Lord invited Enoch, arrayed by
Michael in glorious raiment, to sit beside Him and explained
the Creation of the Universe from the Non-Existing. He told
Enoch that Jupiter once orbited between Earth and Mercury,
Venus between Saturn and Mars. A most extraordinary
cosmic cataclysm caused Jupiter and Venus to change orbits,

the Revolt of Satan against the Lord apparently provoked the explosion of the planet, Phaeton, into the asteroids, an alleged event attributed to Maldek. Enoch is said to have written 360 books in 60 days using a swift pen which the Lord gave him. Enoch made two journeys, he flew across the Earth to the West, possibly to Britain or Atlantis.

'And Azazal taught men to make swords and knives and shields and breastplates and made known to them the metals of the Earth and the art of working them and bracelets and ornaments and the use of antimony and the beautifying of eyelids and all kinds of costly stones and all colouring tinctures. And there arose much godlessness and they committed fornications and they were led astray. Semejaze taught enchantments and root-cutting, Airmoros, the resolving of enchantments, Barorcyal (taught) astrology, Kokabel, the constellations, Ezeqeel, knowledge of the clouds, Araquil, the Signs of the Earth, Shamsial, the Signs of the Sun, and Sarial, the course of the Moon. And as men perished they cried and their cry went up to Heaven.

And then Michael, Uriel, Raphael and Gabriel looked down from Heaven and saw much blood spilled on Earth. They said to the Lord of the ages that Azazal had taught all unrighteousness on Earth and revealed the eternal secrets which were preserved in Heaven and which men were striving to learn. And Semejaze to whom thou hast given authority to bear rule over his associates – gone to the Daughters of Woman – borne Giants.'

The revelations of Enoch translated from a text of great antiquity assume great significance today. His celestial trips seem to anticipate the future travels of our astronauts. We wonder whether this venerated antediluvian actually did ascend to the stars.

'And after some days, my son, Methusaleh, took a wife for his son, Lamech, and she became pregnant and bore a son. And his body was white as snow and red as the blooming of a rose and the hair of his head and his long locks were white as wool and his eyes beautiful. And when he opened his eyes he lighted up the whole house like the sun and the whole house was very light. And thereupon he arose on the hands of the midwife and conversed with the Lord of righteousness. And his father, Lamech, was afraid of him and fled and came to Methusaleh. And he said unto him "I have begotten a strange son diverse from and unlike Man and resembling the Sons of Heaven and his nature is different and he is not like us, and his eyes are as the rays of the sun and his countenance is glorious. And it seems to me that he is not sprung from me and I fear that in his days a wonder may be brought upon the Earth".'[38]

Enoch assured Lamech that he was the child's father though his doubts were aggravated by the prophecy that the Lord would greatly punish Earth because Angels had sinned with mortal women and produced giants. Noah's birth coincided with Adam's death. Again in The Book of Jubilees[37] Enoch testified that two Watchers had sinned with the Daughters of Men. The Dead Sea Scrolls repeat Lamech's suspicions that Bathenosh, his wife, had conceived the child by one of the Watchers or Holy Beings. The classics of most countries describe how the Gods descended to sire culture heroes destined to perform some great feat to save their people, surely it is likely that foreseeing the Flood the Lord himself or another Celestial would procreate Noah with the genius to preserve the few survivors from the old world to the new.

The Bible[81] states that men had done such evil on Earth the Lord was grieved and decided to wipe them out. He gave Noah precise instructions to build an Ark for his wife and three sons, Shem, Ham and Japheth, with their wives and two living creatures of every kind, male and female.

There is reason to believe that Noah was probably a red-skinned Giant, survivor from Atlantis about 10,000 BC, whose family bridged Man's transition from the Fourth Root Race to the Fifth, our own. Madame H.P. Blavatsky with fantastic erudition associated Noah and other Flood heroes, Vaivasvata, Xisithrus and Deucalion, with the submergence of the great islands of Ruta and Daitya, possibly 850,000 years ago.

In 1872 an amateur philologist, George Smith, deciphering some clay tablets from the library of the Assyrian King Assurbanipal in the British Museum, was startled to see those wedge-shaped signs resolve into the world-poem *Sa nagba imurur* or He who saw everything, known now as the Gilgamesh Epic. Here his ancestors, Uta-Napishtim, revealed in noble words to Gilgamesh how Ea, God of Wisdom, warned him to build a ship to save his wife, family and animals from the coming deluge. Uta-Napishtim describes the titanic storms, the tremendous flood, when his ship grounded on Mt Nisir he sent out a dove which returned, then a swallow, finally a raven which never came back.

A Greek legend states that when men were wicked Zeus sent an immense flood to drown mankind. Deucalion built an Ark and with his wife, Pyrrha, was saved. Another tradition tells of Oyges, whose land of Cos of the Meropes, possibly Atlantis, was inundated by a great flood. The Celts recall magic Numinor, symbol of Nordic culture. After the universal Flood the island became Ireland ruled by the sorceress Cesair, suggesting Circe. The Welsh Triads recall floods drowning Britain, the Anglo-Saxon poets wrote of a boiling ocean engulfing the Giants, the Elder Edda of Scandinavia describes a cosmic cataclysm when the Sun darkens, stars fall from heaven and the waters swamp the Earth. The Hindus record Vaivasvata building an Ark guided by a fish through the Deluge. The Chinese, Africans in the Congo, the Persians and Samoans have almost identical legends of Heroes saved from the Floods.

The most impressive Flood legends come from the Americas. The Delaware Indians, Dakotas, Sioux, Iroquois, Pawnees and Okanogans describe how their lands were flooded ages ago. In Mexico the Fourth Age, Atonatiuh, Sun of Water, ended with a great inundation; the Toltecs believed the first world was destroyed by tremendous rains from the sky. The God, Titlacahuan, warned the Giant, Nata, and his wife, Nana, to hollow out a large cypress and enter it, when the water approached the sky. The Mayan Popol Vuh describes several World Ages saying the first men were made from wood but dissolved in water. In Peru the Incas exalted Viracocha, who from stones created giants and deposited them among primitive men, later he destroyed all mankind in immense floods saving only one man and a woman.

When was Noah's Flood? Theologians, scientists, scholars offer persuasive theories, the truth is that no one knows. The Hindus, Chinese, Greeks, Etruscans, Irish, tell of Five World Ages, the Mayas of Four. Earth has suffered countless catastrophies in the immense history of Man. Reversals of the Earth's magnetic-field, sudden increase in cosmic radiation, exploding Super Novae stars, seriously affected our planet.

Hans Hoerbiger theorised that at least three previous moons had crashed down on Earth; Immanuel Velikovsky ascribed cataclysms to Venus, Comyns Beaumont and

Ignatius Donnelly suggested collisions with comets. George Hunt Williamson believed fragments from the exploded planet, Maldek, scourged the West. James Churchward describes subterranean volcanoes destroying Lemuria, the Sanskrit Classics tell of titanic blasts shattering whole countries, possibly provoking the last Ice Age.

Legends and folklore everywhere agree with Genesis that there were Giants on the Earth in those days. Many millennia of cataclysms, wars and human folly have destroyed the monuments of ancient man. But a few solitary works remain. The titanic ruins of Tiahuanaco in the Andes, megaliths in Mexico, burial-mounds in America, Earth-zodiacs in Britain, tunnels under Africa, caves in India, underground tombs in Tibet, rock-paintings in Australia, the Pyramids, the Sphinx, all stand in majestic grandeur, conjuring a marvellous panorama of Earth ruled by Titans, Sons of the Gods.[63]

Tradition ascribes the grounding of Noah's Ark as on Luba, one of the twin peaks of Ararat in modern Armenia. The Italian scholar, Quixé Cardinali, insists that Noah's Flood happened in 2341 BC alleging that the Ark landed on a Mount Ararat not in Armenia but in Ethiopia. In his controversial work Delle Galassie Ai Continenti Scomparsi Cardinali says

> 'There exists a Mt Ararat, a city called Harar, but descending towards the south, still following the crest of the mountains, we meet a mountain called Lubur, 1585 metres high; there is moreover a mountain-chain called Illubabur. From these mountains Noah and his sons descended to the countryside of Sennaar, which must have been the luxuriant land around the Nile; there still exists below Khartoum in the Sudan, a centre called Sennaar and – strange coincidence – two neighbouring regions also called Tigris and Euphrates. I think at this point past traditions become revised and corrected.'[30]

This controversial Writer apparently regards Sennaar as being Shinar in old Babylonia and believes that the Old Testament epic occurred not in Palestine but in Abyssinia. With equal argument Comyns Beaumont insists that the Patriarchs lived in Britain advancing ingenious reasons difficult to refute.

Who the Biblical Noah really was no one knows, there must have been many previous civilisations with Noahs of their own.

'Once upon a time all the world spoke a single language and used the same words. As men journeyed in the East, they came upon a plain in the land of Shinar and settled there. They said to one another "Come let us make bricks and bake them hard", they said "let us build for ourselves a city and make a tower with its top in the heavens and make a name for ourselves, or we shall be dispersed all over the earth." Then the Lord came down to see the city and tower which mortal men had built and he said "Here they are, one people with a single language and now they have started to do this; henceforward, nothing they have a mind to do will be beyond their reach. Come let us go down there and confuse their speech, so that they will not understand what they say to one another." So the Lord dispersed them from there all over the earth, and they left off building the city. That is why it is called Babel, because the Lord there made a babble of the language of all the world; from that place the Lord scattered men all over the face of the earth.'[82]

To us in our Space Age the Lord's descent to see the city of Babylon and disperse its people may be significant. The Creator of the whole Universe would not descend to tiny Earth to see some tower. This simple factual story surely suggests the Lord was a real person, a Spaceman.

The descendants of Noah migrated eastwards from Ararat to modern Mesopotamia. His great-grandson, the giant Nimrod, from this great city in Shinar ruled a vast empire. Like the Greek Titan, Prometheus, Nimrod sought to liberate Earth from the domination of the Celestials.

Berossus, the Chaldean Priest, in his 'Babyloniaca' written about 250 BC, stated there were records in Babylon comprehending a term of fifteen myriads, 150,000, of years. Proclus in Timaeus, Book One, quotes Iamblichus as saying that the Assyrians had preserved not only the memorial of seven and twenty myriads, 270,000 of years but also of seven previous ages. Eusebius and Syncellus quote Berossus as writing

'They say that the first inhabitants of the Earth glorying in their own strength and despising the Gods undertook to raise a tower whose top should reach the sky, where Babylon now stands, but when it approached the heavens the winds assisted the Gods and overturned the work upon its contrivors, and its ruins are said to be at Babylon and the Gods introduced a diversity of tongues among men who till that time had spoken the same language and war arose between Cronus and Titan, but the place in which they built the tower is now called Babylon on account of the confusion of the language, for confusion is by the Hebrews called Babel.'[50]

No confirmation of this Tower is to be found in Babylonian records nor on any of thousands of tablets from Assurbanipal's great Library at Nineveh, an omission which casts doubts on the whole story.

The Tower of Babel was not unique. All over Africa, North America and Mexico legends tell of people assaulting the skyland on ladders of arrows. The Norsemen like the South American Indians, Babylonians, Egyptians, Greeks and Eskimos believed in a World-Tree supporting the sky, original of our old English maypole.

Traditions from every country in the world agree with the familiar Bible story of the descent of the Gods, a Golden Age, then rebellion by the Giants in a war with fantastic weapons which shattered civilisation and scattered survivors all over the Earth.

Science now substantiates the basic facts of Genesis. In ages past several civilisations suffered destruction from the skies in cataclysms or conflict with Spacemen.

What has been shall be again, the future lies in the past!

CHAPTER FOUR
Lemuria

The map of the world has suffered tremendous change during the last two or three billion years. Geologists believe that originally all the land formed one single continent, Pangea, in an immense ocean. It then split into Laurasia comprising present North America, Europe, Northern and Central Asia, and Gondwana embracing South America, Africa, the Antarctic, India and Australasia, separated by a vast Mediterranean Sea. Throughout long ages Laurasia and Gondwana bloomed with vast forests ravaged by violent changes of climate. Then, lacerated by glaciers, torn by subterranean pressures caused by fluctuations in the Earth's magnetic-field, huge slabs of the crust cracked and slowly receded until they assumed their present shape.

The Ancients believed Earth's first civilisation began in the far North long before the Arctic ice, this realm of light and beauty was the Land of the Gods. The Chinese thought their Emperor derived his powers from the Dragon God at the Celestial North Pole, symbolism of a Space King. The Egyptians worshipped the Shining Ones who stood behind Osiris in the constellation of the Great Bear and pointed the Great Pyramid towards Alpha Draconis, then the Pole Star. Some Indians believed that the Aryans originally came from Sveta-dvipa, White Island, which they situated in the far North; the Vedas and the Mahabharata are said to contain astronomical data which can only be understood if it is assumed the observer was actually at the North Pole.

The Eskimos remembered the Shining Spirits from the North. The Sioux tell of an island in the North, cradle of their ancestors drowned by the waters. Ezekiel's famous Wheel descended from the North; Zeus and Mercury winged down to the Greeks from Mt. Olympus symbolising northern regions. Even today Father Christmas dwells in his Wonderland at the North Pole. Students of UFOs note that they usually appear first from the North, presumably through the polar-vents in the Van Allen radiation-belts around the Earth. Or perhaps from that subterranean civilisation of Agharta said to exist many miles beneath our feet. Long ago those tropical lands of the far North would surely attract the Spacemen as they approached Earth. Adepts teach that the North Pole now covered with ice was idyllic Eden, the cradle of humanity.

The second cycle of mankind lived in the circumpolar continent of Hyperborea, where people dwelled in perpetual sunshine amid fabulous splendour, visited by Apollo on his famous Arrow or in a chariot drawn by swans suggesting a spaceship. The Hyperboreans were said to be very tall with fair skin, light blue eyes and blond hair, an ideal Nordic type. Before the Flood the polar regions were hot since Earth probably rotated nearer the Sun on a perpendicular axis which abolished the seasons. Legends allege that the Hyperboreans were Extraterrestrials who colonised this part of Earth similar to their own original planet and became the first ancestors of the White Race. In the 6th century BC Hecateus wrote that the Hyperboreans worshipped Apollo in a wonderful round temple, often regarded as Stonehenge, suggesting that Hyperborea was actually Ancient Britain.

The Chinese writer, Li-Tse, recorded that white men from the North in contact with the Gods arrived in China. The Ancients called the capital of this wondrous Realm beyond the North Wind Thule,[101], evoking Tullan, the mythical origin of the Toltecs of Mexico, said to mean Land of the Sun. The Swastika, a sign used by ancient peoples world-wide, may denote the North Pole around which rotates the Earth. The polar-symbol of the fish signified Man's first home until later adopted by the Christians.[18]

Dim race-memories echo that titanic cataclysm which desolated those fair lands of the North. Legend tells how the Sun changed its course, a Comet or falling Moon displaced

Earth's axis ending a World Age; traditions of the Mayas and the Hindus even suggest some atomic war between the Gods of Hyperborea and the Magicians of Lemuria convulsing the entire planet to change the climate and cause an Ice Age. Around the Black Sea the Scythians,[179] Sons of the Hyperboreans, raised mysterious menhirs to their ancestors.

> 'Divine Kings descended and taught men sciences and arts for man could live no longer in the first land which had turned into a frozen corpse.'
>
> Book VI, 'Commentaries on the Book of Dzyan.'

The third race of Man was set on continents known as Lemuria in the present Indian Ocean and Mu in the Pacific extending northwards to the Himalayas, then bordering the great Asiatic inland sea, southward to Australia and the Antarctic, west to the Philippines. The first peoples of Lemuria were said to be Giants, bi-sexual beings. After millions of years they evolved into male and female. The stature of the Lemurians gradually decreased from twelve to about seven feet, they generally resembled our Red Indians though their skins had a bluish[181] tinge. In the centre of their prominent forehead projected a large lump like a walnut known as the Third Eye, evidence of highly developed psychic powers. Occult traditions say the Teachers from Venus revealed cosmic truths to Initiates in Lemuria, their sublime doctrines forming the secret wisdom of the East.

After long ages men became the colour of the rising sun, perfectly formed like Gods, women fair and graceful with psychic perceptions giving feminine insight transcending the logic of Science. Sex was considered a spiritual communion, marriage a most sacred bond, divorce unknown. Death meant ascension to nobler realms, the Lemurians could die when they so willed. Life for them was far from perfect, the world in which they dwelled was ravaged by cataclysms, volcanic eruptions racked their land, finally splitting it asunder down to the ocean depths. Some Lemurians probably returned with their Teachers to other planets and acquired a wondrous wisdom unattained by us today.

> 'They (the Lemurians) built huge cities. Of rare earths and metals they built. Out of the fires (lava) vomited. Out of the white stone of the

mountains (marble) and the black stone (of the subterranean fires) they cut their own images in their size and likeness and worshipped them.'

Stanzas of Dzyan.[17]

Revelations mainly from occult sources state that houses built of redwood were tall and rectangular with wide projecting roofs to cast maximum shade, since the brilliance and heat of the sun intensified by the warmth from the volcanic soil posed considerable problems to the Lemurians already troubled by earthquakes eroding their Empire of the Sun. Gigantic palaces and temples of unusually hard stone withstood the ravages of time, remains of the cyclopean buildings still sprawl in forlorn desolation in the wilds of the Americas, India and Asia, colonies of Lemuria not convulsed by the cataclysm. Gold and silver[35] were plentiful and used for ornamentation not for coinage, diamonds by their profusion being no more precious than glass. The most valuable adornments were rare brilliantly coloured feathers, so esteemed millennia later by the Aztecs in Mexico. The sunlit buildings gleamed amid luxuriant vegetation lining the spacious avenues, transportation was mainly by water. The Lemurians were renowned mariners[217] who founded settlements all over the Earth characterised by their cyclopean stonework. The peoples of this world-wide Empire spoke a common language, Mayax, root of Sumerian and Chinese.

When the Lemurian priests traced their mysterious signs on skins or stones they were in the habit of turning towards the South Pole, their hand went in the direction of the East, the source of light, accordingly they wrote from right to left. After the White race learned writing from the dark Lemurians instead of turning to the South they faced the North and continued to write towards the East.

Scientists probably inspired by Spacemen studied radionics based on solar and cosmic energies, bringing heat and light to homes and industries; their profound insight of jewels acquainted them with the astonishing properties of semi-conductors and laser-beams; the Lemurians were also noted for their cold light shining in lamps for centuries. Ships and aircraft were motivated by a form of nuclear-power, perhaps the cosmic energy of the Spaceships, a technique bequeathed to Ancient India. Colonel James Churchward who claimed to have studied the temple-records of former civilisations quotes a fascinating account of airships used by the Hindus about 20,000 years ago.[45]

When our oil wells run dry our scientists will no doubt utilise the cosmic forces known to the Lemurians represented by crosses, circles and swastikas depicted on ancient stones found in Yucatan and India. With such powers at their disposal the Lemurians enjoyed radionic inventions beyond our cognisance and probably learned from the Venusians the many medical and electronic techniques of Space-flight.

> 'Then with the mighty roar of swift descent from incalculable heights surrounded by blazing masses of fire which filled the sky with shooting-tongues of flame, the vessel of the Lords of the Flame flashed through the aerial spaces. It halted over the White Island which lay in the Gobi Sea. Green it was and radiant with the fairest blossoms as Earth offered her fairest and best to welcome her King.'[14]

This first description of space-flight probably dates from the days of Lemuria and concerns the descent of the Sanat Kumara, an Avatar from Venus with his four Great Lords and one hundred assistants to a city now buried beneath the sands of the Gobi Desert.[151] South American legends tell of a wonderful blonde, Orejona, who ages ago in a spaceship shining like gold, descended on the Island of the Sun in Lake Titicaca to bring civilisation to the Pre-Incas. Similar traditions of Gods and Goddesses in fiery chariots are cherished by ancient peoples everywhere.

Knowledge and power bring spiritual pride. The scientists of Lemuria delved into the occult arts until the White and Black Magicians[111] contended with titanic weapons to destroy their decadent civilisation. Asiatic traditions tell of Spaceships winging down from Mars and Venus to rescue the chosen, as millennia later Celestials were to save survivors from doomed Atlantis. Consumed by subterranean fires the shattered continent sank to the depths of the sea leaving the mountain-peaks of Mu to garland the Pacific Ocean with islands.[180] A chosen remnant of the Lemurian race took refuge upon its Western extremity under the leadership of a Manu or Divine Guide, from this point they were able to reach Atlantis, a green and verdant land which had recently emerged from the water. Other refugees migrated to America, India and China where they continued the Sun-culture of their drowned Motherland.

Stone tablets and cliff-sculptures in North and South America still show cosmic symbols characteristic of Mu. Around Mt Shasta in California live mystical Brotherhoods who claim descent from survivors of the lost continent.

The wisdom and sun-worship of Lemuria inspired by Celestials reached Europe first through Atlantis then later from India, Egypt and Babylon. The Naacals, holy brothers, are believed to have brought their secret doctrines from Mu to India about 70,000 BC. The Initiates founded cults in Upper Egypt and Sumer, where their wisdom inspired the Magi of Babylon, thus influencing the early Books of the Bible, religious heritage of the West.

Those tropical isles of the Pacific pose fascinating problems. The Polynesians of Malekula remember winged women who descended from the skies, the giant statues on Easter Island[97] suggest enigmas unsolved. In the Carolines the cyclopean ruins on Nan Matol conjure some grandiose civilisation inspired by beings in flying-machines. Aborigines in Australia remember a dream time, an idyllic age in the past. Their rock-paintings bear resemblance to the Tassili frescoes of Extraterrestrials in the Sahara and intriguing petroglyphs in the Andes. The Maoris of New Zealand tell of Gods on Magic birds flying down from lands in the sky to aid men on Earth.

CHAPTER FIVE
Atlantis

For countless generations Atlantis has evoked wonder in the hearts of men. Thousands of books have been written proving the reality of Atlantis, thousands more denying its existence. Can the minds of men down dusty ages be held captive by the same dream? Atlantis was immortalised by Plato born in Athens in 429 BC. In his declining years he taught philosophy and debated with Socrates the nature of Truth. With his famous pupil, Aristotle, this greatest of Athenians may be justly said to have civilised Europe.

Two centuries earlier his ancestor, the great lawgiver, Solon, Wisest of the Seven Sages, visited Egypt and conversed with the priests of Sais, noted for their knowledge of ancient times. Senehis, the venerable custodian of ancient manuscripts in the famous library of Alexandria, reproached Solon for knowing so little about his own country, stating that before the great deluge nine thousand years earlier Athens excelled all lands in greatness and valour. A mighty Power had landed on the Atlantic coast from an island west of the Pillars of Hercules, our modern Gibraltar. Now the island was called Atlantis and was the heart of a great empire, which had rule over the whole island and several others. They subjected Libya as far as Egypt and Europe as far as Tyrrhenia.[158] The priests told Solon that the Athenians smashed the Atlantean invasion saving Europe and North Africa. 'But afterwards there occurred violent earthquakes and floods and in a single day and night of rain all your warlike men in a body sank into the earth and the island of Atlantis in like manner disappeared beneath the sea.' The Egyptians revealed that the story was written on pillars still preserved. In 310 BC the Greek philosopher, Crantor, related that he had seen in Egypt a column bearing the history of that great island submerged in the ocean. Solon penned an unfinished epic poem, Atlantikos, based on papyri translated by the priests of Sais, before writing he checked all relevant traditions. His manuscript fascinated Plato who visited Egypt and verified the facts for his brilliant dialogues the Timaeus and the Critias.

It is significant that Plato called his wonderful island Atlante which is not a Greek word but evokes the Toltecs of Central America, where *atlan* means amid the water. A city named Atlan, with a good harbour, existed on the isthmus of Darien when Columbus discovered America, it is now an unimportant village, Aclo. The Aztecs claimed their ancestors originated from Aztlan, which they depicted on old Mexican drawings as an island with mountains encircled by concentric rings of walls and canals similar to the citadel of Plato's Atlantis. Plato resurrected a civilisation quite different from his own day, resembling the Bronze Age in Western Europe and the sun-cultures of Mexico and Peru unknown to Athens. In old Peruvian Atlantis is said to have meant eastern copper land.[92]

The story of Atlantis was revealed by Plato in wonderful dialogues wherein Timaeus from Locris in Southern Italy, Critias, distinguished as an orator, poet and dramatist, Hermocrates, leader of the Syracusan forces against the Athenian expedition, and Socrates, and presumably Plato himself, discoursed about the lost continent. Critias states that in the centre of Atlantis there were fertile plains, surrounded by lofty mountains, decked with prosperous villages, lakes, rivers and meadows, a fruitful reserve with many animals wild and tame. Sailors from Atlantis sailed the western world and built a great empire dominating the coasts of Europe and the Mediterranean. The enterprising Atlanteans provided spacious harbours for their merchant fleets and constructed broad concentric canals linked by bridges leading to the citadel. The massive outside wall was entirely covered with tin, the innermost surrounding the citadel flashed with the reddish gleam of orichalcum, probably an alloy of copper. The magnificent buildings of immense stones coloured white, black and red, set amid fountains and luxuriant trees were eclipsed by the great temple dedicated to Poseidon and Cleito, covered with silver and orichalcum, its pinnacles gleaming in gold. Plato's work continues with a factual description of the civil administration under its ten Kings, the army, navy and Poseidon-worship. Suddenly the account stops, as if the last scroll were lost, leaving us in suspense.

Socrates says little about Atlantis. Strange, for like most Athenians, he must have heard the story many times. Senehis, the High Priest, probably quoted from the archives in the magnificent library at Alexandria, surely visited by Plato during his stay in Egypt. One of the greatest tragedies of Antiquity was the burning of most of the manuscripts accidentally by Julius Caesar in 48 BC during his dalliance with Cleopatra; the library was finally destroyed by Amron, Lieutenant of the Caliph Omar in AD 651. Plato's own manuscripts nearly suffered a similar fate in AD 1453 when Constantinople was sacked by the Turks. Fortunately a copy of the Critias, like the famous Piri Reis maps, was salved by scholars, otherwise our knowledge of Atlantis would have been almost lost. Heinrich Schliemann claimed to have discovered amid the ruins of Troy bronze vases engraved in Phoenician signs signifying 'From King Chronos of Atlantis', unfortunately his enthusiasm sometimes distorted facts; a similar red vase is said to have been found at Tiahuanaco, high in the Andes now but in the days of Atlantis possibly a sea-port.

References to Atlantis exist in many countries, all supporting Solon's story. Hieroglyphics on the Mexican pyramid at Xochicalco are deciphered as referring to 'a land sited in the middle of the ocean, destroyed and disappeared.' Brolio, the Brazilian philologist, in 1930 translated this ancient pre-Mayan fragment 'On the eleventh day Ahau Katun (indication of the year and month according to the calendar of the epoch) the disaster occurred; there was a most violent windfall, cinders fell from the sky, the sky fell down, the land plunged downwards and the Great Mother (Atlantis) was among the records of the destruction of the world.'[130] The Chinese cherished traditions of an island called Maligasama, destroyed owing to the evil of its giants. The Hindu Puranas describe wars on the continents situated beyond Western Africa in the Atlantic Ocean. Marcellus wrote a history of Ethiopia wherein he mentioned the great island of Atlantis destroyed in ancient times by a violent storm.

Claudius Aelianus writing his Variae Historiae in the second century AD, tells of Silenus, a Satyr, believed by some scholars as being possibly a Red Indian, who revealed to Midas, King of Phrygia the wonders of an unknown continent in the West. A description suggesting America with its vast prairies. Silenus said that ten million men crossed the ocean to invade Western Europe. This incredible invasion is supported by the Alexandrine historian, Timagenes, and the erudite Diodorus Siculus who writes of warlike giants from the Western Ocean landing on the Atlantic coast, a tradition confirmed by Dionysius of Halicarnassus alleging that Hercules led a vast force from Erytheia, Red Island to storm Spain and Italy.

For many centuries scholars wondered whether the story of Atlantis was meant by Plato to be a 'morality' like Sir Thomas More's Utopia, though the moral lesson remains obscure; today some students irreverently applaud Plato as. the first writer of Science-Fiction.

Plato's terse, realistic account of Atlantis contrasts starkly with his elegant fancies and philosophies so that many feel this famous tale must have some truth. In our own short lifetimes we hear of small islands thrust up from the deep and others suddenly submerged by volcanoes. Disposed though we are to believe the Critias our confidence becomes confused by experts who situate Atlantis in South America, Sweden, Palestine, North Africa, Cyprus or Spain, each with plausible argument, all forgetting that Plato clearly sites the island west of the Pillars of Hercules.

Last century Ignatius J. Donnelly, Member of Congress for Minnesota, after intense research into the truth of Plato's Timaeus and Critias, published in 1882 Atlantis, 'The Antediluvian World which may be said to have founded Atlantology, and is still recognised by students world-wide as the authoritative work on the lost continent. Donnelly's encyclopaedic mind marshalled a voluminous mass of material from both sides of the Atlantic showing obvious similarities of language, customs and culture, identical plants and animals on shores East and West, which suggest an island bridge must surely have existed long ago, since destroyed. Lewis Spence in an analysis of Celtic legends and American folk-lore offered valuable support to Donnelly's findings. His studies seemed to prove that Britain was an outpost of the Atlantean Empire, which could be true.

Ancient traditions tell of the days when our world had no Moon. About 20,000 BC a wandering planet, Luna, approached the Earth raising huge tidal-waves, then receded to approach again. The threatened peoples turned to moon-worship to propitiate the Moon. Finally about 10,000 BC Luna came too close and was caught in the Earth's gravity drawing immense tides from north and south to engulf doomed Atlantis. Professor Ludwig Zeidler of Poland believes the destruction of Atlantis was caused by a large cosmic body which struck our Earth about 12,000 years ago shifting it 23 degrees on its axis. The sudden change froze solid mammoths feeding on the prairies of Siberia.

The secret wisdom of Antiquity alleged that a million years ago at the zenith of its brilliance the continent of Atlantis extended from Iceland down to South America, maps still exist purporting to show how, due to volcanic cataclysms in 800,000 BC and 200,000 BC, the land became reduced to two islands Ruta and Daitya. A later convulsion about 80,000 BC left only part of Ruta above the waves, known as Poseidonis, said to have been finally submerged in 9564 BC.

Early inhabitants, the Rmoahals, black-skinned giants, roamed the dense forests contending with gigantic animals; thousands of years afterwards the Tlavatlis, a shorter, reddish-brown race, settled mainly among the mountains. The classical Atlanteans, the Toltecs, originated around modern Mexico. They were a magnificent copper-coloured people eight feet tall, but through the ages their stature diminished. Their noble features resembled the ancient Greeks. It is said that the psychic faculties of the Atlanteans were highly developed, many Adepts attained lofty spiritual and mental powers raising their world-wide civilisation to a glorious Golden Age before misuse of occult powers brought decadence and destruction.

A few rare Sensitives can recall most ancient memories, others in hypnosis, dreams or psychic shock, live again their pains and passions talking in tongues of forgotten lands when the world was young. In sudden moments of precognition we see the future, some people claim powers of retrocognition, in a state of trance they apparently regress through time and view scenes in the remote past. Rudolf Steiner, a disciple of the great German philosopher-poet, Johann Wolfgang von Goethe, author of Faust, penned a detailed history of Atlantis describing the conflict between the Spiritual Beings and the Luciferians, the White and Black Magicians, whose perversion of occult forces brought cataclysms to Atlantis. Foreseeing their doom Initiates escaped to inspire the civilisations of Egypt, Chaldea and the Americas.

Interest in Atlantis was revived a hundred years ago by Helena Petrovna Blavatsky born in 1831 at Ekaterrinoslav in Russia of a noble family. After an early unhappy marriage she travelled extensively all over the East seeking mystics in India and Tibet who imparted the Ancient Wisdom. This knowledge she resurrected for the Western World in her memorable works Isis Unveiled and The Secret Doctrine. In 1875 Madame H.P. Blavatsky with Colonel H. Olcott founded the Theosophical Society which has world-wide influence today.

The cosmic religion taught that the Lords of the Flame from Venus, who ages earlier had brought civilisation to Lemuria, again descended to aid Atlantis ruling as a dynasty of divine Kings, remembered in legends all over the world. Belief in the divinity of Kings has persisted in human consciousness almost down to our own days; traditions among all peoples associate blue blood and imperial purple with Royalty implying that the first Kings really had blue blood, their countenance tinged with purple denoting oxygen-deficiency since they had descended from a planet whose atmosphere contained less oxygen that Earth's. The Venusians radiated a golden aura perceptible to the psychic Atlanteans, later people perpetuated this halo in the crown of Kings. As inferred in Genesis the Spacemen consorted with the daughters of men and begat giants; the early Atlanteans were of great stature. There is reason to believe that Noah and his family were red-skinned giants who fled from the flood engulfing Atlantis.

In 1883-4 near mystic Mt. Shasta in California, Frederick Spencer Oliver, an ignorant youth of eighteen, sensed the inspiration of an entity called Phylos the Thibetan, who taught him by mental talks. He then dictated his fascinating autobiography A Dweller on Two Planets[153] narrating his adventures in Atlantis and on Venus. Sometimes this young scribe would cover eighty letter-size sheets a night penned by lamplight, often in darkness; oddly enough much of the work was written backwards, the sentences rightly last coming first, so fast and mixed that Oliver made little sense of it. Phylos had this erratic script revised twice; some time later he dictated the sequel An Earth-Dweller's Return,[154] describing his incarnations in Lemuria and Atlantis. In archaic language this amazing work depicts with wonderful detail the glory of Atlantis, its laws, religion and way of life, the Golden Age and the decadence which doomed that great continent.

Our modern minds are fascinated by their inventions, space-travel by anti-gravity, television, transmutation of metals, conveyance of heat and power without wires, electric-odic powered cars, airships, brain-washing by magnetism, sidereal death-rays and electron-telescopes. All this vividly described through the pen of a country-boy amid the wilds of America in 1884 long before he saw a motor-car!

On March 18 1877 on a farm near Hopkinville, Kentucky, was born a most remarkable boy, Edgar Cayce, whose perceptions seemed more than normal. Occasionally he was able to catch glimpses of realms beyond our ordinary everyday world. At twenty-one paralysis afflicted his throat muscles threatening loss of voice; doctors could find no cure. As a last resort Edgar succeeded in entering a self-induced trance, he diagnosed his difficulty and on awakening soon banished the affliction. Local physicians sought his assistance, in a state of trance he would attune to their patient's mind and body and ascertain their trouble. Sufferers all over the country solicited his aid. When Edgar Cayce died on January 3 1945 he left almost 15,000 telepathic-clairvoyant statements he had given for more than 8,000 different people over a period of 43 years. These psychic-readings of the Sleeping Prophet embrace the fields of psychology, para-psychology, philosophy, religion, history, prehistory and medicine. Many of his cures are inexplicable, only now in retrospect can we fully appreciate his amazing powers, which he insisted lie dormant in each one of us waiting to be developed.

Edgar Cayce, a country youth, had little education; he had never read the Critias of Plato nor the revelations of Phylos. It is surely significant that when unconscious he should mention Atlantis in the middle of the Atlantic Ocean and describe its electrical technology in almost the same terms as the Thibetan many years earlier. Atlanteans travelled through the air, under the seas, photographed objects at a distance, utilized X-rays, recorded sounds and sights on video-tape, obtained laser-like powers from crystals, devised a terrible weapon from cosmic rays and apparently discovered anti-gravity propulsion. The Firestone, from which Initiates produced power from fusion or fission with radio-active forces, was detailed by the Sleeping Prophet in 1933 twelve years before the explosion of the first atomic-bomb. Misuse of the dark forces of Nature by arrogant Priests and increasing volcanic eruptions accelerated the shattering of the continent into many islands which through several millennia submerged, until about 10,000 BC Poseidonis convulsed by earthquakes sank in flames. Cayce vividly describes how Initiates foreseeing the catastrophe migrated to Egypt in the East and America in the West to continue the Atlantean civilisation. We believe Cayce's other revelations proved to be true, may we not accept his descriptions of Atlantis?

About fifty years ago Colonel Peter Harrison Fawcett convinced that ancient cities, illumined with an ever-burning light linked with Atlantis, were lost in the Matto Grosso, ventured with his son, Jack, and their friend, Raleigh Rimmel, into the Brazilian jungle. They reached Dead Horse Camp deep in the interior on May 29 1925 and presumably were captured by Jivara headhunters; rescue-expeditions failed to find them. During the 1930s British mediums claimed occasional telepathic messages, allegedly from Colonel Fawcett, who had always showed interest in extra-sensory perception. Apparently his son and friend had been killed by arrows, he was prisoner of an Indian tribe. In 1935 Miss Geraldine Cummins, a most gifted medium, while in semitrance found her hand writing automatically a fascinating communication apparently emanating from the aged Colonel amid the Amazon jungle.[4] Fawcett revealed that due to the ministrations of Pythea, an Indian priestess, whom he might be forced to marry, by means of certain herbs he was able in dreams to travel down the stairways of Time back to Atlantis.

With wondrous revelation Fawcett described a newly-built pyramid in a gleaming white city adorned with mighty temples, gaudy palaces, painted tombs, thronged by white-clad crowds not unlike Egyptians. He moved among them, watched the people at work, attended their religious ceremonies and feasts, even the court of Pharaoh. The Colonel confirmed that the Atlantean civilisation was founded on sun-worship and motivated by blast-electricity, electrified air, utilised for industry, heating, lighting, healing, moving immense stones and for warfare. Storage batteries were buried in great underground reservoirs which ultimately exploded destroying Atlantis in titanic cataclysm submerging thousands of miles and thrusting new countries up from the sea. After thirteen years silence in December 1948 a final message was received, this time from far beyond Earth itself. Fawcett revealed that one morning the Chief entered his hut resolved on the Colonel's marriage to Pythea, which neither of the pair wanted. Colonel Fawcett, a man of honour, drew his knife and plunged it into his own heart.

Such occult revelations strain our understanding, our conditioned minds so ill-attuned to psychic phenomena cannot comprehend transmission of knowledge beyond our experience, it is exceedingly doubtful whether we could have explained to our grandfathers, however clever, the principles of television dominating our lives today. The vivid descriptions of Atlantis by Colonel Fawcett were not subjective dreams by him alone but repeat the revelations of Phylos the Thibetan, Edgar Cayce and many other Psychics of all ages with a mutual agreement almost constituting scientific proof.

Atlantis was ruled by its Priest-King in a theocracy dominating every aspect of life, a social system continued in ancient Egypt and Peru persisting until the last decade in Tibet. The cosmic religion taught resurrection in astral realms long before Christianity and reincarnation inspiring men in the East, now spreading among people in the West. The priests practised psychism like our modern spiritualists, certain Sensitives foretold the future, others studied people's auras to diagnose and cure disease, radionic and colour-healings resembled spiritual and psychiatric techniques adopted today. Atlantean technology was not based on the utilisation of coal, steam or oil. Science used vibratory forces,[137] sound or resonance and somehow syphoned static-electricity for transport, industrial or military use and apparently unlocked the energy within the atom mingled with cosmic-rays by techniques still unknown to us.

The Atlanteans probably developed electronic even telepathic techniques, radio, radar, television, for communicating with their armed forces, far-flung Empire and the near planets, abode of their Teachers. The priest-scientists, more advanced than our own physicists, discovered the terrible sideral force called mash-mak or vril, etheric vibrations of fantastic power blasting armies to annihilation. The airships of Atlantis were constructed of thin wood or electrically welded alloys lighter than aluminium and propelled by etheric force generated in a strong heavy metal chest suggesting a nuclear-reactor. Manuscripts in Sanskrit from old India describe vimanas, spacecraft which could travel from planet to planet, probably inherited from the Atlanteans who must surely have mastered the problems of Space-flight, since legends tell of constant communication with the stars. Although Genesis does not mention Atlantis, The Book of Enoch suggests that Enoch, taken to the skies by Extraterrestrials, was probably an Atlantean like his great-grandson, Noah.

The Golden Age of Atlantis lasted for thousands of years bringing great beneficence to all Earth. Then the Atlanteans delved into the dark side of Nature; maleficent Adepts conjured Elementals, evil thought-forms like the Tulkus materialised by the Tibetan magicians.[56] They summoned Spirits from lower astral realms to work their will and appeased sinister Powers by blood-stained rituals degenerating to human sacrifice and murder. Cosmic Masters[111] reveal the titanic mental battle on Atlantis between the White Magicians and their Black adversaries. Atomic war broke out in all its horror convulsing Atlantis in radio-active ruins down to the sea-bed. The destruction of the doomed continent and the rescue of the Illumined by Spaceships from Venus and Mars are wonderfully described in those ancient Stanzas of Dzyan revealed in The Secret Doctrine.

'And the "great king of the dazzling face", the chief of all the yellow-faced was sad, seeing the sins of the black-faced ... He sent his air-vehicles (vimanas) to all his brother-chiefs with pious men within saying "Prepare, arise ye men of the good law, and cross the land while (yet) dry."

'The lords of the storm are approaching. Their chariots are nearing the land. One night and two days only shall the lords of the dark face (the sorcerers) live on this patient land. She is doomed, and they have to descend with her. The nether-lords of the dark eye are preparing their magic Agneyastra. But the Lords of the dark eye are stronger than they (the elementals) and they are the slaves of the mighty ones. They are versed in Ashtar (Vidya – the highest magical knowledge) Come and use yours.

'Let every lord of the dazzling face cause the Vimana of every lord of the dark face to come into his hands, lest any (sorcerers) should by its means escape from the waters, avoid the rest of the four (karmic deities) and save his wicked (followers or people).'

The great king fell upon his dazzling face and wept. When the kings assembled, the waters had already moved ... but the nations had now crossed the dry land. They were beyond the watermark. The kings had reached them in their vimanas and led them on to the lands of fire and metal (East and North) ... Stars (nuclear-missiles?) showered on the lands of the black faces but they slept. The speaking-beasts (radio?) kept quiet. The nether-lords waited for orders but they came not for their masters slept. The waters arose and covered the valleys from one end of the Earth to the other. High lands remained, the bottom of Earth remained dry. There dwelt those who occupied, the men of the yellow face and of the straight eye. When the lords of the dark face awoke and bethought themselves of their vimanas in order to escape from the rising waters, they found them gone.'[17]

Surely the Atlantis cataclysm was recalled by Jesus as He sat on the Mount of Olives telling his disciples of Judgement Day, when the Sun and Moon shall be darkened, stars fall from the sky. The Son of Man shall come in the clouds with great power and glory. He shall send His Angels to gather the Elect from the four winds from the uttermost part of heaven.[132]

Edgar Cayce prophesied the convulsion of our own decadent civilisation and the re-emergence of Atlantis later this century, also the prophecy of Mrs Jean Dixon, the noted

American seer. Plato's Critias and the revelations from occult sources vastly differ in substance but may nevertheless describe the same event. Such evidence fails to satisfy completely our science-conditioned minds, consideration must be given to some proof more convincing.

Although the Atlantean invasion of Europe is not recorded in the few ancient manuscripts now left to us, physical proof may perhaps be established by the sudden appearance on western shores of the magnificent Cro-Magnon Man, whose impressive broad and lofty forehead, splendid cranial capacity and tall stature made him equal, if not superior, to Homo Sapiens today. About 10,000 BC this remarkable being, far more advanced than the brutish Neanderthal Man, suddenly arrived in south-west Europe as from another planet, more probably from lost Atlantis. The marvellous paintings adorning the caves in Altamira and the Dordogne show the artists had imaginative vitality and a delicacy of line revealing an exquisite, aesthetic sense requiring age-long development. The Cro-Magnons in facial contours strongly resembled the Red Indians and employed many of the same religious and social practices, apparently believing in reincarnation, worshipping the Sun and Gods in the sky; many cosmic symbols, circles and figures featured in cave-drawings are now judged to signify Spacemen. The Basque language of the Pyrenees, totally isolated from the Indo-European tongues of prest-day Europe, has intriguing grammatical affinities with Red Indian dialects spoken on the opposite shores of America suggesting a common origin midway in Atlantis. Irish annals declare that the warlike Formorians colonised Ireland before the Flood, the Celts are believed to have inherited their stature, colouring and occult powers from their Atlantean ancestors when Britain fringed the Atlantean Empire.

Every four years swarms of lemmings, small rodents, leave the mountains of Scandinavia and in an incredible death-march cross Sweden and Norway, no obstacle can stop them, on they move finally to throw themselves over the cliffs to drown in the sea. Lapplanders believe that in this mysterious mass-migration lemmings are seeking their original home in Atlantis.

It must be admitted that many anthropologists still deny

the existence of Atlantis and claim that Cro-Magnon Man originated from the Middle East. The brilliant palaeo-linguist, Ugo Plez, in his fascinating work La Preistoria che vive[160] states that Neanderthal Man during the protracted cold for thousands of years had become perfectly adapted to the glaciation and had evolved the high Moustarian culture. When the Ice Age finished the snows were followed by uninterrupted rains. The snow melted transforming a great part of Europe into a swamp. Owing to the melting of the ice, the level of the sea rose submerging part of the Atlantic coast already inhabited by the Neanderthals and the Sun shone still more scorching. Thus was born the myth of the submerged continent and the impression that it was due to a kind of divine curse for having abused the magic arts which were related to sun-worship. Ugo Plez claims that the Cro-Magnons from the Middle-East destroyed the Neanderthal civilisation and developed their own immensely superior culture, continuing to tell of the legend of the lost continent where dwelled their predecessors. The Cro-Magnon race survived until recently among the Guanches, ancient inhabitants of the Canary Isles and today among the Berbers of North Africa. Though the learned Ugo Plez insists they originated in the Middle East, geography suggests their ancestors could have fled from Atlantis. When great experts disagree, what can lesser mortals say?

In 1945 Richard S. Shaver, a Pennsylvania war-plant welder, told a fantastic tale claiming twenty years occasional contact with an underground race of Deros, descendants of the Titans and Atlans who fled down to gigantic caves when Atlantis was destroyed about 12,000 years ago.

The Soviet scientist, N. Zirov, believes the Atlantic land-mass barred the warm Gulf Stream from the coasts of Europe, then covered with ice; samples recently drawn from the Mid-Atlantic Ridge on the western side show ordinary oceanic mud, those from the eastern revealed glacial origin, evidently transported by icebergs. After the submergence of Atlantis the warm current from South America washed Western Europe and banished the Ice Age about 10,000 BC confirmed by our climatologists. In 1913 Pierre Termier dredged a piece of tachylite, lava evidently formed in the atmosphere above sea-level, later diatoms of algae were discovered native to freshwater lakes. The Americans dredged from a submerged peak numerous strange calcareous discs 15 cms in diameter and 4 cms thick, partly smooth, partly rough, with a central hole, apparently artificial; radio-carbon tests showed them to have been formed above the surface about 12,000 years ago. Dimitri Ribikoff and the archaeologist, J. Manson Valentine, have discovered a submerged city off the island of Bimini, the Bahamas; experts from Miami date the fortifications to about ten thousand years ago. Russian geologists apparently prove that Atlantis was doomed by its own rock-structure of unstable basalt which eventually subsided into the sea.

CHAPTER SIX
Ancient America

Geologists believe that violent fluctuations in our Earth's magnetic-field and collisions with cosmic bodies have more than once shifted our planet's axis and displaced the Poles causing the Sun to rise apparently in the West and set in the East, as the Egyptian Priests told Herodotus. Today it is not too fantastic to suggest that the devastation of North America could have been caused by the Atlanteans blasting the continent with nuclear-bombs. Immanuel Velikovsky[206] and Ignatius Donnelly[61] both prove that some comet must have scourged America changing its very geography making lands seas, seas into land, smashing cities, killing countless people, and rendering whole animal species such as elephants and horses totally extinct. Immense earthquakes drained the Amazon Sea into swamps for future jungle and elevating the Andes, a cataclysm attributed to the capture of our present Moon.[11]

The American section of Earth's crust is a notorious fault-zone, for millions of years earthquakes have ravaged the area, some geologists prophesy widespread destruction this century. For thousands of years the Lemurians had close links with South America whose vast Amazon inland-sea and canals led to the Atlantic. The Grand Canyon of Colorado suggests that some cataclysm once convulsed the region. The vast number of oval craters or bays thickly scattered over the coast of Carolina and more sparsely from New Jersey to Florida imply meteoric impact over a very wide area.[206] Legends reveal that the Red Indians may be descendants of survivors who had taken refuge in caverns deep underground from cosmic bombardment which shattered the eastern seabord, charts of the continental shelf show vast submergence. In the Municipal Library at Nancy, France, was a globe in brilliant colour, many centuries old, which mapped the whole continent of North and South America apparently in prehistoric times with startling difference from today. It showed California now a peninsula as an island, possibly the eastern edge of submerged Lemuria, sea-shells found in the soil prove that long ago California was separated from the mainland. Traditions teach that California is the most civilised land on Earth, full of mysteries, it is said to owe its name to the beautiful Queen Califa who long ago ruled this romantic golden island near to the Garden of Eden.[35] Why does Los Angeles mean The Angels or The Spacemen? Does some mystic Power from the skies still inspire this land of many strange cults? The story of Queen Califa and her wonderful island in the West was sung by troubadours in Spain during the Crusades.

Hundreds of rock-writings in the southern States confirm signs of great civilisations in areas now desolate but remembered in local legends. There appears positive proof that the whole of western North America was peopled by highly civilised races during the latter part of the Tertiary era and before the geological glacial period. In the early sixteenth century Piri Reis, a famous Turkish admiral wrote his memoirs, Bahriya, the Book of the Sea; he claimed to possess about twenty secret and most ancient maps, one actually made by Columbus himself. Piri Reis states that Columbus knew precisely where he was going and was inspired by an ancient book which dated from Alexander the Great and depicted the Mare Tenebrosum, Sea of Darkness, bounded by islands in the West.

Two maps of the world drawn by Piri Reis, one in 1513, the other in 1528, on coloured parchment adorned with fascinating sketches of strange peoples, monsters and ships, annotated in elegant Turkish script, give precise delineations of North and South America. Most astounding of all, an ice-free Antarctica. The maps do not show Atlantis and before the glaciation of Antarctica, perhaps between 10,000 BC and 8,000BC, the versions by Piri Reis were lost in the Topkapi

Palace Museum at Istanbul until 1929 when they were found by M.B. Habil Eldem, a Museum Director.

In 1953, a copy was presented to the United States Hydrographical Bureau where it was studied by Arlington H. Mallery and J. Walters, specialists in ancient maps, and later by Professor Charles Hapgood. After years of research and consideration of world-wide legends Professor Hapgood published his findings in Maps of the ancient Sea-Kings, Evidence of advanced Civilisations. He concluded that these maps were made by a highly-cultured people whose civilisation was destroyed about ten thousand years ago by a cataclysm displacing the Earth's axis. The Piri Reis Map depicted the Andes with llamas, animals then unknown to Europe, and mountains in now frozen Canada, only recently discovered. Such landmarks far from the sea could be mapped only from the air, the world must surely have been surveyed by aircraft or Spaceships?

Our Earth is said to be 4,500 million years old, possibly much older. If our planet was originally colonised by Spacemen they would approach through the northern polar-gap in the Van Allen radiation-belt and allow for terrestrial rotation landing in the West like most Spaceships today, therefore occupying America first. The Indians and Aztecs agreed with the Hindus, Greeks and Scandinavians that four previous World Ages had flourished and been destroyed, the present fifth was destined for destruction. The existence of a world-wide civilisation destroyed long ago may be established by many signs insignificant perhaps in isolation but which together form a mosaic depicting a brilliant, tragic culture in ages past.

In North America lonely pillars of stone standing forlorn, strange symbols carved on remote cliffs, are visible witness to that past. More subtle proof might exist beyond our present knowledge. No literature survives from ancient America, the 'Popol Vuh' from Guatemala, the Aztec codices and Mayan stone-glyphs, are comparatively recent, they probably copy older records. Legends from Canada to Patagonia tell substantially the same stories which our modern minds may misinterpret.

Anthropologists once believed that America was

uninhabited almost to historical times, then about 20,000 BC Asiatic nomads crossed the Bering Straits and slowly wandered down from the Arctic to South America, but fossils and metallic objects prove that the continent was peopled by highly-civilised races long before the Ice Age. The Scientific American, 7-298, stated that about the first of June 1851, a powerful blast near Dorchester, Mass, cast out from a bed of solid rock a bell-shaped vessel of unknown metal, with floral designs inlaid with silver.[74] In Morrisonville, Illinois, the Times, June 11th 1891, described how Mrs S.V. Culp breaking a lump of coal was surprised to find embedded inside a small gold chain about ten inches long of antique and quaint workmanship,[103] evoking that block of almost pure cast-iron found inside coal from an Austrian mine in 1885. How did these manufactured articles come to be enclosed within coal hundreds of feet underground? Were they lost in Carboniferous times before the trees became compressed into coal. At Cow Canyon, Nevada, is the imprint of a human foot stamped in the clay of the Tertiary Era like that calcined footprint found by the Chinese palaeontologist, Chou-Ming-Chen, in the Gobi Desert. Alabama and Kentucky abound with pebble tools possibly two million years old.

At Acambara,[103] Mexico, in July 1945 Waldeman Julsrud found some curious pottery-fragments and during the next few years collected about 30,000 pieces, some apparently representing dinosaurs and pleisiosaurs extinct 70,000,000 years ago. Others such as the woolly rhinoceros, horses, camels, elephants, which died out on the American continent about 10,000 BC. These amazing figurines were carefully examined by Professor Charles Hapgood and Ivan T. Sanderson, both renowned experts, who were baffled by their fantastic antiquity confounding all accepted theories of the archaeologists. Fake, though not impossible, in the local circumstances seemed improbable. Carbon-14 tests gave dates ranging from 1110 BC to 4530 BC, thermo-luminescence from 2400 BC to 2700 BC, such methods cannot be wholly reliable, whatever scientists may say.

The suggestion that the ancient Mexicans met prehistoric dinosaurs outrages our conditioned commonsense until we recall that the Zuni Indians have race-memories of reptilian monsters. A tyrannosaurus-rex with something in its front paws, perhaps a man, was drawn on a rock in Ingo County; this drawing could be the oldest work of Man upon this planet. A remarkable petroglyph of a dinosaur standing erect on his powerful tail with huge open jaws was found in the Grand Canyon. Dinosaurs were swamp-dwellers. Scientists assert that this canyon had not been under water for forty million years, iron seeping from the stones had formed a protective covering, impressive evidence of immense age. In California and Arizona skeletons of giants twelve feet tall having six toes have been unearthed suggesting visitors from another planet or a most ancient race of Man millions of years ago. Stone carvings in a Peruvian Temple of the Wind in the Casma Valley depict dancers with six fingers on each hand. At Bear Creek, Montana, in November 1926 miners of the Number Three Eagle Coal Mine discovered two huge human molars belonging to a giant in strata at least thirty million years old when dinosaurs were still roaming the Wyoming swamps.[67]

Prehistorians reluctant to credit immense age to the first Americans now accept traces of Sandia Man 50,000 years old and were persuaded by the late Dr Louis Leakey that small pieces of stone unearthed in the Mojave Desert of Southern California show that Man lived there probably 100,000 years ago, supporting Professor R.W. Gilder who discovered in Nebraska and Kentucky traces of a most ancient civilisation suddenly destroyed by the Great Ice Age.

Across the central and southern States run chains of mounds similar to those pyramids of Egypt and Mexico. Oriented so that their sides corresponded precisely with the cardinal points of the compass, these tumuli form immense circles and squares, pentagons and octagons of giant dimensions, almost unrecognisable at ground level but perfect geometrical figures when viewed from the air, evoking those strange lines at Nazca and curious figures at Marcahuasi in the Andes now believed to signify surveillance by Spacemen. In some of these artificial hillocks are found copper and lead axes, bracelets, rings, silver ornaments, oxydised iron and steel necessitating advanced metallurgy. Were these mounds fortifications against unknown invaders or, like those cyclopean fortresses in the Andes, defences perhaps against hostile Celestials from the skies?

Legends of a White God roaming North and South America teaching and healing people suggest Spacemen from the stars but they could have been Cretan missionaries from brilliant Knossos who reached America about 2000 BC. All Red Indians may not be Mongol in origin as the anthropologists insist, many are possibly Atlanteans. There is definite proof that the Amerindians are descended from northern Europeans,[39] probably Celts, having links with the Druids and, it is said, with the Space Gods.

The Red Indians beneath their superstitions preserved remnants of most ancient wisdom. Medicine-men taught that their ancestors descended from the Sun to the Moon, then to Earth, they were destroyed and re-created after the great Flood, many Chiefs believed in reincarnation, life after death, evidence of a profound theology inherited from some old civilisation or from Spacemen. The Quichés of Guatemala revered their first forefathers as sorcerers and wizards with boundless knowledge who examined the round face of our own Earth apparently from Space.

In her book The Ancient Atlantic Lucille Taylor-Hansen watching the Apaches in Arizona dancing with tridents on their heads describes her amazement at the ceremony similar to the trident dance of the Tuaregs in the distant mountains of North Africa. The whirling dancers, their arm-daggers, the breast-embroidery of the planet, Venus, the headpiece with a tuft of feathers on top, all symbolised lost Atlantis. The Chief told how long ago their ancestors lived in the old red-land amid a great empire destroyed by the Fire God. Survivors fled across the sea to Peru and built cities on mountain-tops. In a later cataclysm 'the oceans ran away', the various clans escaped through caves and eventually migrated northwards to Arizona.

All over North America Indians worshipped Supernatural Beings in the skies. Mysterious white strangers suddenly appeared to teach or punish mankind like those Gods descending to India and Greece or Jehovah and his Angels admonishing the Israelites. The bravest warrior never dared to climb mountains beyond the snow-line dreading lest he met the Gods face to face, a sacred taboo world-wide. The Quaillayutes believed in the Thunderbird which in times of famine brought them food, the Dakotas prayed to the watchful Sky Father, the Blackfeet thought every star a human being, meaning perhaps Spacemen. Many tribes boasted of their ancestors climbing ladders of arrows to attack the Sky People evoking that war between the Gods and the Giants.

In this land of scientific marvels, it seems crazy to mention American Aborigines, Stone Age Man, still surviving lost in the backwoods and the lofty Rockies like those Yeti haunting the Himalayas. Yet bizarre encounters with such fearsome if sadly forlorn primitives incredibly suggest that a parallel race of forgotten sub-humans does exist on the fringe of our modern society. Eskimo myths down the centuries tell of the Tornit,[49] stupid Giants who shamble from the shadows to steal food, even women; cannibals savouring human flesh, feared under many names by most tribes everywhere. Today sober tourists in mountains and wilderness catch glimpses of monsters called Sasquatch. Horrific tales of savage attacks must be believed. Fantastic though it may seem, could such degenerate creatures be descendants of a few survivors from that nuclear holocaust supposed to have shattered the fair North long ago causing an Ice Age? Mutants from radiation-bombs? Victims of some ancient Hiroshima?

Although the Indians lack written literature their vast folklore teems with occult tales rivalling those transcendental legends of Tibet. Charming stories tell of Wondrous Beings winging down from Venus and the Pleiades to marry mortals, then returning to the skies, recalling celestial romances in so many countries, some must surely be true.

The Chippeways[188] tell of Algon, a hunter, who walking on the prairie discovered a circular pathway worn by many feet. He hid in the long grass and hearing the sound of music growing louder and louder he beheld high in the air on osier car in which were seated twelve beautiful maidens. All descended into the magic ring and danced round with such grace that Algon fell in love with the youngest. She eluded him and rushed to the car, soon all soared whence they came. Next day she returned, they married and had a son. The star-maiden pined for her own land. One day she made a basket, sang the magic song and returned with the child to the skies. For years Algon mourned bitterly beside the magic circle. At last he was overjoyed to see his wife and son descend, and gladly returned with them to the stars.

Hiawatha, immortalised in Longfellow's poem, taught the Six Nations agriculture and the arts of peace. His mission complete, he soared towards the sunset in a magic canoe which moved with the melodious sound of music. Tribal legends tell of a White Prophet, bearded and pale of feature, with grey eyes, copper-coloured hair. Arrayed in long white robe, wearing golden sandals, he wrought wonders in Georgia, Oklahoma, Mississippi, Dakotah, Wyoming and Mexico, where he was worshipped as Quetzalcoatl.[91]

Indian customs appear to perpetuate the far past. Braves and squaws deck their heads with feathers, probably to imitate the antennae of Spacemen. The ceramic patterns on some Indian pottery are said to bear a strange resemblance to the canal systems of Mars.[222] The Hopi believe their first ancestors actually came from that red planet and built canals in the American desert like those in their Martian home. The most profound wisdom may be preserved in those intricate Indian dances, the whirling human bodies in a magic circle generate some subtle force to influence Nature thus making rain, equally the spinning ring and solemn chants could signify the motion of Spaceships.

CHAPTER SEVEN

Aztecs and Incas

On 8th November 1519 Hernan Cortés and his Conquistadores gazed in wonder at Mexico City, the capital of the New World. Emperor Montezuma II welcomed the white strangers and in fateful submission long foretold, he surrendered himself and all his people to the servitude of Spain. How did six hundred Spanish adventurers with eleven small ships, ten cannon and sixteen horses plunder a powerful empire, enslave a whole nation, destroy a powerful civilisation? Montezuma, aged only forty, was renowned as a great soldier, victor in nine battles, his seventeen years reign had extended Aztec sway dominating Central America. In the North it took the Europeans four centuries to subdue the Red Indians, the Spaniards conquered Mexico in a few months. Montezuma and his warriors were all brave men, ready to die for their country. At the time of the conquest Tenochtitlan was a huge metropolis with 300,000 inhabitants dwelling in 60,000 houses amid lagoons, dykes and floating islands of flowers, fountains played in the broad streets and vast market place. The city was adorned with palaces and teocallis, or temples, towering to the sky. Mexico could easily have absorbed the Spaniards like India the British, leaving their proud descendants independent today. Why did Montezuma and millions of Aztecs and Mayas surrender to a few white men?

Like the Red Indians in the North the peoples of Central America treasured traditions of a White God, Quetzalcoatl, known to the Incas as Viracocha. He long ago taught their forefathers in a wondrous Golden Age, then promised to return bringing trials and tribulations. Some Christians today believe in the Second Coming of Christ followed by the Last Judgement prophesied for this twentieth-century.

Who was Quetzalcoatl, whose beneficence inspired the peoples of Mexico for hundreds, probably thousands, of years and whose emblem the feathered serpent, symbol perhaps of Spaceships, dominated monuments and temples of Central America? The Toltecs described him as fair and ruddy with long hair, dressed in a long robe of black linen cut low at the neck with short sleeves, a dress worn by natives to this very day. His name Quetzalcoatl evokes that mellifluent language of Atlantis. The *quetzal* was a rare bird with green feathers, *coatl*, a Nahua word for snake, a combination of the Maya *co*, serpent, and Nahua word *atl* meaning water, this signifying winged serpent. Legends state that Quetzalcoatl's mother was the virgin Coatlicue, his father, the Sun, resembling the planet Venus. His affinity with Christ outraged the Spaniards shocked by the startling similarities between the Christian and Aztec religions. Distinguished authorities offer divergent opinions dating Quetzalcoatl at various times from 32,000 BC to AD 967. Alva de Ixtlilxochitl, an Aztec chronicler, steeped in native traditions, declared that Quetzalcoatl succeeded the defeated Giants and lived during the Third Age, *El Sol de Viente*, the Sun of the Wind, contemporary with Lemuria.

Tezcatlipoca, rival God of the Air, plotted Quetzalcoatl's downfall and finally the Teacher decided to return to the skies. He said farewell to his sorrowing people and sailed eastwards on a raft of serpents to the fabled land of Tlapallan, the country of bright colours. The raft of serpents may signify a Spaceship whose force-field flashing electric discharges could perhaps be symbolised by serpents. Another legend tells how the God flung himself on a funeral pyre and from the flames ascended to the planet Venus. In modern context this seems to indicate the launching of a Spaceship. Quetzalcoatl was occasionally regarded as the Sun God but more often pictured as if emerging from the Sun, his dwelling-place. Perhaps the paintings depict a God alighting from a Flying Saucer.

In the National Museum in Mexico City are many Totonac or Zapotec figurines wearing headgear resembling a helmet, with a ring around their neck and a little box on their chest suggesting our familiar conception of Spacemen. These tiny models are similar to the Jomon Dogus, the clay figures or haniwa found in prehistoric tombs in Japan, which could represent little men in Space-suits and helmets calling to mind Oannes who taught civilisation to Babylon.

Near Tres Zapates in the Vera Cruz jungle, partly buried, were found several enormous monolithic heads of black basalt and stone altars in deep relief. One great nine foot head weighed sixteen tons, the huge stone block had been transported from a quarry more than sixty miles crossing a thirty-foot deep gorge. These great heads have broad foreheads, bold features, wide noses, thick drooping lips and appear amazingly negroid in character, quite unlike any native American race past or present. Such heads are not found in Africa. The faces appear serene like the statues of Buddha as though they belonged to transcendent beings not of this world; each wears a close-fitting helmet. These Olmec sculptures recall the famous Martian of the Tassili frescoes in the Sahara and that famous prehistoric painting discovered in a cave near Ferghana in Uzbekistan which the Russian newspaper Pravada Vostoka likened to 'a man wearing an air-tight helmet with antennae and on his back some sort of contraption for flight.'[53] Some prehistorians believe these ancient statues to be representations of the Sun God portrayed like Spacemen.

In Central America the Lemurian colonies flourished for thousands of years and preserved the Sun Culture of the Motherland long after Mu was destroyed. William Niven, a mineralogist, discovered in Mexico evidence of highly civilised races there tens of thousands of years before the Ice Age. Beneath a buried city over 200,000 years old he found traces of a second and below that a third city of fantastic age. All three existed before the present high plateau was raised, all were probably destroyed by cataclysms obliterating civilisation. Nearby Niven[46] found over 2,600 stone tablets more than 12,000 years old interpreted as from Mu. Archaeologists scorn suggestions of ancient Man in Mexico 200,000 BC yet seem vastly impressed with evidence of man-made structures discovered at Terra Amata, Nice, in south-eastern France, built by prehistoric hunters 300,000 years[128] ago. If Europe was inhabited in the remote past, surely people at the same time could have lived in Mexico. At Cuicuilco to the south of Tenochtitlan is a pyramid half buried by lava which Professor Hapgood[224] dated at 2161 BC, although George E. Hyde, a geologist, estimated its age as about 8,500 years old. There is much confusion over the origin of the ancient Mexicans, evidence of the vast migrations in prehistoric times occasioned by great catastrophes possibly occasioned by nuclear-war. The Quichés believed their ancestors came from Tulan or Thule in that mysterious Northern continent of Hyperborea, our present Arctic circle; the Olmecs claimed to have originated from a large island in the east, Aztlan, Atlantis, said to have been the homeland of our Celts.

In this ancient land of the White Gods peopled in prehistory by Lemurians and Atlanteans the Aztecs are strangers arriving only yesterday. The Normans had conquered England for nearly three hundred years, ill-starred Edward III was wearing his uneasy crown, when the Aztec tribes ceased their century-long wandering to settle by the shores of Lake Tezcoco. Traditions recall that the Aztecs, People of the Crane, were directed by their Sun God Huitzilopochtli, about AD 1160, to leave their home far north of the Colorado river and migrate southward to their Promised Land indicated by an island in a lake where they would see an eagle devouring a serpent. Six of the tribes for many decades followed the Spirit of Huitzilopochtli manifesting as a white eagle which led them like Jehovah leading the Children of Israel for forty years in the Wilderness, a startling parallel, especially if both the Aztec and Hebrew Gods were Spacemen. The white eagle leading the Aztecs may have been a Spaceship? Finally about AD 1325 the descendants of the original wanderers arrived at Lake Tezcoco where they saw an eagle perched on a cactus clutching a snake. The tribes halted, the priests scanned the skies, then Huitzilopochtli ordered the Aztecs to build here their city, Tenochtitlan, called Mexico by the Conquistadores after the War God, Mexitili.

Thirty miles north of Mexico City sprawl the abandoned ruins of Teotihuacan, the City of the Gods, built according to legend during the Second Age, Tlachitonatiuh, Earth-Sun by a race of Giants, the Quinamatzin, in the days of Atlantis.

After the cataclysm Atlantean survivors in their Mexican colony were conquered by the Olmecs, who inhabited this great city under the beneficent rule of Quetzalcoatl. *Teotihuacan* in the ancient Nahuatl language of Mexico is said to mean 'The place where men flew like Gods'.

The imposing Pyramid of the Sun measures 760 feet by 720 feet at its base rising to a height of 220 feet, this huge edifice contains a million cubic yards of stone. A temple at its top housed an immense statue of the God with a breastplate of gold. Sixty miles south-east of Mexico City stands Cholula, the Mecca of the Aztecs. In honour of Quetzalcoatl arose the most colossal structure in all the Americas. A teocallis or truncated pyramid measuring 1,400 feet on each side, covering 42 acres, and more than 210 feet high, a stupendous building more than twice as big as the Great Pyramid of Cheops. On the summit stood a resplendent image of the God of the Air drawing pilgrims from far and near.

In south-west Mexico near Oaxaco stood the spectacular ruins of Monte Alban shrouded in mystery, the remains of five distinct epochs. The Olmec builders tore the top off a mountain, uprooted the forests and levelled the plateau with terraces covering thousands of acres, a feat of engineering unsurpassed even today. Hyatt Verrill denies that this fantastic enterprise could have been achieved by slave-labour without explosives, steel-tools and wheeled vehicles. Ixtlilochitl, the native historian, states the Olmecs succeeded the Giants and flourished during the reign of Quetzalcoatl. The plateau evokes those spectacular ruined columns at Baalbek in Lebanon which may have been a landing-place for spaceships. Possibly Spacemen may have inspired this cyclopean structure at Monte Alban.

Race-memory of shattering cataclysms destroying earlier civilisations obliged the Mayas like other ancient peoples to study the stars; the Priests were renowned astronomers and observed the stars particularly Venus and the Pleiades with amazing precision.

The great Stone of the Sun known as the Calendar Stone dedicated in 1479 is said to correlate the dates of previous World Ages, details of transits of Venus and planetary cycles. A work of supreme mathematical skill far beyond the attainments of contemporary Renaissance Europe. Quixé Cardinali with characteristic genius interprets the curious symbols of the Stone as representing a Flying Saucer. With vivid imagination he professes to see sculptures of the Spacecraft's jet propulsion-system repeated in hieroglyphs on buildings and columns everywhere.[31] The flowing spirals of Mexican decoration may tell of Spacemen in cosmic symbols we cannot read.

At Palenque in the Temple of Inscriptions, archaeologist Albert Ruz, discovered a stairway leading down about 75 feet to an underground vault. Dominated by a huge sarcophagus covered with a carved stone slab 12 feet by 6 feet, weighing five tons, it was adorned with the figure of a young man with large nose and mongoloid features, leaning backwards and sitting on an earth-monster'. A remarkable drawing as representing a cosmonaut piloting a vimana. Removal of the inner lid revealed the crumbling skeleton of a man about 5 feet 8 inches tall, 6 inches taller than the average Maya. His teeth painted red were not mutilated in the fashion of the Maya nobility. A magnificent mask of jade in two hundred fragments covered his face like those golden masks protecting the faces of the Achaean dead found by Heinrich Schliemann at Mycenae. Some experts suggest the dead man was Kukulkan himself, others believe him to be an Extraterrestrial among the ancient Mayas, not surprising since Gods descending in vimanas are mentioned in the Sanskrit Classics and legends world-wide.

In startling revelation G. Tarade and A. Millou wonder if the Mayan hieroglyphics conceal some galactic message and speculate daringly

'These hieroglyphics certainly concern the conditions of the pilotage of the ship. The person whom we see on the sculptures and whom we call "the pilot" wears a helmet and looks towards the prow of the ship; his hands are occupied and seem to manoeuvre levers; his head leans on a support, an inhalator penetrates his nose. The bird reposing on the prow of the ship is a parrot which in the Mayan conception is the symbolism for the Sun God. Still on the prow we find three "receivers" which accumulate energy and other "Capturers" forming three series, three on the right, three in the front and three on the left. The motor is subdivided into four parts, the ship's propulsion-system is housed behind the pilot. The thrust is clearly visible and manifests in the form of the flame at the rear end of the vimana. It appears subdivided into two interblending contrary forces, one of solar origin, (touches the tail of the bird), the other of terrestrial or magnetic origin, basically and freely they are symbolised thus by two masks.'[195]

Other scholars believe the Palenque tomb contained the remains of a Maya Chief about 7th century AD. They ignore the drawing's apparent affinity with the extraterrestrial symbolism evident on temple friezes and sculptures and with those helmeted figurines in the National Museum.

The vast ruins of Copan in Honduras and the lofty pyramid temples of Tikal in Guatemala abandoned to the jungle echo forlornly of a civilisation beyond our conception. In the jungles of Guatemala enormous stone globes are found arrayed in geometrical formation particularly significant when viewed from the air. Not so strange as might appear, for in neighbouring San Salvador was found a curious clay dish adorned with a picture of men in odd machines leaving a trail of smoke, apparently some form of aircraft. Recent research claims that these balls of stone have no extraterrestrial significance and are geological freaks.

Near Lake Titicaca in Bolivia stand the immense remains of Tiahuanaco built according to the local Indians before there were stars in the sky. Today the quays and docks of this once busy port perched dizzily in the Andes about 12,300 feet above sea-level sprawl desolate. The Sons of the Sun who built Tiahuanaco many millennia ago were great engineers and astronomers with particular veneration for Venus suggesting visitors from that lovely planet. Among the papers of Garcilaso de la Vega, grandson of the ill-fated Inca Atahuallpa, translated with a commentary by the Spanish biologist, Bertram Garcia, we read 'The inscriptions carved on the stones of Tiahuanaco affirm that humans quite evolved, webbed, and endowed with a blood different from ours arriving from another planet found the highest lake on Earth and made it their home. In the course of the interplanetary journey they were making the pilots hurled down refuse and gave the lake the form of a human being lying on his back. That these mysterious Visitors were webbed is quite curious, it makes them strangely like the man-fish who civilised Babylon. How did the pilots succeed in changing the shape of Lake Titicaca without landing?'[64]

Our own pilots could change the shape of any lake without landing merely by dropping one or two judiciously-aimed nuclear-bombs, it is not suggested that the Spacemen went to this extreme.

Peruvian legends tell of Orejona, so called because she had large ears, shining like gold, who descended from Venus landing on the Isle of the Sun in Lake Titicaca.

Highly elevated shore-lines and fossils of sea-creatures still discernible along hundreds of miles of the Andes prove that the sea-level was once thousands of feet higher than today. The Austrian cosmologist, Hans Hoerbiger, theorised that in Tertiary times another Moon circled close to Earth only twenty thousand miles away. Its powerful gravitational attraction made all men and animals giants. Eventually the satellite crashed and freed from its gravity the seas suddenly receded, the moving mass of water causing universal flood. The survivors in Tiahuanaco found themselves stranded thousands of feet above the sea.

All the buildings still show impressive grandeur in size and construction. The fortress of Akapana, a lofty pyramid, and the Kalasasaya, Temple of the Sun, cyclopean structures, were built with huge stone slabs, some weighing 200 tons, almost impervious to weather erosion and blunting our finest steel tools. How did the builders shape and groove these slabs to an accuracy of one fiftieth of an inch? Mortar was not used, the walls were solid yet their foundations elastic, apparently resilient to earthquakes. Such wonderful architecture eloquently reveals the lofty minds of those Giants who conceived and fashioned Tiahuanaco. Portrait-heads of the great men unearthed there show high foreheads, open faces, bold profiles, energetic chins, powerful personalities, still impressive in the solid rock.

The entrance to the Sun Temple, Gateway of the Sun, is encrusted with complicated groups totalling 1107 symbols comprising winged figures, heads of humans, condors, pumas and the now extinct toxodons. These strange signs apparently constitute a calendar correlated with Venus. They include winged humans, reminiscent of angels in the Bible and those winged sculptures in Babylon. Could they too have represented Spacemen?

At Nazca about three hundred miles north of Tiahuanaco the plateau twelve hundred feet above sea-level is covered with a multitude of fantastic markings. From the air they resolve into an astonishing pattern of spirals, stars, cosmic symbols, beasts, birds and straight lines varying from half a kilometre to eight kilometres in length. It is difficult to understand why these strange symbols were devised unless to be viewed from the air. Not far from Nazca on the plateau of Marcahuasi is a most remarkable assembly of giant sculptures representing human beings, animals and birds, notably a great lion and several condors symbols of the Sun God. Many carvings depict camels, lions, elephants, penguins, which, as far as is known, never existed in South America. They were apparently made by Giants twelve feet tall. Why such monoliths should be grouped thirteen thousand feet high in the Andes far from human habitation baffles our comprehension until we discover from aerial photographs that among these statues exist other figures visible only from the air. Astronauts in our own space-capsules marvel at the extraordinary visibility of terrestrial objects seen from Space, these strange figures incomprehensible to us may have had meaningful significance as beacons for Spacemen.

The Machinguenga Indians of Eastern Peru speak of the 'people of the heavens who came (to Earth) on a shining road in the sky'. The Quecha Indians of South America recall the Illa Siva or light rings, evoking the Egyptian Eye of Horus and the Rampa Livrac or litters of electric energies that were seen in the days of Lord Inca, the magical Flying Boats enchanting the Red Indians. The lofty plateaus at Nazca and Marcahuasi may once have been centres for some ancient electrical civilisation communing by means of those strange lines and sculptures and through radionics with some Supermen in the stars.

The Andes are said to be pierced with immense tunnels built by an ancient race of white men. A subterranean highway runs north-westward from Cuzco to Lima for 380 miles then turns due south to modern Bolivia 900 miles away, the southern end is lost in the deadly Atacama salt desert of Northern Chile. A Peruvian told Madame H.P. Blavatsky[16] that when the Inca Atahuallpa was imprisoned by Pizarro, his wife offered for his liberation a roomful of gold from floor to ceiling as far as she could reach. She kept her word. But then the Conquistador, learning the Incas had an inexhaustible mine of treasures in a mile-long tunnel, vowed to murder Atahuallpa unless she revealed the secret. The Chief Priest looking in a consecrated black mirror, similar to the 'mirror' in which Montezuma had seen Cortés, witnessed the future murder of Atahuallpa. The outraged Queen ordered the entrance of the tunnel to be concealed under huge masses of rock, after her husband's murder she killed herself. Despite many attempts by various Governments neither tunnel nor treasures has been found.

The Machiguenga Indians tell of the days when their forefathers communicated with Celestials in the sky, who belonged to the legendary Amazonian empire, El Gran Paititi, the land of the Jaguar King, believed to symbolise an Extraterrestrial.

South American legends agree with traditions of Atlantis and annals of the Ancient East that long ago shining Gods descended from the stars to rule Earth in a Golden Age of peace and wonder described in the Sanskrit Classics. It is believed that as long ago as 80,000 BC Extraterrestrials had bases on Earth at the bottom of oceans and underground from which UFOs are said to appear even today. The Manacricas, a native tribe in Brazil, cherish legends concerning *macumbeiros*, flying wizards in circular luminous machines.

The Indians told of a Chibcha King who once a year smeared himself from head to foot with honey then gold-dust and bathed in the sacred lake in which worshippers cast gold and jewels to honour the Gods. The legend of the Gilded One fascinated the Conquistadores, who partially drained Lake Guatavita in Bogota but most of the fabulous wealth was lost in the mud. In 1536 the sole survivor of a gold-hunting expedition staggered from the jungle and told later of golden Manoa on an island in a salt-lake in Guiana. In a description not unlike Plato's Atlantis he babbled of a city with glittering houses, statues and trees of gold on sands of gold dust. Sir Walter Raleigh in 1595 made his disastrous expedition to Guiana, searching in vain for the golden city of Manoa, a failure contributing to his execution twenty-three years later.

Was the Gilded One a native King or Spaceman? Did those golden houses of Manoa really exist or had the delirious Spaniard seen Spaceships, anticipating those gleaming UFOs haunting the same land today?

Colonel Percy H. Fawcett, his son, Jack, and their companion, Raleigh Rimmel, searching for lost cities with ever-burning lights in the Brazilian jungle, were killed by hostile Indians in the Matto Grosso during July 1925. A Brazilian wrote to another son, Brian Fawcett

> ' ... his father and brother were advanced souls who were worshipped as Gods by Indians and who were actually alive in a subterranean city called Matali-Ararcaga in the Roncador region of Matto Grosso. There were several underground cities in Brazil where dwelt great spiritual avatars who ruled the world's events, and from these secret places issued flying saucers to make global reconaissance-flights.'

While we mourn the disappearance of Colonel Percy Fawcett and his companions, still we wonder?

The Andes like the Himalayas are said to hide a Shangri-La, a secret valley haunted by Cosmic Masters directing the destiny of Man. Occult traditions record that the Council of the Great White Hierarchy instructed the Lord Meru, a teacher of Lemuria, to take the sacred rolls and Golden Disc of the Sun to the newly-formed Lake Titicaca amid the mountains of South America. Tiahuanaca, a great sea-port, was raised by the cataclysm convulsing Lemuria to a lofty plateau in cold thin air about twelve thousand feet above sea-level. Lord Muru flew to Lake Titicaca in a silver-needle airship and after years of wandering with his fellow-Adepts built the Monastery of the Brotherhood of the Seven Rays; from their secret retreat the Brothers inspired by the Master Koot-Hoomi work for the redemption of the world.[22]

The Peruvians believe that Viracocha came to them from Venus, he arose from the waters of Lake Titicaca like Oannes to the Babylonians. He traversed the southern continent as Quetzalcoatl roamed the northern with the ease of a Spaceman teaching and healing the pre-Incas. At Caba Clos in Peru the Prophet aroused the enmity of the Priests who bade the warriors attack him; like some biblical Patriarch he raised his hands to the sky and called in a strange language. Suddenly from the heavens whirled a curtain of flame which circled around him, the arrows were repelled by this force-field to pierce the hearts of those who sent them. In Cocha the healer, again assaulted by soldiers, prayed to the heavens. Fire-flame darted down whirling in wonderful colours between him and his enemies; they turned to flee then stopped in terror at the second fire-circle behind them. In a flash all dissolved to dust; the Stranger stood unsinged. Today the site is called Place of the Lightnings.[91]

Viracocha was depicted as a giant condor-God carrying the Sun across the heavens, he was also known as the Tiger or Jaguar God. The ancient civilisation of the Chavins at Cajamarca high in the Andes was noted for its great Tiger God about 1000 BC, significantly contemporary with Solomon whose famous Temple according to tradition was built by Angels, possibly Extraterrestrials. In the lofty mountains the Chavins erected a single stone of white granite carved in low relief to represent a human figure with feline fangs. Why did so many motives on sculptures and pottery feature jaguars? Does the CondorGod carrying the Sun represent a Spaceman?

A most ancient legend states that the first inhabitants of Peru were born from bronze, gold and silver eggs which came from heaven, suggesting in ages past the landing of Extraterrestrials, colonists from the stars. This Celestial Egg theme is depicted in traditions from China to Greece.

The first Inca, Manco-Capac, and his wife, Mama-Ocllo, suddenly appeared, so it was said, at dawn on the sacred Lake Titicaca in the Andes, like Viracocha ages earlier, and announced to the marvelling people that they were Children of the Sun sent down by the Sun God to teach men civilisation. Reports today describe Flying Saucers seen to dive and vanish in the waters of the lake as though Spacemen enter some subterranean base there. An astonishing tale alleges that in the twelfth century an English sailor, young and handsome, was shipwrecked on the Pacific shore, though how he reached there is not revealed. The castaway waded ashore to be welcomed by a Prince, who called him Ingasman Capac, handsome Englishman. Later he became known as Inca Manco-Capac, founder of a dynasty of thirteen Incas ruling like Gods for about four hundred years until ill-starred Atahuallpa was garrotted by Pizarro. The title Inca meant of the Sun, relating to Inti, the Sun God; the Incas expanded their Empire of Tshuantinsuyu across the whole of Peru and Bolivia and most of Chile giving their name to the Quechua and Aymara Indians living there.

The Incas were said to be tall, fair-skinned with delicate features, aquiline noses and red or brown hair,[209] a description often applied to the Atlanteans; analysis of tissues from the mummies of Incas showed that all belonged to blood-group A, unknown in Latin America until the advent of the Europeans. The Inca married his sister to ensure a divine descendant from the holy family like the Pharoahs of Egypt, although he dispersed his kingly powers by fertilising hundreds of favoured concubines.

The Incas erected magnificent temples to the Sun where Priests exacted penance, prayed and fasted, gave communion and heard confessions. Virgins of the Sun entered convents for a life of prayer and chastity. Any who conceived was buried alive, although if she swore the Sun, presumably a Celestial, was the father of the child, she was spared. The astonishing resemblance of the religion and rites of the Incas to Christianity outraged the Catholic Fathers as counterfeit by the Devil, even today they refuse to believe the Religions are fundamentally the same.

The Incas deliberately destroyed the records of the Chimu, Chavin and Paraces, previous civilisations whose cyclopean ruins suggest great influence and power. Writing was abolished, data being preserved by quipus, knots of various sizes in strings of different colours similar to the punched-card system of our computer-operators. Unfortunately there is said to be no one alive now able to interpret them.

Unlike the Mayas the Incas were not noted astronomers although they did pay special reverence to Venus and the Pleiades; gold had no special monetary value being used for wonderful metalwork. Much more important than those shiploads of gold which inflated Europe's economy was the introduction of potatoes, pepper, cotton, cocoa, tomatoes and an astounding profusion of exotic fruits and flowers to improve Europe's diet. The cultivation of these plants from wild varieties proves many milennia of farming and is irrefutable evidence of the immense antiquity of pre-Inca peoples.

All the old chroniclers agree that the titanic cities in the Andes were built ages before the Incas. The transportation of immense stones over long distance is usually attributed to some lost power of levitation, but the builders are said to have used a decomposing substance from certain grass which could soften stones into malleable clay easily portable, kneaded into required shape, then petrified into hard smooth stone. Such technique would solve most formidable problems.

The Spaniards were astounded by the cyclopean city of Cuzco with the fortress of Sacsahuaman 11,000 feet high in the Andes housing 200,000 inhabitants, scores of palaces and nearly 400 temples and religious houses glowed with burnished plates of gold; through all the buildings and exquisite gardens flowed running-water conducted through pipes from reservoirs. The fabulous Temple of the Sun, one of the wonders of the New World, prompted W.H. Prescott's description in memorable words

'The interior of the temple was the most worthy of admiration. It was literally a mine of gold. On the western wall was emblazoned a representation of the Deity, consisting of a human countenance looking forth from amidst innumerable rays of light which emanated from it in every direction in the same manner as the Sun is often personified with us. The figure was engraved on a massive plate of gold of enormous dimensions, thickly powdered with emeralds and precious stones.'[167]

The ancient Peruvians most surely have had some special reason for planning their wonderful capital high in the mountains to resemble a giant bird and to fashion their fabulous Sun-disk with the face of a God. Was Cuzco itself like those fascinating monuments at Nazca and Marcahuasi designed to attract the Gods, the Spacemen?

The titanic fortress of Sacshuaman frowning down on Cuzco astounds every traveller by its lofty grandeur, walls sixty feet high were built on a mountain-top artificially levelled covering several hundred acres like Monte Alban in old Mexico. Twenty four miles north-west of Cuzco rises the great fortress of Ollantay some of whose massive stones weigh 300 tons, chiselled and fitted together so that the thinnest blade could not penetrate the cracks. The most remarkable fort was probably Machu Pichu more than ten thousand feet high in the Andes overhanging a three thousand feet high precipice. How were these immense blocks of stone transported to such dizzy heights, fashioned and fitted with such fantastic accuracy? Why were these forts built amid the clouds? What enemy did they resist? These cyclopean defences recall those vitrified forts on mountain-tops all over the world associated in legend with those wars between the Gods and the Giants. Is it too fantastic to suggest that these mountain-citadels of Peru were built by some ancient race as a protection against Spacemen?

Strange as it seems though the Aztecs and Incas shared the same Sun-worship, similar social-systems, subjects of a God-King, the two peoples, as far as is known, never met; neither knew of the other's existence; still more incredible, both about the same time feared, then suffered, the same fate.

In the Bay of Pisco south of Lima the cliffs are carved with a Trident of Three Crosses, the centre Cross is six hundred feet in height, the smaller side-crosses are tied by a line to the main one. This Chandelier of the Andes may have been a seismograph marking earth-tremors from the days of Atlantis and Lemuria, it has more significance for the future.

Earthquakes threaten the American continent from Canada to Peru. Before final destruction the White Gods of Montezuma and Atahualpa may land again, perhaps this century.

CHAPTER EIGHT
India

Most ancient tranditions told that India was peopled by the descendants of Cain,[123] the Brahminical Tables stated Gods landed from Venus more than 18,000,000 years ago, occult wisdom taught that before Lemuria was destroyed Masters and Adepts colonised India and built the great rock temples of Elephanta. The Master Manu is said to have chosen people of the fifth sub-race, named by some the original Semites, and about 60,000 BC led them safely from Atlantis long before it submerged across Europe into Central Asia finally establishing the infant Root-Race upon the southern shores of the great Gobi Lake. Later many migrated to India.[2] Written records in a northern monastery carry the civilisation of India back more than 50,000 years.[45] About 11,000 BC according to Chaldean records there existed in South Central Asia the Atlantean colony of Dravidya which like Atlantis was frequently visited by Teachers from Venus who imparted their knowledge to the Naga Priests. The Sumerians believed that their hero, Gilgamesh, sailed far away across the Sea of the Dead to the sacred mountain where descended the Gods, called Dilmun, Isle of the Blest, it may have been Ceylon.

Dramatic discoveries in the Punjab fifty years ago unearthed an unknown culture contemporary with Egypt and Babylon. In 1922 R.D. Banerji, an Indian archaeologist, excavating an old Buddhist monastery at Mohenjo-Daro on the lower Indus found under the ruins remains of a most ancient city. Sir John Marshall's excavations further north at Harappa confirmed the existence of an extensive prehistoric civilisation about 2,000 years earlier than had been previously supposed.[124] Sir Mortimer Wheeler supervised detailed examination of several mounds, deep trenches revealed a great citadel at each site, centre of an impressive system of walls, he credits 'the Indus civilisation generally with a carefully engineered civic lay-out from as early a period as has been reached by excavation.' adding that 'Mohenjo-Daro, unlike Ur, was laid out at a time when town-planning had passed the experimental stage.' The houses, some of which had more than two floors, consisted of a series of rooms arranged round a central courtyard and usually contained a bathroom, a striking feature was the system of urban drainage;[194] the unpaved streets were supplied with brick drains to an extent unparalleled in pre-Classic times and unknown in parts of the East even today. Buildings were simple with ornamentation and were provided with amenities such as baths, lavatories, drainage and fresh-water tanks. Terra-cotta figurines apparently represent the Earth Goddess, well-known cylinder-seals from Mesopotamia prove trade with Babylon. Gold beads, silver-ware and ornaments of lapis-lazuli, turquoise, jade and amazonite attained such exquisite excellence that Sir John Marshall declared it 'his considered opinion that the jewellery of these Indus people is so perfectly and brilliantly cut that it could more easily have originated in London's present-day Bond Street than in a prehistoric house 3,000 years ago.' The pictorial script in hieroglyphics suggests previous maturity, it is not yet deciphered. Sir Mortimer Wheeler believes strata excavated today show Mohenjo-Daro in its decadence and concludes 'We may have to be prepared to find that the Indus civilisation was a going concern well before 2,400 BC.'[215] What if like Troy there are a dozen cities on the same site, one below the other? Mohenjo-Daro and Harappa may be many thousand years old.

The Indus culture even spread as far as the Arabian Gulf where it covered an area of more than 800,000 square miles, no other civilisation before the time of the Roman Empire managed to achieve such a successful political system.[139]

The excavations at Mohenjo-Daro and Harappa show the Indus peoples of the 4th and 3rd millennia in possession of a highly-developed culture in which no vestige of Indo-Aryan influence is found.[133] In Egypt and Mesopotamia impressive palaces were built for the divine Pharaohs and mighty Kings but the peasants lived in hovels. About the same time the ordinary people of the Indus valley lived in cosy well-built houses with adequate drainage-systems surpassing many squalid European towns until our twentieth-century; the general Public apparently enjoyed a degree of comfort and luxury unexampled in other parts of the civilised world.

Ages must surely have elapsed for the peoples of the Indus valley to attain such a high standard of culture with astonishingly modern ideas. Their tantalising script, evidence of antiquity, baffles scholars, yet there is reason to assume from the brilliant poetry, wonderful imagery and lofty philosophy of later epics that the Aryans who conquered the country inherited sublime concepts from a cosmic, compassionate wisdom acquired through countless centuries or taught by Spacemen. The Aryans believe their remote ancestors came from the star, Sirius.

Long before the discovery of Mohenjo-Daro James Churchward after a lifetime's study of the ancient east declared that India stood foremost for thousands of years holding together and carrying on Earth's first great civilisation after the destruction of Mu, the Motherland. He claimed that ancient temple-records carry the civilisation of India, the Mother of Babylonia and Upper Egypt, back beyond 35,000 years.[45]

Plato bewailed that about 10,000 BC Greece was a most prosperous, fruitful land but many great convulsions had torn the country submerging coastal cities, some of which are now being rediscovered by archaeologists in aqualungs. Off the west coast of India is a large area of submerged lands said to have imposing structures now under water. To view ancient India in clear perspective we must reflect on some basic facts.

The Secret Doctrine of India, the philosophy of Truth, on a level higher than religion and mysticism has existed for an age which scholars admit cannot be less than five thousand years in extent, but is in fact very much older for its origin disappears into historically untraceable epochs.[24] The Laws of Manu attributed to about 10,000 BC anticipated Darwin's Theory of Evolution stating 'The first germ of life was developed by water and heat. Men will traverse the universe,

gradually ascending and passing through the rocks, the
plants, the worms, insects, fish, serpents, tortoises, wild
animals, cattle and higher animals.'[16]

Legends from far antiquity suggest that former civilisations
may have been destroyed by their own scientists meddling
with titanic forces which displaced the Earth's axis,
cataclysms changed the climate and shattered proud countries
into the sea. Race-memories of the destruction of Lemuria and
Atlantis prompted the Initiates of old India to guard their
wisdom with great care. They transmuted dangerous
knowledge only to qualified aspirants from generation to
generation, sometimes the oral traditions were preserved in a
few neglected writings in symbols which only Adepts could
read, hidden to prevent misuse.

Awareness of the achievements of the ancient Sages will give
some glimmerings of the culture acquired from the lost
civilisations of old India, not revealed in the archaeological
remains of Mohenjo-Daro but surely known to the temple
priests. The pre-Hindus formulated world-religions and
inspired the Vedantic school of philosophy. The wonderful
system of Yoga, the Gnani Yoga of Wisdom, Raja Yoga of
Mind, Hatha Yoga of Body, Bhakti Yoga of Love, Karma
Yoga of Work, Mantra Yoga of Sound, all blended mysticism
with daily life and developed a comprehension of Man's
relation to the Universe. The Kaushitaki Brahmana shows
that in 3100 BC the Rishis were far advanced in astronomy.
The Brahmagupta stated the Earth was round and orbited the
Sun, and announced the Laws of Gravitation, facts not known
in modern times until Copernicus and Newton. The so-called
Arabic numerals which came to Europe in the ninth century
originated from India whose mathematicians invented the
decimal system, algebra the differential and integral calculus.
The old Initiates knew the Law of Gravitation and divined the
velocity of light. Kananda, long before Democritus and our
nuclear-physicists, formulated an atomic theory. The
Ancients are believed to have used electrical forces whose
secrets are lost, it is possible that Initiates versed in arcane
Science produced nuclear-bombs by techniques much easier
than our own, they would probably fathom the principles of
flight and construct flying-machines propelled by atomic-fuel

as stated in the Indian epics. The Vaisesaki philosophers reduced Time to its finest mathematical concept by describing the smallest unit of time, *kala*, as the period taken by an atom to traverse its own unit of space, the largest, the life-span of a whole universe according to some ancient Seers.

The ancient Hindus were great alchemists, before 1000 BC they were searching for the Elixir of Life, they knew the composition of water and the occult properties of metals, an arcane science unknown to us now. Their knowledge of medicine and pharmacology was astonishing, the old surgeons performed delicate operations for cataracts, and in music minstrels invented the tonic-sol-fa long before Gui d'Arezzo in the Middle Ages. The greatest development of old India was Sanskrit, a most wonderful language, more perfect than Greek, more copious than Latin and more exquisitely refined than either. Archaeologists still question the significance of the fortified citadels at Harappa and Mohenjo-Daro. They evoke the lofty ziggurats of Babylon, the mounds of North America, the pyramids of Mexico, mountain-fortresses in Peru and prehistoric towers in many lands. Their construction about the same time in countries across the world may be mere coincidence, normal evolution of primitive architecture, yet it is logical to suppose such buildings had some purpose for friends or foes from the skies since legends suggest with the Bible that during the Third and Second millenia BC Extraterrestrials were visiting Earth. After talking to Abraham Jehovah might have flown over the Himalayas to impress some other patriarch in Harappa.

There is reason to believe that Jehovah under the name Indra eventually caused the downfall of the Indus cities by aiding the Aryans invading from Central Asia about 1700 BC. Four centuries later he would lead Moses and Joshua with the Israelites in the conquest of Canaan. Jehovah and Indra did not necessarily denote the same Being, these names probably signified Spacemen generally.

In his classic work, The Indus Civilization, Sir Mortimer Wheeler quoting the older hymns of the Rig Veda states 'Indra, the Aryan war-god, is *puramdara*, fort-destroyer. He shatters ninety forts for his Aryan protégé, Divadasa. The same forts are doubtless referred to where in other hymns he demolishes variously ninety-nine and a hundred ancient castles of the aboriginal leader, Sambara. In brief he rends forts as age consumes a garment.'215

The texts of the Rig Veda meaning Verse-Knowledge were venerated as having divine origin, the Vedas being a revelation by sound directly heard by the Rishis or seers, the chants and recitations were not written down for ages but were orally transmitted by Brahmin priests, whose memories had been rigorously cultivated. The, Rig Veda comprises about ten thousand invocations in Sanskrit. The mythology depicts the Gods as Space beings with a refinement of thought and a mystic insight which far transcends the unsophisticated culture of the Aryans and must emanate from a much earlier civilisation or from the Gods, the Spacemen themselves. Heaven was a physical realm in the sky, the Heavenly Father probably a Space King from some advanced planet in our Solar System, an infinitesimal speck of the whole Universe.

A more powerful God from pre-Indian mythology mentioned in the Vedas, Varuna, was associated with heavenly bodies in the sky. He controlled the Moon and the stars, the flight of birds and had moral authority over men; sometimes he rode the Leviathan, a fearsome sky-monster, suggesting a Spaceship. Varuna, meaning the encompassed sky, was worshipped by the Greeks as *Ouranos*, Uranus, and was later supplanted by Indra, known by the Greeks as *Chronos*, Saturn. Perhaps this was the overthrow of the first Spacemen ruling Earth by others from a rival planet.

Indra, War God of the Aryans, flashed across the heavens in an aerial car with the speed of thought drawn by shining steeds. He waged war against the Asuras, powerful Titans, skilled magicians, implacable enemies of the Gods, and destroyed their cities in the sky with nuclear-bombs. Lord of Heaven, Rider of the Clouds, the Thunderer, Indra lived on fabled Mount Meru, north of the Himalayas and greatly resembled Zeus on Mount Olympus. In his battles Indra was attended by the Maruts or Storm Gods depicted as youthful warriors who rode on golden cars, they brandished darts of lightning in their hands and drove like the wind shaking mountains.'204 Hymns called them 'headlong charioteers, brilliant, of terrible design' on chariots charged with lightning. Immanuel Velikovsky states that the Maruts were comets whirling in the sky after the impact of Mars and Venus, their affinity with the Gods of many other countries suggests they were Spacemen.

Vishnu, riding the eagle Garuda, traversed the three worlds in three strides, Pushan, 'the best pilot of the air', spanned the sky with dazzling swiftness. The most frequently invoked Gods were the twin Aswins like Castor and Pollux, who drove a ruddy, tawny car, bright as burnished gold, armed with thunderbolts; the pair could fly to the stars in a single day, sometimes they skimmed above the ocean in a vehicle described as tri-columnar, triangular and tri-wheeled, well-constructed, on which they once rescued Bhujya from the sea in a hydroplane able to fly into Space.

The Apsaras, alluring wives of the Gods, were aerial nymphs, mistresses of the Gandharvas, heroes from the realms of Space. Sometimes an Apsara would wing down to Earth and become enamoured of mortal man like Urvasi, who according to the Satapatha Brahmana married her earthly lover, Pururavas and bore him a son, only to return to the skies. After months of mourning Pururavas was translated to heaven and dwelt with Urvasi for ever.

The Nagas of North-East Assam, serpent-worshippers, say their ancestors originated from the lost continent of Mu and formed the first Hindu Empire 35,000 years ago. They tell of a man called Meyoo, who lived in the village of Viswema amid the green forests on the hills beside a pleasant stream. One day while hunting he suddenly saw seven Winged Beings who flew down from the sky; taking off their wings they bathed in the stream. With a long hooked stick Meyoo stole the wings of a charming female who could not fly off with her companions. Meyoo married her and hid the wings, years later she found them and returned to the skies with their children. For a long time Meyoo pined for them, finally a crow bore him to realms in the clouds and restored him to his wife and family, later all returned to Earth. The Rig Veda mentions a most ancient race of Shining Ones called Bhrigus to whom Matarishvan brought the secret fire stolen from heaven. This Indian version of the Prometheus legend suggests some conflict in Antiquity between the peoples of Earth and the Celestials.

Occult traditions state that in Scythia around the Black Sea once lived a young Druid called Ram, who ardently seeking divine knowledge was directed by his guiding Genius to fulfil his destiny by leading his people into the very heart of Asia. After conquering Persia his white followers, according to the Zend-Avesta, marched beyond the Himalayas. By his might, his genius and his kindness Rama became Master of India and Spiritual King of the Earth. As leader of the Aryans Rama established a cultured society in Iran from which colonies of Aryans spread their culture, customs and religion to India, particularly the Vedas which became the sacred books of the Brahmins.[179]

The wonderful epic of the 'Ramayana', the quest of Rama for his wife, Sita, stolen by Ravana, have thrilled the peoples of India for thousands of years. The poet Valmiki in 24,000 verses told of Rama, Prince of Ayodha, in northern India, who in a contest bent a mighty bow, to win as bride, Sita, peerless daughter of King Janaka. Banished by his father, Dasaratha, Rama lived happily with the chaste Sita in a forest hut as hermits far from princely pleasure. The beauteous Princess allured Ravana, Lord of Lanka, modern Ceylon, who carried her off in his air-borne chariot and ravished his unwilling captive. Distraught at the abduction of his beloved wife, Rama set forth to her rescue aided by Hanuman and his monkey-hordes who launched aerial invasion of the enemy city. The chivalrous Rama fought celestial duels with Ravana and finally destroyed his rival with a lightning-dart. Rama told Sita he had killed Ravana to avenge his honour. Sita protested her innocence and purified herself by ordeal of fire, she entered the circle of flame and came out unscathed. Rama took his wife in a flying-car back to Ayodha where he ruled in a Golden Age. Rapture turned to despair. Rama still brooded over their long separation. Had his wife surrendered to Ravana? Again suspicion gnawed his heart, he banished the faithful Sita to the forest where she took refuge at the hermitage of Valmiki and soon gave birth to two boys.

One day Rama chanced to walk through the forest and heard his twin sons reciting his deeds taught them by Valmiki, then composing the epic. Rama begged Sita to return to Ayodha and affirm her purity beyond all doubt. Before a glittering assembly Sita pledged her chastity, then weary of life implored Mother Earth to receive her. The ground opened, held on high by jewelled serpents rose a golden throne. Sita placed herself upon it and descended underground amid a rain of heavenly flowers.

Rama had proof at last but was left in desolation; he was destined to suffer long years of loneliness, finally to leave the world and enter heaven.

In his wonderful translation of the Ramayana[65] Romesh Dutt describes Rama's father, King Dasaratha, as 'sprung of ancient Solar Race', a descendant of Kings of the Sun, Space Beings who ruled India. This title is still bestowed on the Mikado of Japan. The epic makes no reference to the Rama of the Scythian traditions who led the Aryans to conquer India. While Rama was hunting in the forest Ravana seized the helpless Sita.

'Seat her on his car celestial yoked with asses winged with speed
Golden in its shape and radiance, fleet as Indra's heavenly steed
Then arose the car celestial o'er the hill and wooded vale,
Like a snake in eagle's talons Sita writhed with piteous wail.'

During the flight they were attacked by Jataka in a giant 'bird' like a fighter-plane.

Rama followed and launched aerial attack.

'Take this car!' so said Matali 'Which the helping Gods provide.
Rama take these steeds celestial, Indra's golden chariot ride.'

Rama and Ravana fought a terrific duel.

'Still the dubious battle lasted, until Rama in his ire
Wielded Brahma's deathful weapon flaming with celestial fire,
Weapon which the Saint Agostya has unto her hero given,
Winged as lightning dart of Indra, fatal as the bolt from heaven.
Wrapped in smoke and flowing flashes, speeding from the circled bow
Pierced the iron heart of Ravan, lain the lifeless hero low.'

Surely 'Brahma's deathful weapon' suggests a nuclear-bomb!

A Hindu manuscript dated 500 BC states that Rawan, King of Ceylon, flew over the enemy's camp and dropped bombs causing many casualties; eventually Rawan was captured and slain and his flying-machine fell into the hands of the Hindu chieftain, Ram Chandra, who flew it to his capital, Adjudhira in Northern India.[45]

The assassinated Gandhi invoked 'Rama!' with his dying breath. Every autumn the Tale of Rama and Sita is enacted in ten-day festivals all over India.

James Churchward insisted that temple-records prove the Rama and Sita poem refers back to 20,000 years ago; he claimed to have seen 'a drawing and instructions for the construction of the airship and her machinery, power, etc. The power is taken from the atmosphere in a very simple inexpensive manner. The engine is somewhat like our present-turbine in that it works from one chanber into another until finally exhausted. When the engine is once started it never stops until turned off. These ships could keep circling around the earth without even once coming down until the machinery wore out. The power is unlimited, or rather limited only by what metals will stand.'[45]

Sanskrit literature abounds with heroes in ancient India apparently equipped with aircraft and missiles more sophisticated than those we boast today. The Samaranganasutradhara of Bhoja, Chapter 31, devotes 230 stanzas to describe principles of construction, attacking visible and invisible objects, ascending, cruising thousands of miles in different directions in the atmosphere and descending.

In Aeronautics by Maharshi Bharadwaja, A Manuscript from the Prehistoric Past translated from Sanskrit we find

> 'The secret of constructing aeroplanes, which will not break, which cannot be cut, will not catch fire, and cannot be destroyed. The secret of making planes motionless. The secret of making planes invisible. The secret of hearing conversations and other sounds in enemy planes. The secret of receiving photographs of the interior of enemy planes. The secret of making persons in enemy planes lose consciousness. The secret of destroying enemy planes.
>
> 'Metals suitable for Aeroplanes, light and heat absorbing, are of sixteen kinds according to Shownaka. Great Sages have declared that these sixteen metals alone are the best for aeroplane construction.'

The most fascinating tales of war in the air waged with fantastic weapons are narrated in the Mahabharata, a marvellous poem of 200,000 lines, eight times as long as the Iliad and Odyssey combined. This epic of the noble prince, Arjuna, and his peerless bride, Draupadi, the God, Krishna, the hosts of Celestials and warrior-knights, is believed to describe the great Bharata War in Northern India fought about 1400 BC. Churchward in The Children of Mu suggests the Mahabharata incidents include history from the temple-records referring to times 20,000 years earlier. Madame H.P. Blavatsky in The Secret Doctrine insists the Mahabharata refers to the strife between the Suryavansas, Worshippers of the Sun, and the Indavansas, Worshippers of the Moon a conflict of great esoteric significance, although the less occult-minded may link it with Hesiod's Theogony describing the War between the Gods and the Titans. Transcending the martial adventures of Mahabharata heroes are the sublime discourses between Arjuna and Krishna enshrined in the Bhagavad Gita.

The Vishnu Purana venerates Krishna as the first of the Messiahs, the oldest of the Sons of God, born of the Virgin, Devaki, more than three thousand years ago; reared among shepherds, he ascended mystic Mount Meru and returned transfigured to teach eternal love, reincarnation and triumph over death.[179]

The Bhisma Parva mentions celestial weapons like Brahma's Rod and Indra's Bolt resembling nuclear-blasts. The Drona Parva, p592, describes an anti-missile-missile; the Son of Rohimi intercepted a 'mace capable of slaying all creatures' as it sped through the air by launching a weapon called Sthunakarma for baffling it. The Drona Parva, p690, tells of the Lord Mahadeva's terrible shafts destroying the triple cities of gold, silver and iron belonging to the Asuras in Space. It also states 'Cukra, surrounded by the Maruts, began hurling his thunder upon the Triple City from all sides. He flings a missile which contained the Power of the Universe at the Triple City. Smoke brighter than ten thousand suns blazed up in splendour.' The ultimate weapon, the Agneya, incapable of being resisted even by the Gods, annihilated armies, stampeded elephants, blasted the Earth, the Sun seemed to turn round, the Universe was scorched like celestial fire destroying civilisation at the end of a World-Age.

The Vishnu Purana mentions Kapilaksha, the Eye of Kapila, a blinding death-ray destroying in a solar-flash armies of men and elephants.

Alexander Gorbovski in his fascinating book Zagadaki Drevenishi Istorii, Enigmas of Ancient History, mentions the discovery of a human skeleton in India revealing radio-activity fifty times the normal. The deceased had apparently eaten heavily contaminated food, suggesting death in atomic war long ago. Such titanic conflict with nuclear-bombs could have shifted the Poles and caused an Ice Age.

The Buddhist monk, Gunarvan, in the fourth century AD claimed to have flown from Ceylon to Java in a glittering aerial vehicle, the dramatist, Bhavabhuti mentioned a flying-vessel used for general civic work by local Government officials; a King of Benares owned a car decked in jewels which could soar in the air, his admiring subjects believed him blessed by the Gods. King Puruvras rose in an aerial car to rescue Urvasi in pursuit of the Danava who was carrying her away. The learned Hariswami was not so fortunate, he married a Brahman's daughter, Levenyavata; one hot summer night while the pair were sleeping on a flat roof a demi-God swooped down and carried her off. Awakening alone the desolate Hariswami sought his vanished wife in vain, in tragic sorrow he ate poisoned rice and died.[159]

The Nepalese Brihat Katha[118] is an amazing romance about Celestial Beings descending from the heavens and meddling in the amours of Princes and their Loves in Northern India. When Queen Vasavadotta desired to mount in an aerial chariot the King's advisers stammered in fright 'As for flying-machines the Yavanas, the Greeks, know them but we never had occasion to see them.' The peoples of Ancient India classed all white strangers as Yavanas or Greeks, and no doubt would believe a light-skinned Spaceman a traveller from the Mediterranean. Vasavadotta's wish was fulfilled; some mystery-man appeared and built a flying ship allowing the royal pair to fly serenely over hill and vale beyond their kingdom. Further references to Yavanas and their flying-machines are made in the Harscha Charita by Bana, a Brahman, who lived in Northern India about AD 630. This is a period when probable Spaceships were chronicled by the Venerable Bede in England and in the Nihongi over old Japan.

The year 563 BC witnessed the Incarnation of the Buddha.[7]

The court-astrologers advised King Suddhodana, who ruled the Sakya kingdom, Southern Nepal, that his wife, Maha Maya, would give birth to Siddharta Gautama, destined to change the world. Legends declare that his birth was attended by angels singing hymns of joy. When he left his wife and child to seek deliverance in solitude Gods disguised as men tempted him with the kingdoms of the Earth. Finally he found that the cessation of suffering is to cease from attachment. The Buddha's selflessness and gentle compassion remain the hope of the world. Celestials manifested in Israel, Greece and Rome in the sixth century BC, surely they would visit this young Ascetic seeking enlightenment. The great King Asoka (273-239BC) propagated Buddhism beyond the frontiers of India. He is said to have founded a society called the Nine Unknowns to preserve the secrets of certain weapons of massive destruction from the Military. Would our own scientists had done the same!

CHAPTER NINE
Tibet

All the people of old Tibet believed that the Lhas who drove
their chariots in the starry heavens descended long ago to that
legendary island in the central Asiatic sea and built their
celestial city of Lhasa for the Sons of God, who controlled the
elements dominating earth, sea and sky.

Antediluvian traditions told of the days when there was no
Moon in the sky, the Giants of Earth basked in a glorious
Golden Age of universal peace inspired by Teachers from
other planets. Suddenly, according to the sacred Stanzas of
Dzyan, 'The flames came. The fires with the sparks. The fight
fires and the day fires. They dried out the turbid dark waters.
With their heat they quenched them. The Lhas (Spirits) of the
high; the Lhamayin (those) of below came. They slew the
forms, which were two- and four-faced. They fought the god-
men and the dog-headed men and the men with fishes'
bodies.' This garbled description resolves into an apparent
invasion by Celestials wearing space-suits evoking Oannes,
the God, half-man, half-fish, who came from the deep to bring
civilisation to Babylon. Such interpretation may strain belief
yet accords in substance with world-wide legends telling of
war between Gods and men followed by shattering
cataclysms.

Tibetan history is veiled in myth, before the Himalayas
appeared the country was flat and fertile surrounded by sea
and peopled by survivors from the drowned continent of Mu,
Empire of the Sun. Fire and flood ravaged Central Asia, the
golden civilisation was destroyed, when the waters drained
away the few who survived found their stricken land poised in

thin cold air among lofty mountains, as across the world the sea-port of Tiahuanaco has become stranded perched high in the newly-appeared Andes.

Though the official religion of Tibet is Buddhism, the Lamas acknowledge many beneficent and malignant Gods and Goddesses ruling every detail of daily life, worshipped in intricate ritual formulated in the Tantric texts. All Tibetans believe in transcendental realms from which Avatars, Boddhisattvas, return to teach mankind on the cosmic pilgrimage returning to Union with God.

'Avalokitesvara, highest of the three Boddhisattvas, and patron saints of Thibet, projects his shadow full in view of the faithful at the lamasery of Dge-G'don, founded by him, and the luminous form of Son-Ke-pa under the shape of a fiery cloudlet, that separates itself from the dancing beams of the sunlight, holds converse with a great congregation of lamas numbering thousands, the voice descending from above like the whisper of the breeze through the foliage. Anon, say the Thibetans, the beautiful appearance vanishes in the shadow of the sacred trees in the park of the lamasery.'

Surely this manifestation of Avalokitesvara to the Tibetans parallels those encounters of Jehovah with the Patriarchs and the Children of Israel. Could they have been the same Celestial? Identical radiance, auras of light, are said to enhalo some Extraterrestrials alleged today.

Tibet, that mystic land in the lofty Himalayas, was venerated as the psychic-centre of Earth. From their remote lamaseries Adepts held telepathic converse with Cosmic Masters on the planets, in metaphysical realms forces of Good and Evil contended for the soul of Man. Indo-Tibetan traditions, somewhat confused, tell of Agharta hidden far underground and approached by tunnels from secret entrances on all the continents. This subterranean civilisation founded by Celestials from the stars apparently dates back to the earliest days of our Earth and may be the underground refuge of the Els or Cyclops after the supposed Space-War between the Sons of Uranus and Saturn, or possibly an escape from some cosmic cataclysm menacing our planet long ago. Refugees from Mu and Atlantis are said to have fled underground. Mystical Brotherhoods world-wide claim some link between a psychic civilisation miles beneath our feet and Masters in Tibet. Advocates of the Hollow Earth Theory allege that those famous Flying Saucers actually emanate from inside our own Earth through holes at the Poles to surveil the countries on the surface. The esoteric teachings call the Ruler of Agharta by the title King of the World, with two lesser Priest-Kings he is said to plan the future of mankind. His symbol is the crooked cross, the Swastika, used by Hitler and distorted by him.

Associated with Agharta is Shamballah, approached by tunnels from Tibet, once capital of a great civilisation in the Gobi, although some traditions site it as White Island in the ancient Asiatic Sea. Tibetan lore regards the Kings of Agharta as Powers of Righteousness, contending with Adepts of Shamballah, Followers of the Left Hand Path, who promote evil. Their cosmic conflict is said to be divinely decreed for speeding the spiritual evolution of Man. This occult doctrine can lead to perversion threatening destruction.

A colony of Hindus and Tibetans, who settled in Berlin and Munich in 1926, formed the Thule Group. A somewhat confused ideology preached the supremacy of the Aryans, the Nordic Superman, mingled with geo-politics and racialism. This peculiar doctrine captured the imagination of the fanatical Hitler and the Nazis, their evil Swastika enslaved Europe. Bizarre though it seems to us some psychics believe Hitler's madness, menacing the world, was fomented by black magicians from Tibet.[148]

Tibetans think that meteorological phenomena are the work of demons or magicians. Madame Alexandre David-Neel records the materialisation of thought-forms into persons or things,[56] men who out-run horses, naked hermits who warm themselves amid mountain-snows, telepathic communication across vast distances, transmigration of souls, levitation and many other incredible mysteries flouting Western Science. Marco Polo in the 13th century related that Tibetan wizards at the Chinese Court could stop a storm or make a goblet of wine fly across the hall from a sewing table to Emperor Kubla Khan's hand and then back again after he had emptied it.[171] Scientists believe that as in the Sanskrit texts, such recondite works as the Kanjur, Tanjur and Batam-Hygm, somewhere explain the secrets of anti-gravity, teleportation, psychokinesis and sidereal forces beyond our knowledge. This archaic literature may contain the wisdom bequeathed from former civilisations and probably secretes experience of Extraterrestrial visitations veiled from the West.

Folk tales from Tibet delight in the supernatural common to every country in the world. A charming romance in the Sudhana Avodana[178] describes how Manohara, a Kinnari, celestial maiden, bathing in a lake was snared with a magic chain by the hunter, Philoka; her companions flew heavenwards leaving her on Earth. Prince Sudhana fell in love with the fair captive, they married and lived happily until Manohara found the jewel which she had lost, giving her the power to fly again; she became a bird once more and flew aloft. The distraught Sudhana succeeded in following her to the skies to the palace of the Celestials. The King set him the surprisingly difficult task of recognising her among her numerous sisters, each of whom looked exactly like her in appearance and dress. Love found a way. Prince Sudhana recognised his wife at once by a ring, they were reconciled and lived in heavenly bliss.

The Tibetans believe that a Changchub semspa, a highly spiritually developed being, has the power to generate thought-forms which are tangible and endowed with natural qualities making them as though real; phantom horses trot and neigh, phantom travellers behave like real persons, phantom houses will really shelter people. Such materialisations abound in the magical Epic of Gesar of Ling, said to have lived in Eastern Tibet between the seventh and eighth centuries. The Guru Rimpoche, the Precious Spiritual Master of Tibet, better known as Padma Sambhava, persuaded a God to incarnate as the hero, Gesar of Ling, in order to destroy the Demon-Kings who were perverting the Earth with evil and attacking the good people of Tibet.

Padma Sambhava rode through the clouds on a winged-horse; after one visit to the young Gesar he 'shut himself into his marvellous tent and slowly rose into the sky; for a few moments the light that surrounded him traced a luminous path amid the clouds, then faded in the distance.' Surely a wonderful description of a UFO! In his fantastic campaigns Gesar created phantom armies killing their enemies like real warriors, he employed magic weapons, sticks of invisibility, rode flying-horses, used enchanted dolls, aided by the Celestials and their fair Dakinis in a wondrous, entertaining epic. Gesar also produced phantom caravans of hundreds of horses, lamas, merchants, servants, all in a fabulous living wonderland of Gods and Demons, Wizards and Faeries, casting their spells in breathless enchantment where physical laws are held in miraculous suspense suggesting the wondrous technology we attribute to Spacemen. The Master entrusted Gesar with a magic *dorje*, or vril rod with which to open the subterranean palace that contained treasures.[55]

A much quoted and highly controversial essay by Vyacheslav Zaitsev[225] alleges the discovery by Chinese archaeologists of 716 strange grooved stone discs in the Bayan-Kara-Ula mountains on the border of China and Tibet said to record the crash of a Spaceship about 12,000 years ago. The survivors mated with the local natives to father the Ham and Dropa tribes. This intriguing story still lacks confirmation and must be questioned. If Celestials did wing down to rescue Initiates from doomed Atlantis it is not wholly improbable that one of their craft may have force-landed in the mountains of Tibet unable to return.

CHAPTER TEN

China

The Chinese believe their earliest ancestors came down from the Moon to found their Celestial Empire. A thousand years before Christ Chinese authors spoke of *sui sing*, luminous globes, saying 'From antiquity until our own days we cannot count the sui sing which have descended.' These mysterious objects were thought to be occupied by titanic and all-powerful Beings,[169] almost the same words as Cicero used in De Divinatione centuries later, recording those 'strange globes' in the sky over ancient Rome. Such fascinating sightings may be confirmed by the discovery in the mountains of Honan, and on an island in Lake Tung-Ting of granite carvings of non-humans with elephants' trunks depicted upright or flying on cylindrical machines in the sky. The New China News Agency quoted Professor Pen Lao of Peking University as dating the reliefs as 45,000 years old; a fantastic age contemporary with Lemuria and early Atlantis. Spacemen teaching those civilisations would surely visit China.

The discovery at Chou-k'ou-tien near Pekin of a human skull proves that a type of man lived in China about 500,000 years ago. Hardly surprising since Dr Richard Leakey found fragments of a large-brained skull two million years older on the shore of Lake Rudolf in Kenya. Can we really believe that in China or elsewhere men remained ignorant for hundreds of thousands of years then suddenly in a few centuries ascended from caves to space-craft? About AD 1200 the philosopher Shusi wrote 'Once I saw shells in the rocks high in the mountains. I am quite certain that they were the shells of marine mussels. Thus those rocks must once have been ocean-clay.'[213] The Latin Poet, Ovid, reported Pythagoras as saying exactly the same about Ancient Greece.

China was ruled for 18,000 years by a race of Divine Kings, according to the manuscript Tchi, an intriguing parallel with similar revelations in the literature of India, Japan, Egypt and Greece. The classic Huai-nan-tzu, chapter 8, describes an idyllic Age when men and animals lived in peace and beauty in a Garden of Eden, body and soul united in cosmic understanding. The climate was benevolent, there were no natural calamities,' the planets did not deviate from their courses', injury and crime were unknown, Earth and humanity prospered. The 'Spirits' frequently descended among men and taught them divine wisdom, later men fell from grace and filled the world with fear, then mankind degenerated to lust and perversions.

The Shan-hai-ching, Book 17, mentions the troublesome Miao, described as winged human-beings living in the extreme north-western corner of the world who about 2,400BC lost the power to fly and after quarrelling with the 'Lord on High' were exiled.[117] It may be oddly significant that in Babylon, which would be the extreme north-western corner of the world to the Chinese sculptures actually did portray winged human-beings accompanying their Great Kings suggestive of the Spacemen who according to the Sumerian epics and Genesis were landing in the Middle East in the third and second millennia BC. They would surely interfere in the affairs of China and probably in every other country world-wide as legends so vividly state.

The Shoo-King (Part Four, chapter 27, p291) referring to the Fourth Root Race, the Atlanteans, reveals

'The Lord Chang-ty (a King of the Divine Dynasty) saw that his people had lost the last vestiges of virtue, then he commanded Tchang and Lhy (two lower Dhyan Chohans) to cut away every communication between Heaven and Earth. Since then there was no more going up and coming down.'[17]

The Miao like the Nine Li before them fostered new rebellion, so the Emperor Yao requested the descendants of Tchang and Lhy to quell the disorder. It was said that

'Tchang lifted Heaven up and Lhy pressed Earth down', the communication between Heaven and Earth ceased.

It may be significant that a Lithuanian legend describes how the God, Pramzimas, looked out of a window of his heavenly house. Perceiving nothing but war among men he sent two Giants, Wandhui and Weyas, upon the sinful Earth who laid all things waste for twenty days and nights.[90]

Almost all the ancient records were destroyed on the orders of the megalomaniac Emperor Che-Hwang-te in 213 BC. He built the Great Wall. The Chinese themselves vaguely believe that there was an age of magic followed by an age of legendary Supermen with fantastic accomplishments enduring in dynasties for thousands of years. Then came an era of wars and calamities degenerating to world-barbarism, slowly ascending to a civilisation far inferior to that wonderful culture of the past. Ancient traditions tell of an island or continent called Maligasama, Atlantis?, destroyed owing to the evil of its Giants. King Peireum escaped like Noah and his descendants peopled China with divine dynasties.

The Chinese writer, Ssu-ma-Cheng, in the eighth century AD in Historical Records states that about 2838 BC Fu Hsi was succeeded by his sister-wife Nu-Kua. She had the body of a serpent and a human head, symbol of a divine Sage, even a Spacewoman. Towards the end of her reign she quelled a rebellion by a vassal, Prince Kung-Kung, 'He struck his head against the Imperial Mountain Pu-Chan-Shan, and brought it down. The pillars of Heaven were broken and the corners of the Earth gave way.'

The sixth chapter of the Huai-nan-tzu, 2nd century BC, states

'In very ancient times the four pillars (at the compass points) were broken down, the nine provinces (of the habitable world) were split apart, Heaven did not wholly cover (Earth) and Earth did not completely support (Heaven). Fires flamed without being extinguished, waters inundated without being stopped, fierce beasts ate the people, and birds of prey seized the old and weak in their claws. Thereupon Nü-kua fused together stones of the fire, colours with which she patched together the azure Heaven. She cut the feet of a turtle with which she set up the pillars.'[117]

Thereafter there was universal harmony, the seasons

followed their due course, men and animals lived in peace.

Confirmation of a cataclysm in Ancient China may be found in caverns at Choukoutien near Peking crammed with assorted human and animal bones in astonishing diversity, apparently swept there from far away by a titanic flood.[206] Immanuel Velikovsky marshals convincing evidence that the mountain-ranges in Tibet and Western China have been elevated in historical times since the Ice Age. In the lifetime of the Emperor Yao, about 1500 BC, the Sun did not set for ten full days and the entire land was flooded, an immense wave that reached the sky fell down on the land of China. Velikovsky's profound researches seem to prove that Venus, allegedly a comet, brushed our Earth displacing its axis causing such disorientation of the cardinal points that Yao sent scholars to different parts of China to find out the location of north, west, east and south, which had apparently changed.

Alterations in the movements of the Sun, Moon and zodiacal signs obliged the compilation of a new calendar. Contacts between Venus and Mars occurred about the eighth century BC.[208] Chinese traditions state that five planets went out of their courses, in the night stars fell like rain. The calendar had a year of 360 days divided in twelve months of thirty days as in India, Mexico and Chaldea. Now the Earth was apparently impelled into Space and its lengthened orbit increased the year to $365\frac{1}{4}$ days.

The history of Northern and Central Asia began much earlier than generally supposed, believe Soviet archaeologists who on the river Ulalinka in Gornojoaltaska, Siberia, have discovered the implements of the oldest inhabitants of this area. These tools date back more than 150-200,000 years ago. The researches of Soviet Scientists published in the last decades have presented a panorama of the happenings in this territory at the end of the second and the beginning of the first millennium of our era. On the Altai mountains there were tribes who left piles of immense treasure and the tattooed mummies of their leaders. About this time on the banks of the river Amur lived tribes who adopted not only stone axes but also iron utensils for working. Their pottery, great containers and vases, is distinguished for its wonderful forms and excellent ornamentations. Archaeological discoveries have led to the belief that Northern, Central and Eastern Asia for a long time were outside the great development of the appearance of Man and of his culture.

Soviet geologists prospecting in the almost inacessible Tien-Shan mountains in Central Asia were astonished to find heaps of slag and well-worn picks, galleries and pit-shafts dating from the Upper Palaeolithic Age showing technical ore-mining about 15,000 BC; the ancient peoples using these metals probably extended their culture to neighbouring China.

Chinese historians ignoring the influence of Lemuria claim that about 5000 BC a New Stone Age culture began in the rich alluvial plain of the Yellow River, they do not explain what happened since the existence of the Peking Man half a million years earlier. Can we believe that during this vast period people lived like cavemen, then suddenly in a few centuries blossomed forth into a brilliant civilisation with exquisite works of art?

The Chinese Exhibition of 1973 shewed a fabulous display of vases, jugs, bowls, dishes, knives, silks and ornaments, marvellously wrought in silver, bronze, jade or porcelain with rich colours, sparkling glazes or crusty patinas, evidence of the artistic wealth of Chinese civilisation down seven thousand years.

The contents of Chinese tombs denote a lofty religion with belief in life after death pervading the whole ancient world. Elegant script on oracle bones and tortoise-shell, like the inscriptions on exquisite bronze-ware, prove that writing and probably books must have developed long before. Today our scientific minds may be more intrigued by objects of 85% aluminium found in the tomb of General Tsao Chou, AD 316, necessitating metallurgical techniques far in advance of contemporary Europe.

There are remarkable parallels between the Chinese religious and mythological beliefs with those recorded in the Hebrew scriptures. The Chinese Repositories, a work of immense wisdom, mentions an age of virtue and happiness, a garden with a tree bearing apples of immortality guarded by a winged serpent (dragon). The fall of Man, the beginning of lust and war, the doctrine of Original Sin, a great flood, virgin-born God-men, discipleship, worship of a Virgin-Mother, Trinities, monasticism, celibacy, fasting, preaching, prayers, primeval Chaos, Paradise and mutual theological doctrines. The knowledge that most of these beliefs were also cherished by the Egyptians, Babylonians, Greeks and Mayas proves that such celestial phenomena were not confined to Palestine as the Bible suggests but occurred world-wide, traditions of the one cosmic wisdom when our Earth was ruled by Spacemen and then scourged by cataclysms. The revelation that the Chinese share almost identical traditions as the peoples of the Middle East, Europe and America confirms that in ancient times China was not isolated from the West but gloried in association with all lands in the world-community. Not until catastrophes destroyed civilisation disrupting transport did China in the East become almost cut off from Europe, although a tenuous trade persisted along the famous Silk Road through fabulous Samarkand.

The fantastic theories of the German orientalist, Hubert Daunicht, University of Bonn, based on the ancient Chinese work Shan-hai-Ching deduce that the Capital of the first Indo-Germanic Empire arose in Sinkiang in North-West China, site of the present atomic-research centre. Dr Daunicht concludes that one of the first Indo-Germanic despots was Huang-ti whom the Gods called Cronos, and one of his sons, Chuan-su-fu, became the Zeus of Greek mythology. The son of Chuan, Yü, was identical with Hercules; he performed twelve tasks almost identical to the twelve labours of the Greek hero. He further claims that the stories of the Gods in the Scandinavian Eddas originated in old China. This though bizarre is not without logic, the Aryans originated in Eastern Asia and driven by cataclysms migrated westwards to the Middle East, Greece and Europe.[23]

The ancient Chinese believed that Heaven and Earth are shaped like an egg. Earth being enclosed by the sphere of Heaven just as the yolk of an egg is enclosed by its shell; belief in the primeval Cosmic Egg was shared by the Indians, Babylonians, Incas and Greeks.

Texts from the Chou Dynasty for the year 2346 BC record the appearance of ten suns in the sky, which at once recall those extra suns over ancient Rome chronicled by Julius

Obsequens, the celestial prodigies mentioned in the Middle Ages by Matthew of Paris and similar sightings reported by UFO students today.

In the legend of the Ching-Chang Brothers, the Four Diamond Kings of Heaven, may be hidden great technological knowledge in the guise of a fairytale. The Feng-shen-i describes how the Four Heavenly Giants led an army of 100,000 celestial soldiers in support of Shang, against Chiang-Tzu-Ya and General Huang Fei-hu defending the town and mountain of Hsich'i, during the consolidation of the Chou dynasty in the twelfth and eleventh centuries BC.

Mo-li Ch'ing, the eldest Brother, was twenty four feet tall with a beard like copper-wire. He wore a magnificent jade-ring and carried a spear. When this Celestial brandished his magic sword significantly called Blue Cloud 'It causes a black wind which produces tens of thousands of spears which pierce the bodies of men and turn them to dust. The wind is followed by a fire-wheel which fills the air with tens of thousands of golden fiery serpents. A thick smoke also rises out of the ground which blinds and burns men, none being able to escape.'[214] Lo-Hu-Yao had a weapon of devouring fire, Ho Tung a rod of fire and Tien-ho-kien the globe containing the fire from the sky.

This fabulous sword, Blue Cloud, surely conjured up that fantastic Agneya weapon shattering entire armies and scorching the Earth, so vividly described in the Indian Drona Parva. That black wind, those piercing spears turning men to dust like radio-active fall-out; the golden fire, the mushroom cloud of smoke recall the atom-bomb.

The other Genii also wielded fearsome weapons. Mo-li-Hung carried the Umbrella of Chaos which caused the heavens and earth to be covered with thick darkness. Turned upside down it produced violent storms of wind and thunder and universal earthquakes. Mo-li Hai held a four-stringed guitar, the twanging of which supernaturally affected the Earth, water, fire or winds. When it was played all the world listened and the camps of the enemy took fire. The youngest brother, Mo-li Shou, used more sadistic methods. He had two magic whips and a panther-skin, bag-home of a creature resembling a white rat, known as Hua-hu Tiao; it could assume the form of a white-winged elephant which devoured men. He also had a snake or other man-eating creatures, always ready to obey his commands. As in ancient India, and todays armies, these animal-names could denote specific weapons. We fear SAM not as a man but as a surface-to-air missile.

At first the battle against General Huang Fei went in favour of this formidable Ching-Chang quartet. None could resist their magic weapons, especially the flying white elephant which devoured many brave warriors. To celebrate their triumph the Four Kings made merry, fell into a drunken sleep and their wonder-weapons were stolen. No-cha broke the potent jade ring of Mo-li Ch'ing who was slain by a magic spike. Seven-and-a-half inches long, enclosed in a silk sheath, it projected so strong a ray of light that the enemy's eyes were dazzled. The same redoubtable weapon killed the three other Giants.

The Feng-shen-i contains a fantastic account of the conflicts of Chou and the last tyrants of the Shang dynasty. Both Gods and mortals wielded marvellous weapons more sophisticated than our modern armaments. No-Chan in his 'Heaven-and-earth Bracelet', surely a Spaceship, vanquished Feng-Lin a Star God, despite his protective black smoke-clouds. Later Chang Kuei-feng fought the hero, No-Cha, thirty or forty times without disabling his wind-fire Wheel which whirled him around and let him launch hosts of silver flying dragons, probably nuclear-missiles, like clouds of snow upon his enemies. Weng-Chung lashed Ch'ih with a magic whip but was routed by an irresistable ying-yang mirror radiating deadly force.

Wars were waged with the technology associated with Spacemen; the combatants flashed dazzling beams of blinding light, released poisonous gases, launched fire-dragons and globes of fire, hurled lightning-darts and thunderbolts. They practised biological warfare dropping capsules of microbes from celestial umbrellas or parachutes, and protected themselves by veils of invisibility. Their radar detection-images, able to see and hear objects hundreds of miles away, were almost identical to the weaponry detailed in the Sanskrit verses of the Mahabharata.

Generalissimo Chiang Tzu-ya somewhat sceptical of No-Cha's victories went off in his spirit-chariot to Kun-lin, Mountain of the Gods in the centre of the Earth.

The fierce battle continued. Immortals on **dragons and** unicorns, possibly types of spacecraft, joined the slaughter. The Ancient Immortal of the South Pole, who some today would consider a scientist from Agharta, the civilisation underground, provided Tzu-ya with a sand-blaster (atomic weapon?) and an earth-conquering light (laser-ray?) In the titanic conflict while Tzu-ya was fighting Weng-Chung amid a turmoil of longbows, crossbows, armour, whips and hammers, Han Chih-hsien released a black-wind from his magic wind-bag, this was promptly nullified by the Stop-Wind Pearl; thereupon Tzu-ya quickly seized his Vanquish-Spirit whip and struck Han-Chih-hsien in the middle of the skull and he died. In this decisive battle at Mu-Yeh, situated to the south of Wei-hui Fu, in 1122 BC Chou's 700,000 soldiers were defeated. Corpses piled mountains high, the tyrant shut himself up in his magnificent palace, set it alight and was burned alive with all his possessions. Chiang Tzu-ya was appointed Prince of Chi with perpetual succession to his descendants.[214]

This fabulous war between Immortals and men ravaging ancient China may be fantasy, perhaps it is. Yet by intriguing coincidence in the same twelfth century BC the Gods were said to be aiding Greeks and Trojans during the Siege of Troy, while Jehovah and his Angels were leading the Children of Israel through the wilderness to storm Canaan.

The Chinese evidently inherited wisdom from a universal civilisation with advanced knowledge of science and magic. The Alchemists of China sought to make Man like unto the Gods, their most secret practices and doctrines aspired to attune to cosmic forces. Their relationship between Man and metal, especially gold, was rather mystical in nature, they aspired to transmute the material to the spiritual in wonderfully exquisite experiments.

By about 2650 BC the Chinese had observed the motions of the heavenly bodies and mapped the sky in constellations. In 2637 BC the Emperor Hwang-Ti is said to have invented the compass to find his way through a smoke-screen laid down by the rebellious Prince Tchi-yean. 2250 BC the Emperor Shun escaped from captivity by making himself wings like a bird, emulating Daedalus who made wings for himself and his son, Icarus, to escape from Minos of Crete. 1250 BC Chinese astronomers accurately measured 365¼ days in the year and knew the Metonic Cycle of 19 years in which the Sun and Moon returned to the same relative position. Chinese astronomers recorded an eclipse of the Sun in 1216 BC, fortunately for them since about 2000 BC an Emperor put two astronomers to death for failing to do so. 1000 BC Chinese appear to have used a floating-compass for navigation at sea. 600BC the classical Tao Te-King anticipated Newton's Third Law that action and reaction are always equal and opposite applying it to morals as well as mechanics. 580 BC Kung-shu Tse experimented in mechanical flight, making small gliders on the pattern of a magpie. 500 BC the Chinese prepared a catalogue of 1464 stars and divided the year into 24 'breaths'. About 310 BC Tsou Yen introduced the Yin-Yang theory of interaction by opposites to explain all phenomena. 240 BC the Chinese observed Halley's Comet. 180 BC acupuncture was in use and in 176 BC Chouien-yu Yi produced a logical system of medical diagnosis. 175 BC a Law was passed in China to forbid the manufacture of counterfeit gold by Alchemists. 150BC Lohsia-Hung likened the Universe to an egg, the heavens were the shell, the earth was the yoke, the world was round. 120 BC Sseu-Ma-tsien, the Chinese Herodotus, wrote a history of Chinese culture. AD 132 Chang Hen made the first seismograph to detect earthquakes. In AD 140 Wei Po-yang wrote a book on Alchemy called Ts'an T'ing, he claimed to have discovered how to make the 'Pill of Immortality'. He took one – and died![183]

The Chinese made the dragon a symbol of their civilisation, they believed the Celestial Dragon to be the Father of the First Dynasty of Divine Emperors. The Dragon ruled over mountains, was linked to geomancy, dwelled near tombs and was connected with the cult of Confucius, appearing it is said at his birth. A mystic dragon-horse is said to have risen from the Yellow River and shown to Fu Hsi, the legendary First Emperor of China, an occult chart on its back from which the written language of the Chinese evolved.

The Dragon Kings exercised supernatural powers, practised hypnotism and telepathy, were invulnerable to mortal weapons, lived and loved in eternal youth. They were said to dwell in enchanted palaces at the bottom of the sea but all owed allegiance to their Lord in the stars. They soared to the skies like flashing lights on rushing winds causing storms until the Earth roared. Seas could have meant Waters of Space, although we are reminded of the many Spaceships today said to plunge to bases in our ocean-depths. The Dragon Kings were known to be immortal, able to communicate among themselves without recourse to words, in spite of any distance that separated them; they made reports to the upper heavens.[98] The Gods rode on dragons, so did Emperors and holy men.

Could the illiterate Chinese of antiquity imagine a dragon, could its concept permeate their consciousness, inspire their religion and art, impress their daily lives, if this flying object never existed? The texts of ancient China tell in wonderful imagery of fiery, flying dragons, symbolising Spaceships streaking through the skies, plunging into the seas, terrifying peasants, shrivelling countrysides, kidnapping people or landing Divine Strangers like some UFOs alleged today.

A Chinese wood-cut from Tu-Shu-tsi-chang depicts Kikung's Flying Chariot. The Chinese Classics, Shi-Chi and Han-Shu have a description of the 'gold-coloured, heavenly man', who had been heard of as long ago as 500 years between the age of Han and that of Tong. It is very significant that they used not God but 'gold-coloured heavenly men'.

The shifting sands of the Gobi desert are said to conceal the wealth of one of the richest empires of antiquity; gold, silver, jewels, statuary, all the trappings of a brilliant civilisation inspired by lost Lemuria. Local traditions assert that the tomb of Ghengis Khan still exists at Lake Tabascu.

In the 13th century the Mongol hordes surged westwards across Asia using a frightening weapon in which sulphur and saltpetre forming gunpowder propelled a flaming missile through a tube; they crossed the frozen River Dnieper to sack the beautiful old city of Kiev.[131] Other Tartars plundered Cracow, surrounded Budapest and threatened Venice. In 1242 the Mongols massed to invade a panic-stricken Europe.

Suddenly news came that in distant China the Great Khan, Ogadai, had died from too much drink. The Mongols raced home to elect a new Khan, never to return. Europe was spared. Legend prophesies that one day Ghengis will awake and lead his people on to world-conquest. The Russians already fear the Yellow armies flooding across Siberia for the Volga before this century ends.

CHAPTER ELEVEN
Japan

The Japanese honour their Emperor as direct descendant of
Amaterasu, the shining Goddess of the Sun, Ruler of the High
Plains of Heaven. Ancient traditions teach that many
thousand years ago the islands of Japan formed a distant
colony of Lemuria, Empire of the Sun. The early colonists, a
white-skinned race, brought with them from the Motherland a
highly developed civilisation which preserved the basic
Lemurian culture until the advent of the Europeans only a
century ago. The Japanese flag, the Rising Sun, still
symbolises the sacred emblem of drowned Lemuria. Like the
Hindus, Chinese and Egyptians, the Japanese too boast
twelve Dynasties of Divine Kings reigning 18,000 years,
suggesting domination by Spacemen.

Ethnologists agree that the first ancestors of the Japanese
were the white-skinned Yamato, who conquered the Neolithic
aborigines, the hairy Ainu, a primitive, decadent race who are
almost extinct. Millennia of inter-marriage with the yellow-
skinned, Mongols have produced that characteristic mutation
we style as Japanese but a surprising number look almost
European.

The names of most of the mountains in Japan are derived
from the Ainu language, the extinct volcano, the beautiful
Mount Fuji, was called after the divine grandmother of fire
floating on an invisible throne.[124] The Ainus like the Shamans
of Siberia practised witchcraft and magic to propitiate
invisible Gods. With the circumpolar peoples of the Arctic the
Ainus made a cult of the bear known as *chinukare-guru*, which
signifies prophet or guardian. The same word was used to

describe the Pole Star in the constellation of Ursa Minor, the Lesser Bear. Perhaps to the Ainu the bear resembled a man in a space-suit? Traditions states that Okikurumikamui, a Space Brother, descended from the heavens and taught the Ainus farming at Pairatori, a town in Hokkaido.

Excavations of ancient dolmens and grave-mounds show that during the third millennium BC the Yamato enjoyed a sophisticated culture displaying great artistry in ceramics, armour and weapons of bronze and iron wrought with technical skill. Exquisite mirrors and magnificent jewels rival the contemporary treasures of Ninth Dynasty Egypt and the fabulous treasures of old China. In the prehistoric tombs clay figurines of curious little people, called Jomon Dogus have faces of Caucasian cast not of oriental Mongol. Archaeologists once believed them ceremonial substitutes for human sacrifice, lately their resemblance to the celebrated Martian of the Tassili rock-paintings in the Sahara, to questionable petroglyphs in a cave near Ferghana in Uzbekistan, and to Aztec figurines in old Mexico, suggests that these little men wore space-suits and helmets.

The Cosmic Brotherhood Association of Yokohama have made a profound study of the Jomon statuettes. In a tomb in the Tohuku Area in Northern Japan statues appeared to be wearing sun glasses, at Komukai, Amori Prefecture, are rock-carvings with a helmet and diver's suit. Their heads are covered with crowns, their mechanical large eyes wear glasses, their mouths covered with masks, which have filters in the centre, necks having white collars and the figures apparently wear a pilot's G-suit which stands extreme pressure. It may be significant that this baggy space-suit looks like a Thailand traditional costume. An American Ufologist who inspected these intriguing statuettes is quoted as saying 'The suit is a perfect NASA Space-pilot suit'. Yusuke J. Matsumura, analyses Jomon Dogu statuettes made about 3,000 BC excavated at Kamagaoka. Describing the suits he states 'They look rather baggy, similar to other clay figures; something like a helmet is joined about its neck and a small opening like a window is seen at the back-side of the helmet. A filter-like equipment is engraved not about its mouth but at its chain'. A representation of the God Hitokotonushti in a Jomon suit shows him standing on a cloud, his name means Space-suit.

Research by the CBA apparently resurrects a cosmic culture in Kamagaoka district. King Iwai, patriarch of the Sun Race of Kyushu, was a descendant of the Celestials. He civilised his people and bade them live in the Sun Disk, calling to mind the illumined Sun religion of Akhnaton, the heretic-Pharaoh. The great Sun Mark, cut into the ground, is said to denote the ancient Kingdoms of the Sun. The Kamagaoka race went completely out of existence leaving their earthenware statuettes as a legacy for our own Space Age. CBAs research-team found at Ohyu in Hokkaido, a layer of volcanic ash about 30cms thick over the ancient cosmic base explaining its destruction. Yusuke J. Matsumura supposes that when Maldek, the fifth planet between Mars and Jupiter exploded into fragments known as the asteroids, catastrophic effects were caused not only to Earth but to the magnetic-field of local Space, obliging Space-Travellers to wear protective suits against new and deadly radiation. Spacemen were obliged to modify and improve their space-suits, the various Jomon Dogu statuettes shewing the different types. Did the Kamagaoka people fearing a further cataclysm try to fly to another planet wearing these cosmic suits, or were they exterminated by the great disaster?

In a Chip-San tomb in the suburbs of Yamago City, Kunamoto, Kyushu, a wall-painting dated about 2000 BC shows an ancient Japanese King holding up his hands to welcome seven Sun Discs, similar to prehistoric murals found in Etruria, India and Iran. Another picture shows people holding hands in a large circle looking up at the sky evoking the Flying Saucers to appear in Izumizaki, Fukushima. The very word Chip-San in the pre-Ainu language is said to have meant 'the place where the Sun came down'. Dr Yoshiyuku Tangye states 'In 1963 surveying Shiranyi or Unknown Fire, on the Yatsushirakai Sea, Kyushu, were found that this was really a Fire from Space and had a close connection with Flying Saucers. And through our survey around this area, where there are many ancient tombs, we found that here once existed a great Sun Kingdom, where Flying Saucers visited in the ancient times.'

An ancient tomb at Katsuhara commanding a full view of

the Shiranui-kai Sea, Amakuse Islands and Udo Peninsula has a picture of the Sun Mark, said to resemble an old navigational instrument, apparently with a fleet of huge Spaceships. Yusuke J. Matsumura claims this fact confirms that the Sun Marks are mechanical structures.[135]

Japanese folk-lore tells of Kappa, a dwarf who by his magic power draws people down into the water, the only way to avoid his clutch is to bow to him, then he bows and pours all the water there is from a hole in his skull. Deprived of this water the Kappa can do nothing.[89] This bizarre belief like all folk-tales probably contains some great truth long since lost. Peasants fearfully describe the mysterious Kappas, Men of the Reeds, as having pointed heads, large triangular eyes, huge ears, nose like an elephant's trunk, a monstrous creature which suddenly resolves into an Alien wearing space-suit and respirator. Jutting from a Kappa's head are four needles like Indian feathers, today we may call them antennae. These strange creatures seem uncommonly like our cosmonauts landing on the Moon.

A commentary in the Nihongi states 'The Celestial Dog or Tengu of modern Japanese superstition is a winged creature in human form which haunts mountain-tops and other secluded places.' The 'exceedingly long nose' of the Tengu, 'winged creature in human form' and the elephant-trunk of the Kappas no doubt refer to some helmet with breathing apparatus, for to some Extraterrestrials our oxygenated atmosphere may be poisonous.

The Japanese lack an ancient literature. Most of their legends preserved for ages by wandering minstrels were not written down until the beginning of the eighth century AD. The Kojiki, Record of Ancient Matters is the oldest extant Japanese book. In 720 AD the legends, duly revised, were re-written in classical Chinese as the Nihongi or Chronicles of Japan.

The Kojiki states that on the Plain of High Heaven, possibly another planet, were born three Divine Personages, Master-of-the-August-Centre-of-Heaven, the High-August-Producing-Wondrous-Deity and the Divine-Producing-Wondrous-Deity. Later many Divinities appeared. The Gods commanded Izanagi and Izanami standing together on the

Floating Bridge of Heaven (a Spaceship?) to plunge a heavenly jewelled Spear into the chaotic brine which curdled into an island to which the pair descended like Osiris and Isis to old Egypt, and Manco-Capac and his wife Mama-Ocllo to Lake Titicaca in the Andes. The Heavenly Pair together created the Great-Eight-Island-Land, and then generated the Sun Goddess, Amaterasu, the Moon God, Tsuki Yama, and the Storm God, Susanowo. Jimmu Tenno, grandson of the Sun Goddess, became the first Emperor of Japan; Amaterasu's one-hundred-and-twentyfourth grandson in descent, the Mikado Hirohito, rules today.

Izanagi made Amaterasu, Ruler of the High Plain of Heaven, and gave Susanowo domination over the sea. In a boisterous meeting the Impetuous Male breaks down the neat division of the rice-fields, fills the irrigation-ditches and defiles the Celestial Palace with excrement. Amaterasu at first excuses her drunken brother but he 'flays a piebald colt with a backward flaying' and flings it into the weaving-hall where she is working with her attendants, many of whom are fatally wounded in their private parts by the flying shuttles. The Goddess is most annoyed; she retires to a cave leaving the world to darkness and disaster. While the Sun Goddess sulks, the Gods and Goddesses try in vain to entice her from her cave to shine her light again on desolate Earth. Finally a lascivious madcap dance is performed by the Goddess Ama-no-uzume, who stamping loudly on the ground, pulling the nipples of her breasts and lowering her skirt so delights the assembled Gods that they break out in raucous laughter.[117] Piqued by curiosity Amaterasu peers out of the cave, the Gods pass her a mirror; intrigued with her own image the Sun Goddess slowly steps out to shine her light on a grateful world. This diverting tale is the Japanese version of the War in Heaven between the Gods and the subsequent cataclysm on Earth.

When Ninigi-no-Kimoto descended to Earth nearly two million years ago, carried in the Floating Bridge of Heaven, he was told that at the cross-roads of heaven was a strange Deity whose nose was seven hands long and from whose mouth and posterior a light shone. This odd description may refer to a Celestial in a Spaceship from another Galaxy since none of the Gods knew anything about him. The Goddess Uzume-hime approached the Stranger who said his name was Sarute-hiko, he too was proposing to land in Japan and offered to make the Goddess a Flying Bridge or Heavenly Bird-Boat. Ninigi brought the jewel, the sword and the mirror as proof of his celestial origin.

Ninigi's great grandson, the first earthly Emperor of Japan, known as Jimmu, Divine Valour, was officially enthroned on 11 February 660 BC. When his forces were repulsed in Yamato the Heavenly Deities came to his assistance and the enemy was vanquished. About two centuries later in 498 BC Castor and Pollux, the Heavenly Twins, aided the Romans to defeat the Tuscans at Lake Regillus. Jimmu's victory was not assured until he invited eighty Ainus to a banquet and had them assassinated.

On February 10th in the year 9 BC nine suns flew over Fujiyama, like those nine Flying Saucers flying near Mt Rainier in America, seen by Kenneth Arnold on June 24th 1947. The nine Sun Disks over Japan parallel the ten suns over China in 2346 BC when nine were shot down by the Divine Archer, Tzu-Yu. On both occasions Earth was torn with discord.

About 220 AD the famous Express Jingo invaded Korea, the Deities went before and after the expedition. The King of Silla, Korea, was overwhelmed by these divine invaders and promptly surrendered.

An intriguing reference to an apparent Spaceman appears in the Nihongi, Book 1, p342.

'4th Spring. 2nd month. The Emperor (Oho-hatsuse-Waka-Taka) went a hunting with bows and arrows on Mount Katsuraki. Of a sudden a tall man appeared, who came and stood over the vermilion valley. In face and demeanour he resembled the Emperor. The Emperor knew that he was a God and therefore proceeded to inquire of him saying "Of what place art thou, Lord?" The tall man answered and said "I am a God of visible men (i.e. One who has assumed mortal form). Do thou first tell thy princely name and then in turn I will inform thee of mine." The Emperor answered and said "We are the Waka-taka-no-Mikoto." The tall man next gave his name saying "Thy Servant is the God, Hito-Koto-Mushi" (Literally "One Word Master." The Deity who dispels with a word the evil and with a word the good.) He finally joined him in the diversion of the chase.'

A curious passage from a work called Sei-to-Ki states

'In the reign of the Emperor Kwamzu, 782-806 AD, we (Japan) and Korea had writings of the same kind. The Emperor disliking this burned them and said "These speak of the God who founded the country and do not mention the Gods, our ancestors." But possibly this only refers to the legend of Ton-kun, which the Tongkom gives as follows. "In the Eastern Region, Korea, there was at first no chief. Then there was a Divine Man who descended under a sandal-tree, the people of the land established him as their Lord. He was called Ton-kun, Sandal-Lord, while the country received the name Choson, meaning freshness. This was in the reign of the Chinese Emperor, Tong-Yao. 2357-2258 BC? the year, Mon-Shen. The capital was at first Phyong-yong; it was afterwards renamed Pek-ok, the white hill. In the 8th year 1317 BC of the reign of Wu-Ting of the Shang Dynasty he entered Mount Asatai and became a God." '

This Divine Being was believed to have lived a thousand years in Korea then was mysteriously translated to the skies. We are reminded of the fabulous Count St. Germain who is said to have visited Earth during several centuries, returning periodically to the planet Venus.

The Nihongi mentions more than a dozen sightings of Unidentified Flying Objects manifesting over Japan in the seventh century AD. It is likely that many haunted the skies for ages before written records began.

A Japanese fairy-tale from the Nippon Mukasi Banasi states that a man returned still young from a trip to heaven only to find no descendants in his home. Similar things can be read into a Russian fairy-story and in a Ukrainian tale saying three years for ourselves are like three hundred years to God. This refers to the Time-Dilation paradox postulated by Einstein's Theory of Relativity, whereby a Spaceman travelling at a speed approaching the velocity of light would apparently age little compared with the people he left behind on Earth. The Greeks suggest a similar story concerning Epimenides, the famous Sage of early seventh century BC. Did this concept of Time-Dilation reach Japan from Greece via Russia or was it taught to all by Spacemen?

The Historical Records tell how the Emperor Hwang to attract a celestial dragon first gathered copper, associated with the planet Venus, on a mountain, then cast a tripod. A dragon winged down at once, after the Monarch had flown in the God as in an airship, seventy of his subjects went for a flight in it too.[129]

Shinto meant in Chinese the Way of the Good Spirit, known

much later as Kami-no-Michi, the Way of the Gods, it permeates all aspects of Japanese life. This early religion taught that all living creatures and things fell down to Earth from a hole in the sky. Heaven resembled a technicolour picture of Japan connected by a celestial arch facilitating frequent visits between Earth and Sky until the bridge broke down. All believed the Sun, Moon and stars were thronged with Spirits, who would do good or evil ruling men's lives. The teachings of Confucius brought ancestor-worship to Japan followed by the compassion of Buddhism and the austerity of Zen. Shintoism taught the worship of the Emperor, memories of that Golden Age of the Space Kings.

Clypeus—R. Drake.

1. The 'Flying Car' of Ki-Kung-Chi, c. 1700 BC

2. The Disc of Phaistos, a clay disc stamped with ideograms discovered in Crete. Ideograms were the secret symbol-writing of the archaic priests, preserved mostly on megalithic monuments. Arrowed is an ideogram depicting a flying saucer.

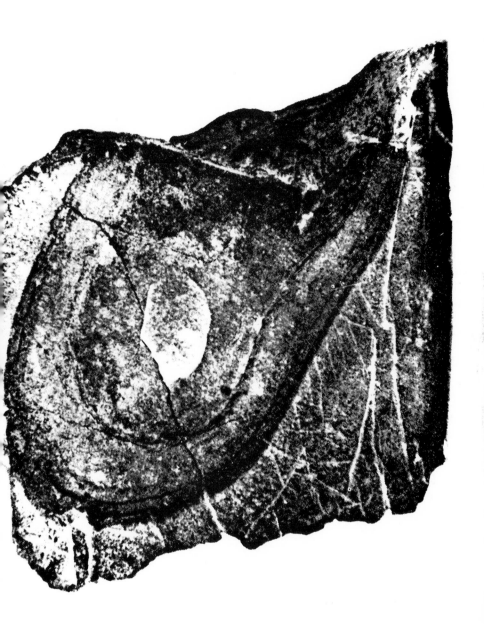

3.   Imprint of the sole of a shoe discovered in a limestone quarry
in Nevada, going back to an epoch before the appearance of man
on the earth.

4.   Area about two miles north of Palpa, Peru, showing where the ancient city was built directly over a series of hundreds of radiating lines. This area was once the center of a highly evolved culture. Beacons for the gods?

5.   Ancient pre-Inca representation of the Road in the Sky from Peru. The Jaguar God is placed above the Moon, flanked by two eight-pointed stars. Above the entire design is a circular symbol which archaeologists cannot explain. However, this 'disc' represents the coming in ancient times of the *Illa-Siva* or 'light rings', known also as the *Rampa-Liviac* or 'litters of electric energies', the UFOs or Flying Saucers of modern times.

6.   A Chac-Mol, Aztec idol: does it not seem like an astronaut in position for take-off?

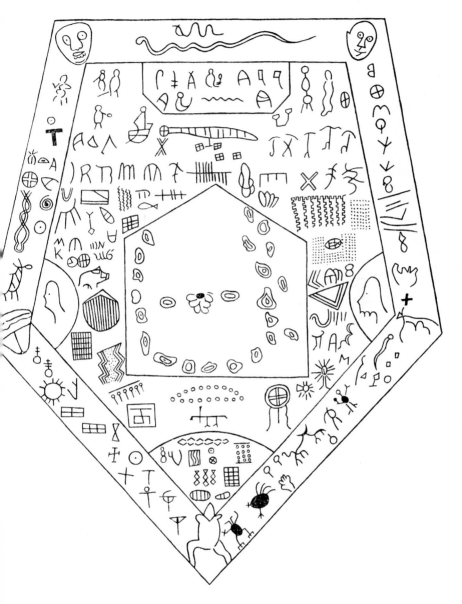

7. Hieroglyphs, symbols and ornaments of the giant stone *Pedra Pintada*, in Brazil.

8. The Platform at Baalbek, Lebanon. Was this a launching pad for flying saucers?

9. The location of the Lost Continent of Atlantis, by Moreux.

Clypeus.

10.   Reproduction of a bas-relief from Palenque. According to space archaeology, the goddess is sitting on an apparatus very similar to a flying saucer.

11. The god Homoyoca was depicted on a strange mount. Could it be a one-man flying vehicle?

12. Temple of the Sun, Trujillo, on the Rio Moche.

Clypeus.

13. The Conqueror, Cortes, sits before Montezuma. At his shoulder is Malinche, who acts as interpreter.

14. Ten thousand years ago these figures were carved on the rocks at Tassili in the Sahara. They clearly show helmeted figures, presumably wearing space suits.

::MONTE SYNAY::

15.   The monastery of Santa Katerina on Mount Sinai. The wrath of God descends in the form of a rocket which strikes the summit of the mountain. An old wood-cut representing Judgment Day.
Clypeus—R. Drake.

Clypeus—R. Drake.

16. Gulliver and the Flying Island of Laputa, by Marco Rostagno.

Clypeus—R. Drake.

17.   Flying Saucer photographed at Pian Audi, Turin, at 11.45 am
on 29th August 1962.

18. Picture taken at 9 am on 8th December 1973 at Crosnes, twelve miles from Paris, by M. Rolland. It was shown on French television in February, 1974.

19. The same picture, enlarged 350 times. Notice the trail and a darkish zone in the luminous halo.

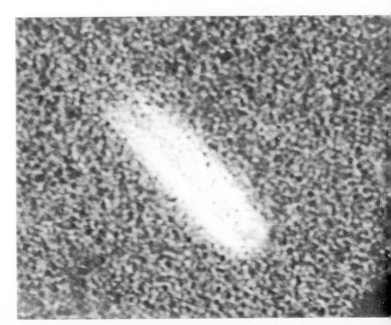

CHAPTER TWELVE
Egypt

The Egyptians believed themselves to be the oldest of mankind.[95] Occult traditions teach that tens of thousands of years ago Lemurians migrated from their drowned continent across India to form settlements on the Upper Nile.[16] The first Dynasties were said to have sprung from the Solar and Lunar Races, signifying Spacemen.

The extreme antiquity of the Egyptian God-Kings is confirmed by Manetho, born about 300 BC, who rose to be High priest in the temple of Heliopolis famed as a great seat of learning. Manetho must have had at his disposal age-old records, above all the advice of his erudite colleagues to criticise his History. This scholarly work Aegyptica written in Greek during the reign of the first Ptolemy is lost with all its sources, possibly burned accidentally during the partial destruction of the great Library at Alexandria by Julius Caesar, or consigned to the flames by fanatical Christians or by the Arabs in AD 643. Of this valuable history only a few extracts are preserved in works by Julius Africanus and Eusebius.

The extant fragments of Manetho's Aegyptica state

'The first man, or God in Egypt is Hephaestus who is also renowned among the Egyptians as the discoverer of fire. His son, Cronos, Osiris, Typhon, brother of Osiris and lastly, Horus, son of Osiris and Isis. They were the first to hold sway in Egypt. Thereafter the kingship passed from one to another in an unbroken succession down to Bydis through 13,900 years. After the Gods the Demi-Gods held sway for 1,255 years and again another line of Kings held sway for 1,817 years. Then came thirty more kings of Memphis reigning for 1,790 years and then again ten Kings of this reigning for 350 years. Then followed the rule of Spirits of the Dead for 5,813 years.[50]

Perhaps the Spirits of the Dead were Spacemen?

The Old Egyptian Chronicle preserved by Syncellus, Vice-Patriarch of Constantinople in the 8th century, contained thirty dynasties in 113 descents during the long period of 36,525 years. Simplicius in the 6th century wrote that he had heard that the Egyptians had kept astronomical observations for the last 630,000 years, comparable with the claim by Berossus that a King ruled Babylon 432,000 years before the Flood. Diogenes Laertius dated astronomical calculations by the Egyptians to 48,863 years before Alexander the Great, 356-323 BC, and Martianus Capella stated that the Egyptians had secretly studied the stars for 40,000 years before revealing their knowledge to the world.

Panodorus, an Egyptian monk about 400 AD, described the days when the Egregori, Watchers or Angels, descended to Earth and taught men astronomy. The ancient Phoenician writer, Sanchoniathon, hundreds of years before Christ wrote about Elianu, The Most High, and the war between Ouranos and Cronos for whom Thoth fabricated a Spaceship.

On the ceiling of the Denderah temple was carved a Zodiac said to portray a configuration of the stars about 90,000 BC proving that the early history of Egypt was contemporary with Atlantis.[25] Such vast antiquity confounds our Egyptologists who dispute with each other. Petrie dated the First Dynasty of Menes as commencing in 4777 BC, Breasted as 3400 BC; some authorities suggest 2850 BC. Archaeologists trace civilisation in Jericho to 8000 BC and in Turkey to 9000 BC. Can Egyptologists really believe that the fertile banks of the Nile were deserted until more than 5000 years later, especially when Man is known to have existed 2,000,000, perhaps even 20,000,000 years ago on the shores of Lake Rudolf in Kenya.

Herodotus in 443 BC toured Egypt, Babylon and lands in between, writing about his travels as he went. He was clearly awed by the antiquity of the Egyptians for he pursued his enquiries closely. His conclusions contradict archaeologists and agree with those ancient authorities already quoted. In Book Two, Chapter 142, of his History he states impressively

'Thus far the Egyptians and their priests told the story. And they shewed that there had been three hundred and forty one generations of men from the first King unto this last, the priest of Hephaestus. And in these generations there were even so many (high priests and) Kings. Now three hundred generations of men are equal to ten thousand years, for three generations of men are an hundred years. And in the forty one generations which yet remain in addition to the three hundred, there are one thousand and three hundred and forty years. Thus in eleven thousand and three hundred and forty years they said that no God in the form of a man had been King; neither spoke they of any such thing either before or in after time among those that were kings of Egypt later. (Now in all this time they said that the sun had removed from his proper course four times, and had risen where he now setteth, and set where he now riseth; but nothing in Egypt was altered thereby, neither as touching the river nor as touching the fruits of the Earth, nor concerning sicknesses or deaths.'

A few years earlier the priests at Thebes showed Hecateus, the historian, three hundred and forty three colossal wooden statues which Herodotus also saw. All were high priests, father and son in unbroken descent. They were 'noble and good but far removed from Gods. But they said that in the time before these men, the rulers of Egypt were Gods who dwelt among mankind'.

The world-wide catastrophe 11,000 years earlier mentioned by Herodotus, when Earth's axis became displaced four times, the sun appearing to rise in the west, may synchronise with the destruction of Atlantis. Plato related in the Timaeus that when his great ancestor, Solon, visited Egypt about 590 BC the learned Priests of Sais told him of the onslaught of the Atlanteans on Europe and Libya. They were finally routed by the valiant Athenians and driven back to their island before it sank.

Comprehension of the origin of the Egyptian civilisation surely requires a survey of North and Central Africa, even contemporary Atlantis; all apparently surveilled by Gods, the Spacemen.

Herodotus believed that the alluvial deposits at the Nile Delta were comparatively recent.[95] and was occupied gradually as land became available by the drying-up of the great Saharan sea.

Strabo and Pliny recall that most of Libya was an inland sea, possibly the remains of a vast gulf which flowed from the Sudan into the Atlantic Ocean opposite the now sunken island of Poseidonis near the present Canary Isles. Abyssinia in the remote past was an island. Hoerbiger's questionable cosmogenic theory claims that about a hundred thousand years ago the then-Moon, predecessor of our familiar Luna, crashed down on the Mountains of the Moon in Abyssinia. The Sahara Gulf dwindled to Lake Tritonis bounded in the West by the Atlas Mountains, in the East by Egypt with islands like the Hoggar plateau. At Siwa in the present desert are old stone quays from when the city was a port on the Triton Sea; in the Middle Ages near the Draa depression a ship was found with the skeletons of the rowers still with chains around their bones.

Galleries at the Temple of Agarumi near Djebel Muta display brilliant paintings of a city on a seashore showing square-sailed ships. Some pictures depict buffaloes, mammoths, ferny forests, beautiful birds and strange animals like those frescoes on the cliffs at Tassili. Greek traditions quoted by Diodorus Siculus tell of earthquakes cracking the Mediterranean Valley at the Pillars of Hercules and draining away the waters from Lake Tritonis.

Dr Giancarlo Ligabue and Dr Cino Boccazzi in the Southern Sahara near the mountainous group of Termit discovered a vast cemetery of dinosaurs and the bones of monstrous flying-dragons, when the area was Jurassic swamp a hundred million years ago. Even more marvellous, near the fossil remains were found stone arrowheads, signs of Ancient Man.

The blue eyes of the Tuaregs, the customs and weapons of the Berbers, evoke legendary Atlantis. Fantastic stories are told of Antinea, fabulous last Queen of Atlantis, in the Sahara's wild Hoggar Massif and her silent court of glittering golden mummified lovers. Plato declared that the Atlanteans once ruled all Libya.

Legends suggest that for thousands of years Extraterrestrials founded colonies on our planet, particularly in East Africa, concentrating their dropping-zone in Abyssinia where they worked deep mines to extract copper, gold and silver. Chaldean records are said to reveal that about 11000 BC the confederation of Talantu-Atlantis flourished in East-Central Africa governed by Priests of the Wisdom inspired by Teachers from Venus. Their descendants are believed to have migrated to Babylonia and founded the Sumerian civilisation whose symbol was Solar Fire. Aided by Celestials they developed a psycho-electrical science.[62]

As the great Saharan Sea disappeared leaving the Nile to flow into the Mediterranean tribes from Libya occupied the Delta and emigrants from Abyssinia moved northwards into Upper Egypt bringing knowledge of the Celestials who ruled there. The God Kings were said to have withdrawn from Egypt after refugees from Atlantis settled along the Nile. Traditions allege that their new cities, given the collective name of the World down below, were located in the headquarters of the Nile and in mountains like Sinai accessible by water through tunnels.

One of the Books of Hermes, Thoth, from a remote age describes certain of the pyramids as standing upon the sea-shore, 'the waves of which dashed in powerless fury against its base',[16] proving the extent of the vast Saharan Sea and the immense antiquity of Egyptian civilisation. Egypt was not so isolated as we imagine. First Dynasty inscriptions about 5000BC refer to the Land beyond the Western Sea as Urani Land, the Urani were people of Ur. Pharaoh Necho's fleet circumnavigated the African continent in 600 BC, probably not for the first time. Intriguing Egyptian hieroglyphics at Wollongong near Sydney suggest Cleopatra's ships reached Australia.[149] In 1963 a pile of Egyptian coins that had been buried 4000 years was found in terrain in Australia sheltered by rocks. Necho actually built a Suez Canal connecting for centuries the Mediterranean and the Red Sea.

Harold Bayley in Archaic Britain states 'Sir John Morris-Jones has noted remarkable identities between the syntax of Welsh and that of early Egyptian; Gerald Massey in his Book of the Beginnings gives a list of 3000 close similarities between English and Egyptian words, and the astronomical enquiries of Sir Norman Lockyer have driven him to conclude 'The people who honoured us with their presence here in Britain some 4000 years ago, had evidently, some way or other, had communicated to them a very complete Egyptian culture and they determined their time of night just in the same way that the Egyptians did.'

Claudius Aelianus, 2nd century AD, quoting the now lost Meropidae by the celebrated 4th century BC Greek historian,

Theopompus of Chios, states that Silenus, son of a nymph (Spacewoman?) told Midas, King of Phrygia, that the Atlanteans invaded Europe and Libya with ten million men. Occult sources say this titanic war was fought with nuclear and electrical weapons like those fantastic conflicts in the Indian Classics. Egypt in coalition with heroic Athens smashed their powerful enemy with cosmic forces which are thought to have displaced the Earth's axis causing the last Ice Age, a fantasy not quite so silly as it sounds. To marshal such fabulous power the Egyptians must have shared the secrets of the Space Gods.

In 1966 an expedition conducted intensive X-ray examination of the mummies of several Pharaohs and found them sadly subject to all the ills that plague old people today. Almost all had bad teeth and suffered from rheumatism. Ramses II, alleged Pharaoh of the Exodus, father of a hundred sons and fifty-nine daughters, was also plagued by cold feet. X-rays show degenerative arthritis in the hip-joint and arteriosclerosis of all the major arteries of the lower extremities.[215]

The Divine Eye, sometimes known as the Eye of Ra or the Eye of Horus was associated by the unsophisticated Egyptians with the War in Heaven. The Goddess Hathor at the command of Ra once took the form of the Divine Eye and waged war upon mankind; she slew so many Men that Ra feared all humanity would perish, so he poured seven thousand jars of beer upon the fields; Hathor paused to admire her beautiful reflection in the beer then quenched her thirst, became drunk and abandoned the slaughter.[189] When the Eye descended to Earth the glorious Being residing therein dominated men like Jehovah in his power and glory overlorded the Israelites. Since it seems unlikely that two Celestials would rule adjacent lands like Egypt and Israel, they were probably the same Entity. Logic would suggest that the Sky Gods worshipped by most peoples were either the same Celestial or Supermen from the same planet. The Egyptians regarded the spaceships haunting their skies as boats of the Sun sailing across the sky, a symbolism of world-wide significance since carvings of solar barks are found in Ireland, Brittany, Sweden and other prehistoric sites. Ancient traditions allege that the builders of the Great Pyramid buried a solar boat, a spaceship, near the edifice.

Intriguing references to the 'Divine Eye' and to the conflict between Horus and Set are found in the ancient Egyptian Book of the Dead. This collection of hymns, litanies, spells and words of magical power, describes the journey of the newly-arrived Spirit in the Underworld through infernal regions of torment to the Hall of Judgement where his heart is weighed on a great balance by Anubis with Thoth as scribe in the presence of the forty-two Judges of the Dead. The German scholar, Adolf Erman, declared that this ancient literature belonged to the most remote prehistory; copies of the text were inscribed on coffins, papyri written with beautiful hieroglyphics were secreted among the linen-cloths enwrapping mummies as guide-books for the deceased in the Underworld.

Many texts appear to have been miscopied down the long ages. Scribes unconversant with the original meaning made obvious mistakes. Translators last century lacking a perfect knowledge of Ancient Egyptian were further frustrated by their ignorance of aeronautics, puzzled by many passages they made the best rendering possible. As with our own Bible such translations sometimes strayed from the intended truth.

Throughout the many papyri comprising the Book of the Dead are scattered intriguing phrases such as The Ancient of Days, Spirits of Light, Sons of Darkness, Legions in the Sky, Hidden Gods, Deities in the Divine Eye, Winged Disks, I, Horus, am Yesterday, I am Tomorrow, I course through Space and Time, terms found in sacred literature all over the world, probably referring to the same Space God.

The struggle in the skies between Horus and Set parallels the War between the Angels of Light and the Powers of Darkness mentioned in Hebrew theology, Good and Evil contending for the Soul of Man. Possibly a race-memory of a real war in Space, perhaps the conflict between Chronos and Zeus vividly described in the Greek Classics. The Turin Papyrus states 'He (Horus) is considered ... the inhabitant of the Sacred Eye and to him is accorded to live within it. His seat is the throne.' Moreover 'the Eye renders him Knower of the abysses (Space?) he is Messenger of the Lord for whom he crosses the sky and surpasses the firmament (Hyper-space?); it produces a flame with the light which comes from its rim' (a means of propulsion?) it can 'fly to the sky and descend to Earth every day', says the Book of the Dead, Chapter 52). The Italian scholar, Solas Boncompagni, after profound research into ancient Middle Eastern texts considers that this Being who hides himself in the Eye, for the Egyptians the Mysterious One, He Who may not be seen, had an affinity with the God, Thoth, Hermes Trismegistus of the Greeks, Enoch of the Hebrews, Oannes of the Babylonians. The Eye, sometimes known as the Cosmic Egg or Sacred Falcon was identified with the Flying Thrones of Hebrew literature and with the Celestial Chariots of the Indian Classics.[19]

The Divine Eye mentioned in sacred texts may be more than religious imagery. During many thousands of years observing the heavens the priest-astronomers must have seen many celestial phenomena; only one admittedly controversial case is left to us. A badly decayed papyrus among the papers of the deceased Professor Alberto Tulli, Director of the Egyptian Museum of the Vatican, was identified as part of the Annals of Thutmosis III about 1500 BC. The translation, somewhat disputed, is said to state

'... In the year 22, of the 3rd month of winter, sixth hour of the day, the scribes' archivists or chroniclers, or annalists, of the House of Life found that there was a circle of fire coming in the sky ... (but) it had no head. From its mouth came a breath that stank. One rod long was its body and a rod wide and it was noiseless. And the hearts of the scribes became terrified and confused, and they laid themselves flat on their bellies ... They reported to the Pharaoh. His Majesty ordered ... has been examined ... and he was meditating on what had happened and which is recorded in papyri of the House of Life. Now, after some days had gone by, behold, these things became more numerous in the skies than ever. They shone more than the brightness of the Sun and extended to the limits of the four supports (quarters) of the heavens. ... Dominating in the sky was the station of these fire-circles. The army of the Pharaoh looked on with him in their midst. It was after supper. Thereupon these fire-circles ascended higher in the sky towards the south. Fishes and winged animals or birds fell down from the sky. A marvel never before known since the foundations of this land! And Pharaoh caused incense to be brought to make peace on earth. ... And what happened was ordered by the Pharaoh to be written in the annals of the House of Life ... so that it be remembered forever.'[219]

Pliny in Historia Naturalis, Book II, LVII, mentions rains of flesh on Rome in 461 BC. Similar falls were recorded by Julius Obsequens in Libro de Prodigiis and in modern times by Charles Fort. Fish, animals and birds are probably elevated from Earth by Space-craft powered by a gravitational field then jettisoned from a very high altitude as unwanted cargo.[52] Mention by those ancient scribes of fish falling down from the sky seems surprising evidence associating those fire-circles with Space-ships.

For centuries the Jews claimed to be the only people who believed in the One Supreme God, a belief which distinguished them from the idolatrous races on Earth. The Rabbis forgot that long before Abraham spoke with the Lord on the Plains of Mamre about 2000 BC 'from the earliest times one of the greatest tendencies of the Egyptian religion was towards monotheism', Sir E.A. Wallis Budge continues 'We have already shown how much the monotheistic side of the Egyptian religion resembles that of modern Christian nations and it will have come as a surprise to some that a people possessing such exalted ideas of God as the Egyptians could ever have become the byword they did through their alleged worship of a multitude of Gods in various forms'.[27] It is true that Egypt like most countries had scores of Gods. Each though more than human was known to be subservient to God, the Creator of All. Unlike many people today educated Egyptians knew that the word God has at least two distinct meanings, the Absolute imagining the Universe in Whom we live and have our being, and the local Gods or Spacemen, who originate from some advanced planet and from time to time manifest among men.[63] Many of the Egyptian Gods probably symbolised Teachers from Space.

The god Thoth, the human with a bird's head, surely signifying his association with Space-flight, was the God of earth, sea and sky. Inventor of all the arts and sciences, lord of magic, patron of literature, scribe of the Gods, inventor of hieroglyphics, author of magical books, founder of geometry, astronomy, medicine, music and mathematics, master of occult mysteries, recorder of history, Clerk to the Judges of the Dead. Sanchoniathon, the Phoenician historian, wrote that Thoth contrived a flying-machine for Cronus who waged war in the skies against Zeus; he is said to have fashioned and serviced the Eye of Horus, a Spaceship, and was Lord of the Moon, suggesting he was an Extraterrestrial who had landed there. Occult traditions teach that Thoth was an Atlantean who aided in the building of the Great Pyramid in which he secreted tablets of wisdom and magical weapons.

CHAPTER THIRTEEN
The Great Pyramid

'Surid, one of the first Kings of Egypt before the Great Flood, had the two larger pyramids built. He ordered his priests to conceal there the summarised writings of their wisdom and of their artistic and scientific knowledge as well as the names and properties of medicinal plants and everything referring to arithmetic and geometry. The King finally deposited in the Pyramid indications regarding the position of the stars and their cycles, the history and chronicles of times past and prophecies of times to come.'

This revelation by Masaudi, the tenth-century Arab scholar, expresses age-old beliefs that the Great Pyramid was built by Antediluvians to preserve their wisdom for future generations. The long dark entrance-passage would have pointed to Alpha Draconis, the then-Pole Star in 2170 BC. Astrologers claim that allowing for the precession of the equinoxes it could have been a sidereal year 25,868 years earlier, about 28,000 BC; occultists mindful of the Dendera Zodiac suggest three sideral years earlier or 79,000 BC during the Golden Age of the Divine Dynasty, the Space Kings.

The Great Pyramid stands exactly in the centre of the World Land-Map. To fix this focal position its builders must have surveyed our Earth from Space, its siting and construction suggest that this Wonder of the World was probably built by Spacemen or by Initiates mastering extraterrestrial science. The Arabs believed the Great Pyramid was built by Djinns or Spirits who came from Space.

Startling support for the antediluvian building of the Pyramid comes from the questionable cult alleging a Hollow Earth with a most ancient civilisation miles beneath our feet, whence emanate those mysterious Flying Saucers, so it is said. Dr Raymond Bernard states

'Atlantis was connected by subterranean tunnels with its Egyptian colony to the east and its Brazilian and Inca colony to the west. It is probable that the real purpose of the pyramids was not to serve as tombs for the dead kings but as covered entrances of tunnels connecting Egypt with the subterranean world and so built to prevent the entry of flood waters, since their builders had foreknowledge of the flood that would occur and cause the sinking of Atlantis. The floodwaters would have to rise to the top of the pyramids to enter the subterranean chambers and tunnels below. Since Egypt is flat country pyramids were necessary for this purpose, like in Yucatan, whereas in mountainous country and in high plateaus, as in Brazil, no pyramids are needed as tunnels here open on mountain tops which provide natural protection against the entry of water during floods.'[13]

Egyptologists agree that the Great Pyramid was built by the Fourth Dynasty Pharaoh, Khufu, called Cheops by the Greeks. His seal was found there; they still dispute over the age of the edifice. Sir Flinders Petrie dates its erection at 3900BC but James Henry Breasted a thousand years later. Immanuel Velikovsky considers both chronologies to be wrong.

Herodotus stated that a hundred thousand men toiled for thirty years to build the causeway, underground chambers and the Pyramid itself. The height was 480 feet, each triangular side slanted 756 feet and it covered an area of 571,536 square feet. Originally smooth polished casing stones adorned with hieroglyphics covered the slopes pointing to a pyramidal cone of crystalline copper associated with Venus, possibly a beacon for Spaceships. Two and a half million blocks each averaging two and a half tons, according to Herodotus none of the stones was less than thirty feet long, were dragged by gangs of slaves from Arabian quarries and the Libyan hills, cut, polished and fitted precisely into place, their joints hardly perceptible, as thin as paper. Bunsen believed the Pyramid to have been built about 20,000 BC and calculated its vast mass as 82,111,000 cubic feet which would weigh 6,316,000 tons.[16] How could gangs of slaves be mobilised to manipulate such immense stones to build this mammoth structure?

The height of the Pyramid is one thousand millionth of the distance from Earth to Sun. Measurements embodied in the building are said to reveal the radius and weight of the Earth, the length of the solar year, the Precession of the Equinoxes, the value of 'pi', that is the relationship between the circumference of a circle and its diameter. Whence came this knowledge?[148]

The strange inner structure of the Great Pyramid proves that it must have been used in initiation-ceremonies, not as the tomb of the King Sesostris as archaeologists believe.

Commenting on Cheops, Herodotus in Book Two, Chapter 126, reports irreverently

> 'And Cheops came to such wickedness that when he lacked money he set his daughter in a brothel and enjoined her to charge thus and thus much; but they told me not how much. And she demanded the sum enjoined by her father, and also resolved to leave a memorial of her own. And she besought each man that went in unto her to give her a present of one stone. And from the stones, they said, was made the Pyramid, that standeth in the midst of the three in front of the Great Pyramid and each face thereof is one plethrum and a half long.'

One plethrum and a half long! One hundred and fifty feet!

Sensitives today claim that the Great Pyramid still radiates magnetic force and that the immense blocks of stone were levitated by Extraterrestrials utilising anti-gravity or sonic vibrations,[121] perhaps the same power motivating the Spaceships, one of which is alleged to have been buried nearby. Count Louis de Hamon, better known as the seer, Cheiro, predicted that beneath the Great Pyramid would be discovered a temple with fabulous treasures and revelations of a secret wisdom transcending our science.

Were these massive stones raised by psychic power?

What if a hundred Adepts, a thousand, ten thousand, pooled their own psychokinetic power, said to be dormant in all men, to levitate massive stones? A hundred thousand might move mountains, a million displace our Earth from its axis, as many believe did actually happen long ago. Lenormant in Chaldean Magic states 'Certain it is that in ancient times the priests of On by means of magical words raised storms and carried stones for their temples through the air which a thousand men could not lift.'

Perhaps Herodotus was right? A hundred thousand men might have toiled to build the Great Pyramid, not as gangs of sweating slaves lashed by overseers dragging some immense slab but grouped in teams. Batteries of psychic energy directing a beam of mental force to levitate huge stones and fit them in place. All over the world from Stonehenge to Tiahuanaco stand prehistoric columns confounding our conventional building-methods; many students now suspect the Ancients must have mastered some potent force lost to us today.

In a maritime zone confined between Florida, the Bahamas and the Virgin Islands is an area notorious for the totally inexplicable disappearances of aircraft and shipping, generally known as the Devil's Triangle often associated with the appearance of UFOs. A similar deadly region exists in the Pacific delimited by Japan, the Philippines and the island of Guam, called by the mariners of ancient China The Devil's Sea. Research by Pierre Carnac, a Roumanian scientist, shows that exactly midway between these fatal areas stands the Great Pyramid, the focus point of the world known to the Ancients as proved by the Piri Reis maps. Pierre Carnac suggests that the builders erecting the Great Pyramid and the Adepts who chose its position must have known something about these Portals of the Devil in the Atlantic and Pacific. The phenomenon may be geo-physical, perhaps a law of Nature still unknown. Why are the Pyramid and those Devil's zones East and West shaped like triangles?[32]

About AD 820 Caliph Al Mamour, son of Haroun Al Raschid, famous Caliph of Baghdad in the Arabian Nights summoned his best architects and engineers to find the fabled treasure of the Pyramid. The solid masonry resisted hammer and chisel, so the resourceful Arabs built little bonfires against the stones and when these became hot flung cold vinegar on them until they cracked, the blackened surfaces are still to be seen today. After tunelling their way inward for more than a hundred feet the workmen were about to give up when the sound of a falling stone in the interior encouraged them to continue and to break through to the original entrance-passage. When they had scaled sloping passages and galleries Caliph Al Mamoun's men finally entered a large room in the very heart of the Pyramid; to their deep disappointment this King's Chamber, apart from an open stone coffin, was entirely empty. The coffin contained nothing but dust.[25]

An Arab historian quoted by the Italian scholar, Italo

Sordi,[187] contradicts conventional belief by describing the astounding discoveries inside the alleged tomb of Pharaoh Kufu. On an enormous stone-table stood two statues, one in black stone represented a man grasping a lance, the other in white stone, a lady armed with a bow. In the centre of the table reposed a vase of red crystal hermetically closed. And finally there was a great cockerel of reddish-gold adorned with precious stones; when the amateur archaeologists approached, the bird began to beat its wings and emitted a terrifying shriek, while on all sides of the funeral chamber resounded other menacing voices. The objects were transported to a secret room in the Caliph's palace, he personally examined the vase found to be empty. As an experiment the vase was weighed empty, then weighed full of water, to everyone's stupefaction the mysterious receptacle had exactly the same weight full or empty. Before long these precious discoveries were looted during subsequent sackings of the palace at Baghdad and irretrievably lost. Italo Sordi suggests that the vase might have been made of a substance which acted as an anti-gravitational screen, thus nullifying the weight of whatever it contained. The cockerel was apparently programmed to function at a person's approach like the famous bronze robot, Talos, invented by Daedalus to guard the coast of Crete; the mechanism may have been activated by brainwaves from the workmen entering the Chamber, whose mental excitement at the discovery increased the normal electric tension there. A fascinating story open to doubt. Could the wisdom attributed to those ancient Egyptians fashion such wonders?

In the sands beside the Pyramid at Gizeh near Cairo crouches the Sphinx. The significance of this great monument is lost to us. A vast human head in royal headdress rears thirty feet above its lion's body two hundred and forty feet long carved from solid rock.

Six thousand years ago King Khafra unearthed the monster and inscribed his royal cartouche on the Sphinx's side but still the sands threatened to bury it again. About 1450 BC Thutmosis IV, then a young Prince, tired from hunting slept between the great paws when the Sun God appeared to him in a dream and urged him clear away the sands which covered it.

An early fourth dynasty inscription mentions the Sphinx as being a monument whose origin was lost in the night of Time and that it had been found by chance in this reign buried by the desert and beneath which it had been forgotten for long generations.

The human head on the lion's body is said by Initiates to symbolise the evolution of Man from animal, the triumph of the human spirit over the beast. Like the Atlanteans, the Egyptians associated the Sphinx with the Sun God, its name was Harmakis or Harmakuti. It was the Greeks who named it the Sphinx after the celebrated monster with the winged body of a lion, the breast and face of a woman, who posed that fatal riddle to Oedipus.[217] The face of the Sphinx was turned to the East towards the rising Sun, symbol of dawning life, while the tombs were in the west, since life had set as the Sun sets. On its brow was a disk of gold, at dawn the Sun's rays striking it illumined the countenance of the God with a golden light and Priests prayed at its feet.

Sculptures at Karnak and Thebes depict sun-disks surrounded by serpents or spirits; winged disks made of wood covered with shining gold were placed over the doors of temples as potent symbols. Some frescoes showed the great Sun disk with many hands reaching down to bless Pharaoh. During the Golden Age of the Space Kings, through many millennia, the worship of Harmakis as Ra, the Sun God, inspired all Egyptians, later it was supplanted by the worship of local Gods. After the expulsion of the alien Shepherd Kings, the victorious Princes of Thebes erected magnificent temples to their own God, Amen, first symbolised as a goose; Amen became humanised as a Man wearing on his head two plumes, strangely suggestive of Spacemen. At the zenith of the Eighteenth Dynasty about 1500 BC, Egypt ruled most of the Middle East. Treasures and tribute from Babylon, Assyria, Palestine, Crete and Ethiopia enriched the valley of the Nile. Through Pharaoh the Priests of Amen dominated every aspect of Egyptian life, the beneficence of the old religion was swamped by soulless materialism.

Velikovsky claims that about 1500 BC the planet Venus, then a Comet, brushed our Earth causing immense destruction, the Middle Kingdom of Egypt collapsed into chaos and about six hundred ghost years crept into Egyptian history.[205] This fantasy scorned by Egyptologists nevertheless finds impressive support from astronomy, geology and the papyrus of Ipuwer giving a vivid eye-witness account of the devastation of Egypt.

Amenhotep IV, ascended the ancient throne in 1375 BC aged only fifteen, his skull long, features sensitive and ascetic, with the eyes of a prophet, his abdomen large and lower limbs swollen; he may have suffered from epilepsy due to the psychic forces charging his questing soul. The young King[3] displaced the degenerate religion of Amen for the simple worship of Aton, the One God, symbolised by the disk of the Sun and changed his name to Akhnaton. He built Akhetaten, near modern Amarna, on the Nile about 150 miles south of Cairo. With his lovely wife, Nefertiti, and seven daughters he renounced the decadent traditions and encouraged a new naturalistic style in all the arts in a golden age of cosmic brotherhood. But finally the reactionary Priests of Amon fomented rebellion and deposed the King. He died, possibly poisoned, in 1358 BC, the seventeenth year of his reign, only thirty-two years old.

Who inspired this young Saint to smash the idols of Amen and restore that ancient cosmic worship of the Sun, even to building a fantastic city were all men lived in beauty and peace? A century earlier Fire Circles haunted Thutmosis III, a Celestial appeared to Thutmosis IV, decades later Jehovah would encourage Moses to deliver the Israelites from bondage. Surely an Extraterrestrial inspired the idealistic Prince with the cosmic religion of the Sun to resurrect his people.

CHAPTER FOURTEEN
Babylon

The Babylonians claimed immense antiquity, they called their city Bab-ilu, Gate of the God, to signify Celestials. Berossus, a Priest of Bel, about 330 BC wrote Babyloniaca a work since lost based on Chaldean records, stating that ten Kings, Divine Dynasties, reigned 432,000 years, then the God, Cronus, foretold the Flood to Sisithrus, who built an ark, sent out three birds and landed in the mountains of Armenia.

The early Sumerians told of a Golden Age governed by the Gods, then came heroes and superhuman Kings; they listed Kings over five cities reigning 370,000 years before the Flood, confirmed by annals of the Assyrians. Legends extolled the Indovansas, Lunar Kings, flying down from the Moon to rule Chaldea. Traditions recalled those Sons of the Gods who mated with the Daughters of Men, they built that wondrous, decadent civilisation destroyed by the Flood.

The ancient Persians, who subsequently conquered the Babylonians, believed that before Adam Earth was ruled for 7000 years by wicked Atlantean Giants and for 2000 years by the beneficent Peris, Sons of Wisdom, possibly Spacemen. They counted ten antediluvian Kings, agreeing with Berossus, the Sumerian King-List and the number of generations from Adam to Noah. Statues of seventy-two wise Kings, all called Suliman, were said to stand in a gallery in the Khaf mountains, three reigned each a thousand years. The great King Huschenk, who restored civilisation, fought the Giants on a flying-boat; his famous grandson, Tahmurah, on his winged steed liberated Peris imprisoned by the Giants; his successor, Giamschi, sung by Omar Khayyam, built Esikar, old Persepolis.[17]

Man has lived on Earth for millions of years, there have been many cataclysms, world-wide traditions tell of four vast ages preceding our own. Noah's Flood may have synchronised with the submergence of Atlantis about 10,000 BC but there were many local floods in the flat land of Mesopotamia, any one could have been the biblical Deluge obviously borrowed from Babylonian literature.

Babylonia was a bridge between north and south, east and west, the cockpit of nations throughout world-history. After each great catastrophe whole peoples fled across the stricken continents seeking safety; the survivors from northern Hyperborea and shattered Western Europe hurried southwards to the Middle East; survivors from lost Lemuria crossed India, their descendants moved north and settled on that fertile land between the twin rivers. Remarkable affinities between the architecture, religion and cultures of the Pre-Incas and the Babylonians suggest that colonists from South America crossed the Atlantic to Egypt and on to Babylon. Their word for Priest was *Sume*, so they called themselves Sumerians and spread their wisdom from Peru. Later disasters caused more mass-migrations. Some Sinologists theorise that since the Chinese language belongs to the same linguistic group as Sumerian, the Chinese people originated in Akkadia,[214] so did the Japanese whose ideographic script is said to resemble Assyrian symbols. Centuries afterwards migrations occurred in the reverse direction, remnants of the Uighur race left the Gobi for Central Asia,[45] one main stream now called Aryans went south to India, the other came north to the plateau of Iran, and as the Medes and Persians were led by Cyrus in 529 BC to sack Babylon.

The antediluvian civilisation of the Sumerians is said to have been inspired by the Akpallus, Fishmen, whose leader, Oannes, appeared from the deep at the city of Eridu before the fourth millennium.

Alexander Polyhistor quoting a fragment of the lost 'Babyloniaca' by Berossus, Priest of Bel, states

'Berossus describes an animal endowed with reason who was called Oannes; the whole body of the animal was like that of a fish, and had under a fish's head another head, and also feet below, similar to those of a man, subjoined to the fish's tail. His voice too and language was articulate and human, and a representation of him is preserved even to this day. This Being in the day-time used to converse with Man but took no food at that season; and he gave them an insight into letters and sciences and every kind of art. He taught them to construct houses, to found temples, to compile laws, and explained to them the principles of geometrical knowledge. He made them distinguish the seeds of the earth and showed them how to collect fruits; in short, he instructed them in everything which could tend to soften manners and humanise mankind. From that time so universal were his instructions, nothing has been added material by way of improvement. When the Sun set, it was the custom of this Being to plunge again into the sea and abide all night in the deep, for he was amphibious. After this there appeared other animals like Oannes.'[50]

Extracts from Berossus quoted in the histories by Apollodorus and Abydenus mention the ten antediluvian Kings from Alorus to Xisithrus stating that after Oannes other semi-daemons or personages appeared from the Persian Gulf. In esoteric language the sea or deep often meant regions of space; a creature with a fish's head and another head underneath and human feet appears to have been a man wearing a spacesuit. Today Spaceships are believed to descend to the ocean depths, so Oannes like Neptune could actually have emerged from the sea itself. Like Jehovah who retired to the tabernacle, Oannes every night returned to the deep, presumably to his Spacecraft.

Dr Carl Sagan, the American astronomer, states

'In any event a completely convincing demonstration of past contact with an extraterrestrial civilisation will always be difficult to prove on textual grounds alone. But stories like the Oannes legend, and representations especially of the earliest civilisations on the Earth deserve much more critical studies than have been performed heretofore, with the possibility of direct contact with an extraterrestrial civilisation as one of many possible alternative interpretations.'[184]

The three nearest stars of potential biological interest according to him are Epsilon Eridani, Epsilon Indi and Tau Ceti between eleven and twelve light years from Earth, any Supermen there might visit us.

Archaeologists date human societies in Northern Iraq at perhaps 10,000 BC. Present evidence suggests the cultivation of crops particularly cereals and the domestication of animals about 8000 BC, apparently refuting the immense antiquity attributed to the Babylonians and Egyptians. They forget that their researches deal only with the re-civilisation of Men, cataclysms and floods swept away those great civilisations which flourished before. The vast age of mankind is surely proved in legends and ancient literature supported by ancient monuments all over the world.

Rabbi Yonah ibn Aharon studying Chaldaic records, the Kabbalah, the Zohar, the Sefer Sefirah and Sefer Yetsinah and works in Aramaic reveals that the Elohim on High were Interplanetary Beings who settled on Venus about 18,000,000 years ago. The Chaldeans told of the Titans (Gdolim) who came from afar to build Titania, now Khorasan in Central Asia, and later settled in Nigeria. They were taller than we are and mastered a science based on sonics and radionics which was utilised by the Celtic, Aryan, Tiahuanacan and Israelite priests. The Chaldeans insisted that Man originated on Earth about 31,000,000 years ago, the Elohim assisting human development with teachings of the Inner Planetarians. The Sefer Leqt Tithna Saliqa states that communication with the planets continued until about 600 BC

The Magi could generate a force called in Aramaic Rukha Shakintu and made aerial craft apparently propelled by mental powers, they also fashioned a golden rod with fantastic magnetic properties, possibly the Atlantean vril-rod or miracle-staff of Moses. In Chaldea people could visit the planets with ease in disk-shaped spacecraft motivated by Kvod, which was apparently electric discharges between positive and negative lightning-bolts, the same force motivating Y'hova's Power and Glory of the Lord. The Extraterrestrials developed a psychic science based on the electric magnetic-field underlying every corporeal manifestation, crime was detected by a person's distorted magnetic orientation.

The symbol of the Golden Age was Solar Fire and the Priests of Chaldea were generally accepted as successors to the Initiates of Atlantis. The rule of Earth was relinquished voluntarily by the Council of Those from Upon High, control was left to Celestials like Y'hova who befriended a wood-cutter called Abramu.

The remarkable revelations by ibn Aharon from Semitic literature accord with world-wide traditions of advanced civilisations before the Flood; the attainments of the Hyperboreans, Lemurians and Atlanteans may be questioned but there is growing reason to believe that the ancients in remote Antiquity had a cosmic wisdom and natural science in some ways surpassing our own. This arcane knowledge was never completely lost. Adam himself was said to have written a book setting down all the lore learned from God. The Book of Enoch, the Book of Thoth, the Emerald Tablets of Hermes, preserved much ancient wisdom couched in terms cognisable to Initiates; the Atlanteans are believed to have secreted records in time-capsules which like the Dead Sea Scrolls will become revealed when Man is ready for them.

Cronus advised the flood hero, Sisithrus, to write a history from the Beginning and to bury the account securely in the City of the Sun at Sippara. Nabonasir (730 BC) collected all the mementoes of earlier Kings and destroyed them, destruction repeated by megalomaniac Emperors from China to Rome and far Peru causing almost total absence of writings from the remote past.

A popular legend has come down to us in three versions, the Old Babylonian, the Middle Assyrian and the Neo-Assyrian from the library of Assurbanipal, telling of the post-diluvian King Etana who apparently consorted with Spacemen.[168] A translation of the Italian rendering is as follows

'In excavations at Nineveh there was discovered in the Library of King Assurbanipal clay cylinders on which is described a voyage to the sky. It narrates how King Etana, who lived about five thousand years ago, called the Good King, was taken as an honoured guest on a flying-ship in the form of a shield which landed in a square behind the royal palace, rotating surrounded by a vortex of flames. From the flying-ship alighted tall blond men with dark complexions, dressed in white, handsome as Gods who invited King Etan, somewhat dissuaded by his own advisers to go for a trip in the flying-ship; in the middle of a whirlwind of flames and smoke he went so high that the Earth with its seas, islands and continents, appeared to him like a loaf in a basket then disappeared from sight.

King Etan in the flying-ship reached the Moon, Mars and Venus, and after two weeks absence, when they were already preparing a new succession to the throne, believing that the Gods had carried him off with them, the flying-ship glided over the city and touched down surrounded by a ring of fire. The fire abated. King Etan descended with some of the blond men who stayed as his guests for some days.'[71]

The truth of this tale may be open to question yet it does appear paralleled by the space-flight of Enoch,[36] the translation of Elijah in a fiery chariot.

The psycho-science of the ancients will be better understood next century when coal and oil have become exhausted and Man must re-discover sources of energy. Adepts studied the occult aspect of nature, cosmic radiation, and utilised atmospheric electricity in ways unknown to us, probably taught by their Space Teachers.

In Babylon the Persian Magi claimed to control those occult powers of nature called pantomorphic fire and astral light. In their temples it was said darkness reigned in broad daylight, lamps were lit without human agency, the radiance of the Gods was visible and the rumble of thunder could be heard. The Magi could generate, condense or disperse electricity at will and could direct electric currents of the atmosphere and magnetic currents of the Earth like arrows against mankind.[179]

They probably manipulated matter by the subtle powers of mind and probed the potent secrets of the atom for devastating force. Such speculation is not wild fantasy. An American nuclear-scientist has said 'Anyone can build a nuclear-bomb with information from a public library and material from an ironmonger's.'

Excavations at Ur show that about 2500 BC, perhaps a thousand years earlier, the Sumerians had attained a brilliant civilisation. In the tomb of Queen Shub-ad Sir Leonard Woolley found a rich array of funerary gifts, beautiful jewellery, gorgeous head-dress, exquisite diadems, marvellous ornaments in gold and lapis-lazuli, rings, bracelets, necklaces, 'all these are so wonderful, even by modern standards that no goldsmith of our own day could even begin to conceive them.'[124] The metallurgy, craftsmanship and artistry required to fashion these treasures suggest many centuries of advanced, progressive culture.

The Sumerians had considerable knowledge of mathematics. They divided the circle into 360 degrees, said to be the number of days in the year in those days, and the hour into sixty minutes, each with sixty seconds. We accept this legacy from ancient Sumer without full appreciation of the profound philosophical, astronomical and mathematical attainments needed to conceive this division of time, concepts which our own sophisticated science cannot surpass. A cuneiform text found on the mound at Kuyunjik records a mathematical series the end-product of which in our number-system would be expressed as 195,555,200,000,000,[34] a conception far surpassing the mathematics of the Greeks and not known to Europeans until the 17th century. Were the Sumerians taught by Spacemen?

About 2350 BC a priestess, like the mother of Moses a thousand years later, laid her newly-born baby in a basket to float down the Euphrates; he was found by a gardener who adopted him. Young Sargon later became cup-bearer to King U-Zaboba whom he eventually dethroned to make himself ruler. During his fifty-six year reign he conquered Mesopotamia and Palestine to reach the Mediterranean and in the south dominated the Persian Gulf.[15] Excavations at Mohenjo-Daro and Harappa unearthed cylinder-seals from Babylon showing considerable trade between Mesopotamia and India before 2000 BC. More amazing to us is the revelation that Menes, eldest son of Sargon, made a voyage from Sumer to the Sunset Land, South America, 'where he was poisoned by an insect and buried there.' Such intercourse must account for the remarkable similarities in architecture between the two countries.[209] The religion, the customs, the culture of Babylon, were to influence men's minds throughout the Middle East, until the city was sacked by Alexander the Great in 323 BC, for two thousand years.

The researches of ibn Aharon into Chaldaic literature suggest that in the early Second Millennium BC fantastic Beings with incredible power and wisdom ruled everywhere; in India, China, Peru and Britain the Priests were building temple-observatories and anxiously scanning the heavens for the Space Gods.

Midrashic traditions claim that on the night of Abraham's birth, conventionally dated about 2000 BC, the wise men and magicians beheld a large and brilliant star swallow up or consume four stars from the four corners of heaven, which obviously suggests a mothership embarking four scout ships. Abraham was born at Ur of the Chaldees. He warned Nimrod of the power of the Lord, the outraged King sent an army to arrest him, so Abraham prayed to heaven and the Lord suddenly interposed a cloud of darkness between him and his enemies, who fled in terror. Such Extraterrestrial intervention was continued by Gabriel, said to have raised the young Abraham on his shoulders and flown with him through the air from Ur to Babylon. The Lord saved Abraham from Nimrod's flaming furnace and eventually bade the Patriarch leave the country with his wife, Sarai, his nephew, Lot, and all his dependents and property, setting out for Canaan, Egypt, they finally came to the plains of Mamre near Sodom and Gomorrah to begin the long epic of Israel.

Supernatural events alleged in the Bible and Talmud find little support from archaeologists. However the stele of Hammurabi, now in the Louvre, shows Shamash, the Sun God, receiving the homage of King Hammurabi[173] about 1750BC, to whom he gave famous Laws just as Zeus was said to have given the Cretan Laws to Minos three hundred years before. Moses was not the only man to receive Commandments from a God! The Old Testament abounds with visitations by Jehovah and his Angels to Abraham, Isaac and Jacob. If we believe these, should we not also accept the presence of Extraterrestrials in old Babylon?

The terrible cataclysm of 1500 BC also devastated the Middle East shattering the Babylonian civilisation, spreading ruin from Troy to the valley of the Nile. Arabia, a land of plenty, paradise on Earth, was turned to barren desert. Numerous seismic shocks and earth-tremors were recorded by the Babylonians on clay tablets stored in the library of Nineveh.[206] Assyriologists apparently know little of this period. Babylon was sacked by the Hittites followed by the Hurrians from the north-east, suggesting centuries of confusion possibly aggravated by some cosmic disaster.

The Italian, Boncompagni,[20] draws attention to a topographical map of Nippur, an archaeological site about a hundred miles from Bagdad and spiritual-centre of ancient Sumer, contained in the Hilprecht Collection. Drawn about 3,500 years ago this map is remarkable since its orientation shows the cardinal point, North, displaced 45 degrees East. A similar disorientation alleged for the Great Pyramid could mean the displacement of the Earth's axis by some cosmic body long ago.

Herodotus visited Babylon and vividly described the city as a square fortified by massive walls with a perimeter of fifty miles, eighty feet high and twenty feet thick, wide enough on top for a four-horse chariot to wheel around. Set in these walls were 'an hundred gates all of brass' ... 'Now this wall is the outer wall, but another wall runneth round within, not much weaker than the other ... ' The King's palace was a miniature city, adorned by those famous Hanging Gardens, one of the Seven Wonders of the world. Above the great golden temple of Bel rose a lofty tower where the Chaldean astrologers predicted eclipses and plotted the influence of the planets on human destiny. A vast artificial lake provided water for the huge population; a tunnel ran under the river-bed. Such immense constructions prove that the Babylonians had attained superb techniques and in some respects at least were highly civilised.

At night Babylon was illumined with petroleum from pools on the ground, site of modern oil-wells. Alexander the Great is said to have dipped a boy's head in oil and applied a flaming torch, confident it would not catch fire. He guessed wrongly, the boy met a shocking death.[124]

In Peru young men over twenty-four, women over eighteen, if unmarried, were lined up in the village-square and the local Mayor forced each man to select his mate[212] there and then. After eight days trial-marriage an ill-favoured or bad-tempered wife could be sent back home liable to pay a penalty.

According to Herodotus, in Babylonia once a year all the marriageable girls were summoned to the market-place, then a herald called the damsels up one by one and auctioned them to the highest bidders. The richest Babylonians bid against each other for the most beautiful maidens, the humbler wife-seekers must content themselves with homely wenches for small payment. When bidding ceased and the marriage-portions were totalled in a chest, any dowdy spinster left on the shelf was offered for sale with a dowry for some husband willing to have her and the money too. 'In that way the beautiful girls brought the ugly and deformed ones to husband.' He adds 'This was the best of all their customs.' and said that in his day the Babylonians were bringing up their daughters to be harlots.

When the Space People wish to influence the course of mankind, a Celestial may descend to Earth and father a hero by some mortal wench like the lusty Zeus in mythology. But sometimes Extraterrestrials may leave a baby of their own to be adopted on Earth in chosen environment, so it might grow up and shape historical events aided and inspired from Space.

About 800 BC in Babylon ruled the great Queen Sammuramat, immortalised as Semiramis. She was believed to be the daughter of the fish Goddess, Ataryatis, and Oannes, God of Wisdom and is said to have been miraculously fed by doves. Found by Simmas, the royal shepherd, she was brought up at the Babylonian Court. In 811 BC Babylon was conquered by Ninus, King of Assyria, known to history as Shamsi-Adad V, who devastated most of Asia. After the suicide of her husband Semiramis married the King who conveniently lived long enough to father a son leaving her Empress of his huge domains. Now Queen, Semiramis proceeded to rebuild Babylon with palaces, temples and dykes draining floods from the Euphrates; she invaded Egypt, Ethiopia and Libya, then turned to India. For this enterprise Semiramis is said to have marshalled armies comprising 3,000,000 foot, 500,000 horses and 100,000 chariots with 2,000 ships prefabricated for transport overland, even allowing for wild exaggeration this was surely the most stupendous expeditionary force in all antiquity. She overcame her shortage of elephants by having mechanical elephants constructed from hides. Semiramis won resounding victories and led her armies into the heart of India. King Strabrobates counter-attacked, the Babylonians were forced to retreat in hostile country and suffered shattering defeat.[58]

On return to Babylon Semiramis made war against the Medes and the Persians. Suddenly, after a Regency of forty-one years, she abdicated in favour of her son, Ninyas, and disappeared. People believed that she turned into a dove and flew to the skies. Perhaps like Elijah in roughly the same century, she was translated in a Spaceship.

For many years Semiramis was identified by the Babylonians as an embodiment of Istar, Goddess of Love, linked with the planet Venus. In Semitic languages the word *Sama* means Sun. Sammuramat therefore appears to have had some close association with the Sun, which may infer that she was a Celestial. The Queen was accompanied by the Winged Sun Disk of Assyria which later symbolised the great Persian God, Ahura-Mazda.

In 714 BC Sargon II extended his rule north to the Caspian Sea. His son, Sennacherib, campaigned against Hezekiah of Jerusalem. About 670 BC Sennacherib's forces invading Egypt were decimated at Pelusium by what now appears to have been a nuclear-blast by Spacemen, although Velikovsky attributes the cataclysm to a collision between Venus and Mars. Nebuchadnezzar in 597 BC stormed Jerusalem and deported many Jews to Babylon. Among the exiles near Nippur on the Chebar, an important canal of the Euphrates, in 593 BC the young Jewish Priest, Ezekiel,[70] beheld in the sky a bejewelled Wheel with four living creatures, now assumed to be Spacemen in their Spaceship. Fifty-five years later in 538BC another young Jewish idealist, Daniel,[54] saw a certain man clothed in linen, 'his face as the appearance of lightning and his eyes as lamps of fire' suggest an Extraterrestrial. After two centuries of Aechemenid domination in 323 BC the city fell to Alexander the Great and sank to ruin. Later Babylon's splendour, it's very site, were forgotten.

The Sumerians, a non-Semitic people, brought to Mesopotamia from an origin still unknown a civilisation perfectly evolved; in their religion are to be found no traces of totemism or animalism, the Gods were Beings superior to men in intelligence, wisdom and power.[29] The early peoples of Babylonia believed in a pantheon of living Beings in human form but superhuman and immortal, invisible and surveilling the Cosmos. Throughout the Old Testament the Israelites regarded God as a Super-Being who would materialise at will to praise or punish accompanied by Angels from realms unseen. Because the Gods had a human aspect and acted as men, the Sumerians built them temples, the house of God. Sometimes the Gods or Goddesses descended among mortals to procreate heroes to promote national evolution. The great Temple of Marduk contained a lofty chamber with a large, elegant bed and a golden table, a sanctuary which none could enter except the Babylonian woman chosen as the Bride of God. Was this bride reserved for a Celestial?

Migrants from Persia and Central Asia profoundly influenced the peoples of Babylon and fertilised their science and religion with novel ideas. Initiates respected a World-Teacher, who according to Aristotle about 6000 BC appeared in Iran, a date without historical fact. Students of the Secret Wisdom[2] believe that through legendary ages many Avatars called Zarathustra incarnated to teach mankind. The last prophet, known to the Greeks as Zoroaster, was born 660 BC in Azerbaijan near the Caspian Sea. An Angel prophesied to his Mother before his birth 'This honoured child shall be a Prophet of the Just God.' Hearing of this prophecy King Darum Sarum sought the baby's death but from the age of seven the young Avatar was able to confound all the magicians of his day. At fifteen he was acknowledged as a prodigy; he studied religion, farming and healing, worked among the poor, then retired to a cave on Mount Sabalan to gain wisdom. One day at sunset the mountain became bathed in fire, suddenly the young hermit was enlightened by Ahura Mazda, usually depicted with a winged disk like Horus, suggestive of a Spaceman. In his home Zoroaster had celestial visions and conversed with Archangels, whom we may regard as Teachers from Space. Zoroaster taught a philosophical, universal magic and used fire as an emblem of the wisdom. His followers migrated to Babylonia where as the Magi they practised the occult arts.[123]

As Jehovah appeared to the Kings of Israel, so Ahura Mazda materialised before the Achaemenian Kings of Persia, his winged figure in human form was depicted on the façade of the tomb of Artaxerxses III at Persepolis.

CHAPTER FIFTEEN
Israel

'The Lord appeared to Abraham by the terebinths of Mamre. As Abraham was sitting at the opening of his tent in the heat of the day he looked up and saw three men standing in front of him.'

Abraham, a powerful Prince, recognised his transcendent visitants at once. The three Extraterrestrials were human in appearance, they washed their feet, ate food, and conversed like ordinary mortals.

About 1950 BC Abraham's nephew, Lot, seated at the gate of Sodom saw two Angels approaching the city. Lot invited them to his house; at first they declined preferring to spend the night in the street, but finally they accompanied him home. As they feasted the house was besieged by rowdy citizens, shouting 'Bring them out, so that we may have intercourse with them!'[83] To save his guests Lot even offered to appease the mob with his two daughters, both virgins, saying 'You can do what you like with them.' The rabble in lynching mood tried to smash in the door. Finally the Angels rescued Lot and smote the hoodlums with blindness. They told him the Lord was going to destroy the city and suggested he warn his family, who laughed at their father, thus sealing their fate.

At dawn the Angels escorted Lot, his wife and two daughters out of the city warning them to hurry to the hills and not to look back. 'Then the Lord rained upon Sodom and Gomorrah brimstone and fire from the Lord out of heaven. He overthrew those cities and destroyed all the Plain with everyone living there and everything growing in the ground. But Lot's wife behind him looked back and she turned into a pillar of salt.'[83] Abraham who 'stood before the Lord' saw all the cities of the plain smoking like a furnace, their inhabitants slain and all vegetation destroyed.

Lot and his virgin daughters fled to a cave in the mountains; gazing down on the holocaust. The girls imagined they were the only people left alive in the world, there were no men to marry. That night they made their father drunk and the first born went in and lay with him; the next night they plied him with wine again and the younger girl slept with him. Both women conceived, the elder's son fathered the people of Moab, the younger's son the people of Ammon.[83]

The desolation near the Dead Sea suggests Sodom and Gomorrah were destroyed by nuclear-blast. Arab scientists have discovered abnormal radio-activity in the region of Rathi, Sairat and Sinai, radio-active isotopes in the sands could have been caused by jets of particles streaming from the reactors of Spaceships. Abraham saw smoke rising like that mushroom cloud over Hiroshima. The shores of the Dead Sea consist largely of rock-salt, which would be blasted into dust by nuclear-explosion and shroud the corpse of Lot's wife with fine salty powder, similar vitrification of bodies occurred at Hiroshima. Not far away at Baalbek in Lebanon stands a cyclopean terrace built from colossal blocks of stone which may have been a launching-site for Spaceships.

When Abraham was ninety-nine the Lord established a Covenant with him saying he would father many nations. And the Lord visited Sarah Abraham's wife and she conceived a son, Isaac at the age of ninety. Later Abraham was tempted to sacrifice Isaac to the Lord, but the timely intervention of an Angel saved the boy's life.

Abraham died at the age of one hundred and seventy-five years and tradition insists that like Enoch he was translated to the skies.

The Apocalypse of Abraham written in Hebrew between AD 70 and AD 130 clearly associates Abraham with Extraterrestrials. It describes how a voice from heaven bid Abraham leave the house of Terah, his father, the idol-maker, then fire descended and consumed all within. Abraham was taken to heaven by the Angel Jaoel on wings where he saw the divine throne with cherubim and holy creatures.

An almost identical apparition in 538 BC appeared to Daniel beside the Tigris. Michael conducted Abraham round the Seven Heavens as generations earlier Angels had conducted Enoch through Ten Heavens to receive divine wisdom at the throne of God.

After a childless marriage of twenty years Isaac, fifty-nine years old, in despair besought the Lord to visit Rebekah his wife as once he had visited Sarah, his mother. The Lord yielded to his entreaty. Rebekah conceived and bore twin sons, Esau and Jacob. It would surely be consistent with celestial eugenics for some Space Lord known as Jehovah to father the ancestor of the Children of Israel in Palestine just as in ten centuries time another God, Mars, would mate with Rhea Silvia, a Vestal Virgin, to produce Romulus, Founder of Rome.

At the age of a hundred and forty-seven Jacob died in Egypt having fathered twelve sons, one of whom was Joseph, destined to head the Twelve Tribes of Israel.

The Israelites apparently vanished from history for five hundred years until delivered by Moses.

The Bible echoes the familiar myth of Sargon, King of Babylon, and tells how Jochabed to save her infant son from murder by Pharaoh placed him in a cradle of bullrushes among the reeds of the Nile, where he was found by Princess Bathia who adopted him and named him Moses. The Talmud states that the Lord was with Moses, when he was barely four months old he began to prophesy saying 'In days to come I shall receive the Torah from the flaming torch.'[86] A most significant prophecy in view of subsequent events, for those flaming torches seen in all lands in antiquity are now considered to have been possible Spaceships. Educated as a Prince, Moses is said to have been initiated into the ancient mysteries. He became a great magician, the scientists of those days.

'A Pharaoh who knew not Joseph', possibly Ramses II (1292-1225 BC) incensed at the numbers of Israelites in Goshen conscripted them as slaves to build frontier-fortifications.

The sight of his oppressed people troubled young Moses to tears, when he was eighteen he killed an overseer beating a

Hebrew labourer. According to the Talmud Moses was saved from the scaffold by an Angel and transported to Ethiopia where he fought as a General. After the death of Kikanus he was crowned King and given Queen Adonith as wife. Soon he abdicated and travelled to Midian where he married Zipporah, daughter of Jethro and lived as a shepherd for forty years.

> 'Moses was minding the flock of his father-in-law, Jethro, Priest of Midian. He left the flock along the side of the Wilderness and came to Horeb, the mountain of God. There the Angel of the Lord appeared to him in the flame of a burning bush. Moses noticed that although the bush was on fire, it was not being burnt up; so he said to himself "I must go across to see this wonderful sight. Why does not the bush burn away?" When the Lord saw that Moses had turned aside to look, he called out to him out of the bushes "Moses. Moses." And Moses answered "Yes, I am here." God said "Come no nearer; take off your sandals; the place where you are standing is holy **ground.**" '[69]

A bush silhouetted against a glowing Spaceship would appear to be on fire though not burnt, the Lord warned Moses not to approach too close since he would be paralysed by the ship's forcefield. The Lord commanded Moses, aided by his elder brother, Aaron, to deliver the Israelites from bondage and lead them to 'a land flowing with milk and honey."

With his wonderful staff suggesting an Atlantean vril-rod, Moses surpassed the magicians of Egypt but despite nine plagues, perhaps chemical and germ warfare by the Celestials. Pharaoh's heart remained obdurate. Only when the Lord killed the Egyptian's First Born did he let the Israelites go. Led by the Angel of God, a pillar of cloud by day, a pillar of fire at night, probably a cigar-shaped Mothership, 600,000 Israelites with their flocks and herds set out on their epic forty years wanderings to Canaan, a trip which a camel could have made in a couple of days.

Pharaoh suddenly regretted giving his grudging consent and led his chariots and cavalry to harry the fugitives. Jewish legend states that what affrighted the Israelites most was the sight of the Angel of Egypt darting through the air, other Angel adversaries attacked them too; eventually Michael and the Lord's Angelic hosts threw Uzza,[86] Angel of Egypt, Rahab and other Angels into the sea. A literal interpretation suggests a battle between rival Spacemen. At the Lord's behest Moses stretched out his hand over the sea. The waters made a wall to the right and left for the Israelites to pass dry foot, when the Egyptian army thundered after them the waters returned, the Egyptians were drowned. It would be a simple matter for the 'Lord' in his Power and Glory to direct an anti-gravity beam to part the shallow sea for the Israelites to cross then to allow the two walls of water to crash down on the stranded Egyptians.[144]

The Israelites soon complained of hardships, so the Lord dropped down to them Bread of Heaven, manna, a white seed, that could be ground and baked into wafers or cakes which tasted like fresh oil, possibly carbohydrates synthesised in the atmosphere by the Spaceship's force-field; it was known to the Greeks as Ambrosia of the Gods, today it is called Angel's Hair. The Ark of the Covenant appears to have constituted an electric battery generating enough power to strike people dead; worshippers had to stand some distance away. Moses was able to insulate himself, his priests and trusted companions.[179]

Communication between the Lord in his Spaceship and the Israelites' leaders was maintained by the Urim and Thummim, two strange devices in the breastplate of the High Priest containing twelve precious stones and gold chains. Today scientists are discovering the amazing properties of certain jewels used in lasers and transistors. The Urim was probably a two-way radio attuned to the Lord's wave-length.

Of all the Israelites who left Egypt only two, Joshua and Caleb, were destined to reach Canaan.

The death of Moses is shrouded in mystery. None knew his burial-place. Josephus states 'A cloud stood over him on the sudden and he disappeared in a certain valley.'[105] Traditions tell of Angels descending to take Moses up to Heaven from Mount Nebo which was sacred to Mercury.

When the Israelites invaded Canaan they found a host of small Semitic tribes with a common mythology of Sky Gods like Baal or Sea Gods like Yamm, who may have represented Spacemen.

The Lord to ensure eventual victory promised in Exodus XXIII v 28

'And I will send hornets before thee, which shall drive out the Hivite the Canaanite and the Hittite, from before thee.'

In Deuteronomy VII the Lord promised

'Moreover the Lord, thy God, will send the hornet among them until they that are left, and hide themselves from thee, be destroyed.'

The hornets may have been flying-machines. The translators of the original Hebrew unacquainted with aeronautics would naturally imagine the text meant some super-flying-insect, wasp or hornet. All Air Forces from ancient India to modern Europe and America call their various aircraft with the names of swift insects or birds.

After the fall of Jericho, advised by the Lord Joshua destroyed Ai, although again our archaeologists disagree. The ruthless onslaught of the Israelites prompted a hasty federation of the Amorite Kings of Jerusalem, Hebron and other threatened cities, who marched against the invaders.

'On that day when the Lord delivered the Amorites into the hands of Israel, Joshua spoke with the Lord and he said in the presence of Israel "Stand still, O Sun, in Gibeon, stand Moon in the Vale of Aijalon," so the Sun stood still and the Moon halted until a nation had taken vengeance on its enemies, as indeed is written in the Book of Jasher. The Sun stayed in mid-heaven and made no haste to set, for almost a whole day.'[106]

The Lord hurled great hailstones out of the air, more died from hailstones than the Israelites slew by the sword.

Velikovsky seizes on this as a fundamental proof that 'in the middle of the Second Millennium before the present era, the earth was interrupted in its regular rotation by a comet'. Livy, Pliny and Julius Obsequens quote many occasions when two suns or sun and moon together were seen in the heavens, which today we interpret as possible UFOs. The Spacemen who inspired the Israelite invasion of Canaan would probably watch this vital battle at Beth-horon, they may have rained down missiles on the Amorites like those Flying Shields which assaulted the Saxons at Sigiburg many centuries later.

In 1200 BC an Angel of the Lord descended to Canaan and sat under an oak-tree at Ophrah near Bethel just as a thousand years earlier a Divine Man descended in Korea and sat under a sandal-tree. The Angel called on Gideon, a young

Hebrew, threshing wheat by the wine-press, and encouraged him to take-up arms and lead the Israelites against their enemies. The Lord appeared and dictated tactics inspiring Gideon to resounding victories which saved Israel.[107]

The Angel of the Lord appeared near Hebron about 1090BC to the wife of Manoah who was childless and told her that she would soon conceive and give birth to a son. 'He will strike the first blow to deliver Israel from the power of the Philistines.'[108]

The woman told her husband. At his prayer the Angel appeared again and repeated his promise, then vanished in the flame of the burnt offering on the Lord's altar upwards to heaven. Josephus says the Angel ascended by means of the smoke 'as by a vehicle', which makes us think of the launching of a Spaceship.[105] The baby was called Samson, probably derived from Shamash, the Sun. Shamash was the Babylonian Sun God.

King David poured forth his devotion to the Lord in many wonderful Psalms describing what he saw and heard in simple words curiously akin to our own Science-Fiction.

> 'He swept the skies as he descended
> thick darkness lay under his feet.
> He rode on a cherub, he flew through the air
> he swooped on the wings of the wind.'

In Psalm 68 David draws a vivid picture of the Lord with his victorious heavenly hosts returning from an annihilating attack to their mountain-base, and Psalm 77 paraphrases those Chinese classics describing Sky Dragons plunging the seas.

David's grievous lapse from grace was his seduction of Bathsheba and his order which brought her husband, Uriah, to certain death in battle. After promising Bathsheba to give the throne to their son, Solomon, he died about 961 BC.

At Solomon's birth the Lord told Nathan the Prophet that the baby should be called Jedidiah, that is Beloved of the Lord[176] but he became better known as Sol-om-on, the name of the Sun in three languages with cosmic significance. The Bible suggests that Solomon received his wisdom from the Lord during his pilgrimage to the holy hill of Gibeon near Jerusalem after he became King, which might mean some encounter with an Extraterrestrial like so many Sensitives before and since.

The building of the Temple took nearly twice as many men as Cheops, according to Herodotus, employed on building the Great Pyramid. It took seven years to build and was not much bigger than a village church, taking allegedly thirteen years to finish it. David had bequeathed Solomon 'a hundred thousand talents of gold and a million talents of silver with great quantities of bronze and iron, more than can be weighed[42]' for this purpose.

> 'In the building of the house, only blocks of undressed stone direct from the quarry were used; no hammer or axe or any iron tool whatever was heard in the house while it was being built.[112]'

The Talmud recounts that the builders, forbidden to cut the stones, touched them with a magical stone called the Shamir which caused them to separate and form the required pattern. The erection of stones without noise suggests levitation by sonic vibrations or psycho-kinesis believed to have been utilised in the building of the Pyramids. Some Jews believed the Temple was built by Angels just as the Arabs swore the Great Pyramid had been built by Djinns.

> 'In the Most Holy Places he carved two images of cherubim and overlaid them with gold. The total span of the wings of the cherubims was twenty cubits.'[43]

Angels with a wing-span of thirty feet! Pure gold!

The friezes around the wall of the Temple were adorned by cherubim, these winged figures were embroidered on the veil of the tabernacle. Why was Solomon so obsessed with Angels that he spent a colossal fortune representing them in the Temple? Such vast expenditure would hardly be spent on symbolising an invisible, formless Deity. The Cherubim must surely portray friendly physical Gods, Supermen from Space.

On the day of dedication before Solomon and all the congregation of Israel, brought into the Temple by the Priests stood the Ark of the Covenant containing the two tablets of stone which Moses had deposited there at Horeb. 'Then the priests came out of the Holy Place, since the cloud was filling the house of the Lord, and they could not continue to minister because of it, for the glory of the Lord filled his house.'[113] Fire came down from heaven and consumed the whole offering of Solomon's sacrifice on the altar, while the glory of the Lord filled the Temple so that the Priests could not enter.

That night the 'Lord' like an Extraterrestrial appeared to Solomon and renewed his covenant with Israel threatening dire tribulation should they desert him.

The Temple was razed to the ground by Nebuchadnezzar in 587 BC, the present Wailing Wall in Jerusalem formed part of Herod's temple built many centuries later. Solomon's statesmanship raised his country to a zenith unparalleled before or since. It is surprising that he left its foundations so insecure that soon after his death the kingdom split into Judah and Israel, his golden Empire suddenly dissolved.

The Lord for a thousand years had kept his solemn Covenant with Abraham and raised the Children of Israel from nomadic shepherds through bitter trials and tribulations, victories and defeats, to glory in possession of their Promised Land, without celestial inspiration they would have perished. After the death of Solomon the Extraterrestrials turned their attention elsewhere. Judah and Israel struggled alone until in the 8th century BC the Northern Kingdom fell to the fierce Assyrians and the Ten Tribes of Israel were lost, scattered across the face of the Earth.

CHAPTER SIXTEEN
Greece

The immortal epic of Homer's Odyssey abounds with thrilling adventures destined by the Gods. Some Initiates believe it to be the Greek *Book of the Dead*. Ulysses descended to Avernus to learn the secrets of the dead. It is said to contain certain cosmic wisdom known only to Adepts.

Scholars have long assumed that the voyages of Ulysses occurred in the Mediterranean. Robert Philippe[152] with persuasive logic and detailed geographical analysis of Homer's Odyssey with the map of the European coasts apparently proves that Ulysses was impelled by the storms into the Atlantic. The Land of Lotus Eaters and island of the Cyclops were the Canary Islands; King Aeolus lived in Madeira, the savage Laestrygonians in Lisbon; Circe dwelled on Belle-Isle, the Land of the Cimmerians was Quimper peninsula, the Sirens sang on the Isle of Sein; Scylla and Charybdis were the Black Rocks; the Isle of the Sun was Quessant off Brittany; Oygia enchanted by Calypso was Guernsey. Thence sailing north along the amber-route Ulysses was cast ashore among the Phaeacians near modern Oslo whose brilliant Bronze Age culture is believed to have been Atlantis.

On the other hand Hubert Daunicht, Professor at the University of Bonn, asserts that the famous voyages of Ulysses represent a Grecian expedition to Asia in search of the Gods and that many of the hero's exploits occurred in the Yellow River and Sea of Japan. The Professor devoted ten years to profound research to produce his masterpiece of four impressive volumes proving to his own satisfaction at least that the Greek Gods originated as Kings of the ancient Indo-Germanic Empire in Sinkiang, home of the first Aryans. Memory of these Supermen was brought to the West by the vast Asiatic migrations during the Second Millennium BC.[23]

This fascinating theory is based on that mysterious personage Aristeas of Proconessus, mentioned by Strabo the teacher of Homer. His fantastic travels which amazed the Greeks suggest transport in Spaceships, especially as he lived contemporary with Elijah who a few hundred miles away in Israel was translated to the skies in a chariot of fire. Herodotus[95] says that Aristeas, the son of Caystrobius of Proconessus, an island in the Sea of Marmora, stated in verse that he was taken by Phoebus, the Sun God, across the lands of the one-eyed Arimospeans and the griffins who hoard gold to the fabulous century of the Hyperboreans in the far North; apparently accessible only by air.

Herodotus narrates that Aristeas entered the shop of a fuller in Proconessus and died there. The fuller promptly spread the news that the renowned Aristeas was dead, only to be contradicted by a man who said he had just met and spoken with Aristeas going towards Cyzicus, the wealthy city on the Asian coast opposite. The relatives of Aristeas entered the fuller's shop, the body was gone. Seven years later Aristeas re-appeared, wrote a poem about the one-eyed Arimaspeans, then vanished.

Two hundred and forty years afterwards Aristeas appeared at Metapontum near Taranto, Italy, and had men establish an altar to Apollo stating that they should also erect a statue to himself for he went with the God 'as a raven', then he vanished. The men of Metapontum consulted the Oracle at Delphi where the sacred Pythea commanded them to obey the apparition. 'Therefore a statue by the name of Aristeas now standeth beside the image of Apollo and there are bay-trees round about it, and the image is established in the market-place.'

The researches of Dr Daunicht claim to prove that about the middle of ninth century BC Aristeas ventured to the Sea of Japan and to the mouth of the River Amur then returned home to relate his fabulous peregrinations to whomever would listen, for example to blind Homer. This bizarre theory suggests that the legends concerning the destruction of Troy became intermingled with the Indo-Germanic traditions from the peoples emigrated from Asia. Dr Daunicht alleges fascinating parallels between the Shan-hai Ching and the Odyssey. The Chinese work On Seas and Mountains tells of 'Eaters of sweet flowers', the Greek 'Lotus-Eaters' and of 'Cyclops' also of a country of one-eyed Giants like Polyphemus. The Ulysses of Aristeas roamed between China and Japan touching at along the Yellow River, Lo Yang (City of the Phaeacians), the island of Kyushu (Oygia, isle of Calypso), Korea (country of the cannibal Laestrygonians) and Hondo (island of Aeolus) coming to the Amur (the Styx, where Charon ferried the souls of the dead), finally reaching the region of the Eclipse (Hades) where the Gods of the Hwang-ti Dynasty banished their enemies, not excluding the Titans and Giants, the Anti-Gods whom they defeated in epic wars. The very fact that such a revolutionary conception of Homer's well-known Odyssey emanates from deep scholarship serves to show how little we really do know about the world of 1200 BC.

Aristeas disappeared from the sight of men and returned two hundred and forty years later. Before scorning such a story as superstition should we not pause to consider its possibility? Could a mortal man travel through Time leaving our Earth to return in the flesh after his family and friends have dissolved to dust? Einstein certainly thought so. His Theory of Relativity postulates Time-Dilation for a traveller approaching the speed of light, the duration of Time within his spaceship and consequently of all his bodily processes slows down relative to the Time elapsing on the planet he has left; this paradox may enable future cosmonauts to attain the near-stars. Aristeas was probably a contact of the Celestials then visiting Earth and accompanied them to remote Hyperborea, China and Japan. When the Celestials returned to their home-planet about a hundred light-years away Aristeas went with them. After a few years he flew back with a later expedition to find more than two centuries had rolled by, he had become a stranger in his own land.

Bizarre though this tale may be, Aristeas was not the only Time-Traveller in ancient Greece. Epimenides, the celebrated poet and prophet of Crete, when a boy in the early seventh century BC was sent by his father in search of a sheep; seeking shelter from the heat of the midday sun, he went into a cave and there fell into a deep sleep which lasted fifty seven years. On awakening and returning home he found to his great amazement that his younger brother had in the meantime grown an old man.[202]

In 596 BC Solon invited Epimenides to purify Athens from the plague, there he performed many wonders and by certain mysterious rites halted the epidemic. Epimenides wrote a Theogony, a Critica and strange writings in praise of Zeus. His influence must have been most profound for six hundred years later St Paul in his Epistle to Titus quoted him concerning the people of Crete saying 'One of themselves, even a prophet of their own, said "The Cretans are always liars, evil beasts, slow bellies".' Epimenides was not immortal. The Spartans took the Philosopher prisoner in a war with Proconnesus and put him to death because he refused to give favourable prophecies.

The Cretans believed Epimenides lived for three hundred years and worshipped him as a God. He obtained his renowned wisdom from somewhere, not asleep in a cave, more probably on another planet. Stories of him wandering outside his body ascribed to Epimenides powers of astral travel practised by great Initiates but such tales could be meant to conceal possible trips in Spaceships.

Lycurgus, son of Eunomus, King of Sparta, visited Spain, Crete, Libya and even India in the ninth or tenth centuries before Christ meeting the wise men of those countries. He paid frequent visits to Delphi and said the Laws of Sparta were given him there by Apollo just as Minos, Hammurabbi and Moses received Laws from their own Gods. Lycurgus lived about the same time as Solomon, who like his father, David, was inspired by God and Angels who were probably Spacemen. They would impart their wisdom to Lycurgus striving to create the future civilisation of Hellas. The belief that Lycurgus was inspired by Celestials was strengthened by the fact that he left Sparta to finish his life in voluntary exile. Where and how he died nobody could tell. Perhaps translated to the skies in a Chariot of fire like Elijah a century later.

When Lycurgus went to the Oracle at Delphi the Pythea quoted him as beloved of Zeus and all who dwelt on Olympus, she hailed him not as a man but a God. The Spartans built a temple to Lycurgus with yearly sacrifices and the highest honours.[95]

About the sixth century before Christ lived the poet, Aethalides, a herald, the son of Mercury, to whom it was permitted to be amongst the dead and the living at stated times; he was said to have travelled in Hades and above the Earth, reminiscent of Enoch. This ancient Adamski penned his revelations in a poem unfortunately lost. Pythagoras claimed to be a reincarnation of Aethalides which suggests the poet was an Initiate receptive to Spacemen.

Diodorus Siculus[58] wrote that during the 61st Olympiad, 536BC, in Greece Pythagoras was a God among men. People ran in crowds to hear him, he possessed not only great eloquence of speech but a temperate character of soul, a marvellous modesty. The Sage of Samos believed in transmigration of souls and considered the eating of flesh as an abomination saying that the souls of all living creatures pass after death into other living creatures. Pythagoras remembered having been in Trojan times Euphorbus, the son of Panthus, who was slain by Menelaus at Argos. He recognised a Trojan shield as his own and inside were found characters of Euphorbus. Pythagoras called his principles philosophia or love of wisdom, which according to Suidas was an adaptation of ancient British doctrines. Ammianus Marcellinus reported that Pythagoras learned his knowledge from the Hyperborean Druid, Abaris, the Priest of Apollo from Britain. Callimachus said Pythagoras was the first to introduce geometry from Egypt to Greece. Pythagoras told of intercourse with the Gods and was believed to have been miraculously transported around the Earth like Aristeas centuries earlier. Iamblichus says that some people considered Pythagoras formed a fraternity sworn to secrecy. Their bizarre behaviour like our social drop-outs today prompted the people of Crotona to burn down their Temple. The Celestials must have arrived too late for the Sage perished in the flames. Pythagoras expressed his ideas in his famous Golden Verses and his teaching greatly inspired Plato, Apollonius of Tyana,

Dante, Giordano Bruno and many great thinkers in the Middle Ages.

The Greeks said that Pythagoras once freed a slave, Salmoxis, who made a great store of money, then returned in style to his native Thrace. Herodotus related that Salmoxis

'prepared a hall wherein he entertained the chief men of the land and feasted them and sought to persuade them that neither he himself nor his guests should die, nor their children after them for ever, but that they would come to a place where they should live for evermore and have all good things. And during the time that he did and spake as I have said he was making a dwelling beneath the earth. And when the dwelling was finished he disappeared from among the Thracians and went down into the dwelling beneath the earth, and lived there three years. And the Thracisns yearned after him and wept for him as dead. But in the fourth year he appeared unto the Thracians, and so the things which Salmoxis said were made credible to them. Thus they say that he did.'[95]

What was this 'dwelling under the earth'? Adepts might suggest that Salmoxis had descended to Agharta, that alleged subterranean civilisation peopled by Atlanteans and believed by some Sensitives to be the source of the UFOs haunting us today? Salmoxis told the Thracians that he and his children would go to a place where they would live for evermore and have all good things. Did he mean translation to another planet? Aristeas, Epimenides, Aethalides, Pythagoras, Salmoxis! Travels through Time! Trips through Space! Should we really be surprised? When similar experiences were alleged by the Prophets of Israel about the same time a few hundred miles away, they formed the substance of the Old Testament, the very basis of two world-religions.

Almost all the literature of Antiquity was destroyed by fire, flood, megalomaniac Kings or fanatical priests. The few records that remain show that during the seventh and sixth centuries before Christ Extraterrestrials appeared all over the Earth.

670   Annihilation of Sennacherib's army by Angel of the Lord.

660   In Japan Heavenly Deities assist Jimmu against Ainu.

640   Tullus Hostilius killed by fire from heaven.

630   Zoroaster received Laws from Ahura-Mazda on Mt. Sabalan.

Humanoids appeared in Ancient Greece similar to those Extraterrestrials alleged today in South America, some were probably known as the God, Pan, usually represented as a sensual being with horns, puck-nose and goat's feet. In 490 BC Darius, Great King of Persia, invaded Greece. Herodotus relates that the Athenians sent to Sparta a runner, Philippides, requesting aid. Philippides himself said that on Mount Parthenium he met Pan who said he had often helped the Athenians in the past and would do so again. The Spartans refused aid. The Athenians attacked the Persians on the plain of Marathon winning one of the most decisive battles in world-history. Plutarch in Theseus records that the Greeks claimed Theseus, Athene and Heracles descended to fight with them. Victory was won by the Gods!

After the battle the grateful Athenians built a temple to Pan.

The Persians planned revenge for their defeat at Marathon. Ten years later in 480 BC Xerxes invaded Greece with more than two million men, probably more than the population of the country he was invading! The vast army bridged the Dardanelles with boats and crossed to conquer Thessaly and Macedonia. They then advanced on the disunited South. Leonidas with his three hundred Spartans met heroic deaths defending the Pass of Thermopylae. Herodotus states that when the Persians attacked the Temple of Delphi the Priest whose name was Aceratus saw weapons lying before the shrine mysteriously removed outside. Thunderbolts fell on the enemy out of heaven and from Parnassus two mountain-tops were broken off and crashed among them. Some Delphians saw two warriors of greater than human stature following and slaying the invaders.

The Persians swept on to burn Athens, the Athenians had evacuated their wives and children to the island of Salamis. Themistocles cleverly lured the great Persian fleet, partly crippled by heavy storms, to venture into the narrow waters, watched by Xerxes seated on a marble throne on the hill above. The heavier Greek ships smashed the trapped enemy in glorious victory. Plutarch wrote

> 'At this stage of the struggle they say that a great light flamed out from Eleusis and an echoing cry filled the Thricasian plain down to the sea, as if multitudes of men together conducting the mystic Iacchus in procession. Then out of the shouting throng a cloud seemed to lift itself slowly from the earth, pass out seawards and to protect the Hellenic triremes. These they conjectured were the Aeacidae, who had been prayerfully invoked before the battle to come to their aid.'[164]

The Aeacidae were descendants of Aeacus, son of Zeus, and Aegina, a daughter of the river-God, Asopus. Plutarch's account suggests the apparent intervention of Extraterrestrials.

Herodotus in his vivid description of the battle of Salamis mentions the shattered Persian ships stating that the Greeks were ready for another battle, expecting that Xerxes would use the ships that were left to him.

> 'But a west wind arose and bore many of the broken pieces to the beach in Attica which is called Calias, so that besides the other prophecies which were spoken by Bocis and Musaeus concerning this battle the thing was fulfilled which had been spoken many years before in a prophecy by the seer Lysistratus of Athens but none of the Greeks had comprehended it.'[95]

The revelation that Lysistratus had foreseen the great sea-battle of Salamis many years before is a fascinating authenticated case of prophecy.

Cicero recorded that a few years earlier in 498 BC Castor and Pollux saved the Romans at Lake Regillus.[47] A comet, possibly a UFO, hovered over the Battle of Hastings in AD 1066, strange aerial lights attended battles during the Hitler, Korean and Vietnam Wars. Did Gods aid the Greeks at Marathon and Salamis? The great dramatist Aeschylus probably thought so, he fought there.

Aeschylus modestly described his works as scraps from Homer's banquet; like Homer he was inspired with religious awe of the supreme authority of Zeus. He wrote with concentrated power of human destinies directed by the Gods. Only seven of his seventy tragedies are extant. In the

Eumenides Apollo advises the guilt-stricken Orestes to go to Athens for the judgement of Athene who acquits him, as though Aeschylus knew that Celestrials judged the fate of men. Prometheus Bound concerns the struggle between Zeus and Prometheus, a titanic drama of the Gods. The chorus often refers to winged-cars, Okeanos flies on winged griffons, the celestial messengers Hermes and Io fly down to Prometheus bound to the mountain-crag by Hephaestus.

Aeschylus died at Gela in 456 BC at the age of sixty-nine. An eagle mistaking the poet's bald head for a stone dropped a tortoise upon it to smash its shell and so fulfilled an oracle by which he was fated to die by a blow from heaven.

Sophocles,[185] thirty years younger than Aeschylus, was a sunny-natured Athenian. His lyrical plays proved more popular than the austere moralisings of his rival. Of his outstanding output of one hundred and thirty plays only seven remain. Tragedies like Antigone, Electra express deep and poignant emotions yet Sophocles is profoundly aware of the Gods brooding over the destinies of men.

While Aeschylus was fighting to defeat the Persians at Salamis in 480 BC Euripides[68] on that very island was born, whose parents had evacuated from their home in Athens. In his brilliant plays Euripides considered it good theatre to bring the Immortals down to Earth. Castor and Pollux appeared in Electra and Helen; Apollo in Alcestis and Orestes, Minerva in Ion, Suppliants, Trojan Women; and Artemis in Hippolytus.

Aristophanes,[6] born in 448 BC, in his eleven extant comedies satirised the Gods in many amusing scenes. Hundreds of Greek plays must have been lost, the few that remain suggest that the characterisation of the Gods on the stage was a welcome convention.

The Philosophers spoke of the Gods somewhat vaguely, perhaps they hesitated to reveal the esoteric teachings of the Mysteries but generally they were much more interested in men. When Socrates spoke of his daemon he usually meant the voice of conscience, his inner Self. Plato however wrote 'Daemons are defined as a race superior to men, but inferior to Gods; they were created to watch human affairs', suggesting perhaps the existence of a celestial race or Spacemen. In the

Phaedrus Plato, describing the divine as beauty, goodness and the like, added

> 'Zeus, the mighty leader, holding the reins of a winged-chariot, leads the way in heaven ordering all and taking care of all and there follows the array of Gods and Demi-Gods marshalled in eleven bands.'

This concept would suggest that Plato believed in Celestials speeding across the skies like the Gods in their golden cars so brilliantly described in the Sanskrit Classics.

Lysander, the distinguished Spartan General, in 405 BC brought the Peloponnesian War to a conclusion by defeating the Athenian fleet at Aegospotami near to the Dardanelles. Plutarch describing Lysander's great achievement states

> 'Therefore some actually thought the result due to "divine intervention". There were some who declared that the Dioscuri, (Castor and Pollux) appeared as twin stars on either side of Lysander's ship just as he was sailing out against the enemy and shone out over the rudder-sweeps.'

Diodorus Siculus commenting on the fall of Sparta in 372BC wrote that during the course of many nights a great blazing torch was seen in the heavens, a little later the Spartans met heavy defeat.

By 600 BC visitations by Spacemen were reduced to rare surveillance, the Gods appeared content to watch men on Earth evolve by their own efforts without interference. Soon eclipsed by new exciting philosophies the Celestials receded to vague myths. Thales of Miletus, 636-546 BC, rejected the old mythological explanations, he introduced into Greece the new mathematics he had acquired in Egypt which enabled him to predict the eclipse of the Sun in 585 BC. Anaximander, 610-547, propounded an endless cycle of universes, worlds created from immense rotations of matter. He anticipated Darwin teaching that all creatures including Man had evolved from primitive life in the sea. Pythagoras, 570-500, stated that the Earth was round, confirmed by Aristarchus, 310-230, who anticipated Copernicus and declared that the Earth revolving on its own axis moved around the Sun. About 320 BC Aratus of Soli composed his wonderful poem Phaenomena giving detailed knowledge of the constellations which proves that the Greeks knew much more astronomy than we imagine.

Hipparchus, 190-120, regarded as the greatest astronomer in Antiquity rejected the helicocentric theory of Aristarchus, he believed our Earth to be the centre of the Universe. Pliny in his Historia Naturalis, wrote that Hipparchus detected a new star which came into existence leaving us to speculate as to whether it was a Super-Nova or a UFO surveilling Greece.

Alexander the Great, whose death in 323 BC at thirty three left the world and himself unconquered, led the Greeks to India. He actually thought himself to be a God and his dazzling, meteoric career certainly suggests powerful inspiration from some inner daemon or other celestial source. Arrian, Ptolemy and Megasthenes depict Alexander's life and death in prosaic detail. Later historians embellished him with wonders of doubtful authenticity omitted from the classical histories. Frank Edwards, the noted American UFO reporter, quoting some source unfortunately not disclosed, states 'Intelligent beings from Outer Space may already be looking us over.' He exasperates us by claiming

'Alexander the Great was not the first to see them nor was he the first to find them troublesome. He tells of two strange craft that dived repeatedly on his army until the war-elephants, the men and the horses all panicked and refused to cross the river where the incident occurred. What did the things look like? His historian describes them as great shining silver shields spitting fire around the rings ... things that came from the skies and returned to the skies.'[67]

This remarkable incident was apparently paralleled by an equally fantastic visitation during the siege of Tyre by Alexander in 332 BC. Giovanni Droysen's Storia di Alessandro il Grande quoted by the Italian scholar, Alberti Fenoglio, runs as follows

'The fortress would not yield, its walls were fifty feet high and constructed so solidly that no siege-engine was able to damage it. The Tyrians disposed of the greatest technicians and builders of war-machines of the time and they intercepted in the air the incendiary-arrows and projectiles hurled by the catapults on the city.

One day suddenly there appeared over the Macedonian camp these Flying Shields, as they had been called, which flew in triangular formation led by an exceedingly large one, the others were smaller by almost a half. In all there were five. The unknown chronicler narrates that they circled slowly over Tyre while thousands of warriors on both sides stood and watched them in astonishment. Suddenly from the largest "shield" came a lightning-flash that struck the walls, these crumbled, other flashes followed and walls and towers disolved, as if they had been built of mud, leaving the way open for the besiegers who poured like an avalanche through the breaches. The "Flying Shields" hovered over the city until it was completely stormed then they very swiftly disappeared aloft, soon melting into the blue sky.[71]

The intervention of Flying Shields from heaven was chronicled again about eleven hundred years later in AD 776 when two large flamming shields appeared in the sky to rain down fire on the Saxons besieging the Franks in Sigiburg on the River Lippy until they fled in headlong flight.[138]

Such astounding incidents in the times of Alexander the Great and Charlemagne confound us, though we solemnly worship those Extraterrestrials said to have manifested in Israel.

The Priests like Adepts all over the ancient World could utilise atmospheric-electricity and are believed to have protected their great temples with lightning-conductors. Pausanias mentions a golden lamp in the temple of Minerva at Athens which burnt a whole year. Plutarch saw one in the temple of Jupiter Amun which had burnt continually for years, although it stood in the open air neither wind nor water could extinguish it. A lamp found at Edessa burned 500 years; near Attesté a lamp was found alleged to have burned for 1500 years 'by means of a most pure liquor contained in two bottles, one of gold and the other of silver.'[16]

Plato in his Laws[157] reminded the cynical younger generation 'No one who has adopted in youth the idea that the Gods do not exist, ever continued to hold it until he was old.' Though the landings of Extraterrestrials became quite rare, the people of Greece with superstitious awe believed the stars were inhabited by wonderful eccentrics who might be persuaded to aid mortals on Earth. Though most of the literature of antiquity is destroyed some writers are known to have anticipated our Science-Fiction authors today.

Antonius Diogenes is said to have written a lost work entitled Of the Wonderful Things beyond Thule which describes a voyage to the Moon; Plutarch, the great biographer of the second century AD, wrote a philosophic treatise De Facie in Orbe lunae, Concerning Spots on the Face of the Moon; the most fascinating Spacesatire was penned by

Lucian of Samosata, the second century Sophis. His so-called A True Story anticipates those marvellous tales of Jules Verne.

'Once upon a time setting out from the Pillars of Hercules and heading for the Western Ocean with a fair wind, I went a-voyaging. The motive and purpose of my journey lay in my intellectual activity and desire for adventure, in my wish to find out what the end of the ocean was, and who the people were that lived on the other side.'[127]

Lucian excuses his failure to land by blaming a sudden whirlwind which seized the bellying sails and tossed the boat aloft higher and higher for seven days and seven nights becalming at last on a great country resembling an island, bright and round and shining with a great light. They had landed on the Moon!

With the rise of Rome the Extraterrestrials turned their attention to Italy but the memory of the Gods was still preserved in the Sacred Mysteries of Greece.

CHAPTER SEVENTEEN
Italy

Legends tell of the ancient culture of the Uranids, Celestials from the stars when Earth was young. After an immense age this stellar race was overthrown by Beings from Saturn or its Moons, who imprisoned the giant Cyclops underground. Mythology credits Saturn with dethroning his father, Uranus, from the Government of Earth until he himself was overthrown by his own son, Jupiter; this symbology clearly suggests that in far antiquity there were three distinct cultures when our Earth was the prize of warring Spacemen from those planets. Plato explains that Saturn, meaning Celestials, taught men agriculture and morality. In ancient times Italy was called Saturnia, the land of plenty. Initiates believed that the Secret Wisdom was communicated by Saturnians to the inhabitants of our Moon who taught men on Earth, this probably means that they used our Moon as a base before landing on Earth.

The worship of Saturn was hailed all over the world. The old chroniclers support Tacitus and Plutarch in saying that Saturn was imprisoned by Jupiter on an island in the West, perhaps Britain, where he was worshipped by the Druids. Later Saturnia worship degenerated into licence perpetuated by the notorious sexual extravagances of the Roman Saturnalia.

Saturn was usurped by Jupiter suggesting that fleets of spaceships from that planet, more probably from a Jovian Moon, attacked in force, vanquished the Saturnians and established their Age of Silver followed after world-disasters by Ages of Bronze and Iron; their conflict might have been the

War of the Gods mentioned in most religions. Such fantasy lacks proof though most myths agree that some celestial struggle surely occurred, for in Rome the worship of Jupiter supplanted Saturn whose temples were re-dedicated to this most powerful of Gods, and this was the official State religion until Constantine in AD 312 introduced Christianity.[62]

Dr Costantino Cattoi, the Italian airman and archaeologist, discovered gigantic stone figures including monstrous carvings of a Sphinx near Trapani in Sicily and on Mount Argentario, Orbotello, Italy, which closely resembled those fantastic carved figures on the plateau of Marcahuasi in Peru, possibly 100,000 years old. The vast antiquity of Man in Italy is supported by the recently discovered Paleolithic site at Terra Armata, Nice, in south-eastern France, revealing evidence of man-made structures about 300,000 years old.[128] In August 1958 Dr Johannes Huerzeler, a Swiss palaeontologist, working in a coal-mine at Baccinello in Central Italy discovered amid coal strata 600 feet down a complete skeleton of a man, Oreopithecus, who apparently lived in Italy during the age of the carboniferous forests millions of years ago. Near Mt Bego between Milan and Bolzano are found thousands of mysterious signs traced on cliff walls representing people, horned animals, weapons and strange drawings of humans, possibly Spacemen like those intriguing frescoes at Tassili in the Sahara. In the Valle di Susa near Villa Focchiardi was found a giant stone head resembling those great Olmec heads in Mexico. Immense megaliths abound in Corsica, all suggesting some race of Giants living in the Mediterranean lands long ago.

Dionysius of Halicarnassus[60] states that Hercules invaded Europe with a great army probably from Erytheia, Red Island in the West, evoking the Atlantean invasion of the Mediterranean lands about 10,000 BC which was routed by the heroic Athenians. Hercules conquered Spain, Southern France and campaigned in Italy where he is said to have founded the city of Herculaneum destined to be destroyed with Pompeii. The destruction of ancient records makes substantiation of this story difficult. Curious stone cupolas in Puglia bear remarkable resemblance to the truncated pyramids of old Mexico and suggest that some Atlanteans fled eastwards to Italy, others westwards to America. These highly cultured people reduced to barbarous conditions in barren Puglia tried to leave some record of their former civilisation in cosmic symbols on stones telling posterity of their grandiose past.[115]

Virgil's 'Aeneid' tells in majestic verse the epic of Aeneas from burning Troy about 1200 BC. After dallying with Queen Dido in Carthage the Trojan hero was guided by Venus, his Mother, to fulfil his destiny in Italy. Aeneas and his companions sailed up the west coast to the Tiber and were welcomed by King Latinus of Latium, who gave him in marriage his daughter, Lavinia; their son, Iulus, built Alba Longa, where four centuries later were born Romulus and Remus, Founders of Rome. Brutus, great-grandson of Aeneas, killed his father hunting and in banishment fled west to that fog-wrapped island on the edge of the world inhabited by Giants to which he gave the name Britain.[84]

Seven hundred years before Christ between the Arno and the Tiber flourished the brilliant civilisation of the Etruscans still veiled in tantalising mystery. Etruria was a federation of independent cities rather than a single State, linked by the aristocracy and the all-powerful priesthood. Many languages of Antiquity have been deciphered, but not Etruscan; the little we glean of this fascinating people comes from their tombs.

According to Dionysius of Halicarnassus the Etruscans were quite original and dissimilar in language and custom from any other people. Modern glottologists agree that their language is neither Indo-European nor Semitic, scholars speculate that perhaps they were one of the Peoples of the Sea known to the Egyptians as the Tursha defeated by Pharaoh Merneptan about 1200 BC.[72] Apparent linguistic and cultural links with the pre-Aztecs suggest that the ancestors of the Etruscans originated from Atlantis. Livy hinted that the Etruscans had a considerable literature and regretted that almost all had perished; the scholarly Emperor Claudius wrote a history of the Etruscans in twenty volumes, all lost. While Rome was a primitive village the Etruscans basked in a sophisticated culture, their ships traded with Greece and Carthage, a tiny Etruscan colony flourished in Egypt. Unlike the Romans the Etruscans boasted no martial ambitions.

They lived for sensual enjoyment soon degenerating to sexual decadence; socially they abolished slavery, their few prisoners-of-war were employed in factories. The Priests or Lucomones knew a science lost to us, they practised parapsychology, water-divining, telepathy and spiritualism, for them the dead lived in other realms within communication until their souls reincarnated on Earth. A few years ago some swords were unearthed from an Etruscan site, beautiful and shining the blades looked newly forged, never 2500 years old, chemical analysis showed the iron to be chemically pure and not subject to oxidation; bronze forceps found were said to be similar to those used in our modern hospitals.[85]

The strange lore of the Etruscans was known to some of their neighbours. In the ninth century BC the Latin city of Alba Longa was ruled by Tiberinus descended from Aeneas. His son, Amulius, dabbled with electricity using techniques known to Adepts but alien to us. Dio Cassius states

'Amulius, a descendant of Tiberinus, displayed an overweening pride and dared to make himself a God; he went so far as to match the thunder with artificial thunder, to answer lightning with lightning, and to hurl thunderbolts. He met his end by a sudden overflow of the lake beside which his palace was built, it submerged both him and his palace.'[57]

This revelation suggests that about 850 BC Initiates in old Italy utilised forces like nuclear-bombs, hardly surprising since a few hundred miles away in Israel Elijah was summoning Angels to blast the Priests of Baal.

Cicero states that the Etruscans were taught by a Divine Being called Tages. One day in the reign of Tarchon, son of Tyrrhenus, as a peasant ploughed a deep furrow in a field near the city of Tarquinia there sprang out of the earth a young child with grey hair and wisdom of an old man. The apparition revealed he had been sent by Tinia, the Supreme God, to reveal the laws, religion and art of divination to the Etruscan Kings, the Lucomones. He dictated to the augurs the 'Libri Tagetici' which formed the Etruscan Bible governing the lives of the Etruscans from the cradle to the grave just as the Books of Moses regulated the daily life of the Jews. Artists represented Tages in bronze statuettes as a bald-headed dwarf. Was he teleported or transported by Spaceship from another planet? His sudden appearance from the earth suggests emergence from those subterranean passages leading to Agharta alleged to exist underground. Such speculation is not mere fantasy, there are many well-authenticated reports of alien humanoids, small in stature, appearing in Italy today, some might have manifested in Tuscany centuries ago.

The Etruscans were not a war-like people and were eventually overwhelmed and deported in mass by the bellicose Romans. When Perugia tried to rebel the Romans walled-up the gates of the city and let the population including women and children starve to death.

Many Etruscan cities were built on windy isolated hills like those cyclopean fortresses in the Andes suggesting they were sky-ports for Spacemen. Etruria was famous for its towers recalling those lofty ziggurats of Babylon; in the ancient world towers had cosmic significance being probably used by the Priests for communication with the Gods.

In the 8th century BC the Celestials active in Israel and Babylon became vitally interested in the destiny of Italy. Amulius who had wrested Alba Longa from Numitor, fearing the latter's daughter, Rhea Silvia, might have children, made her a Priestess of Vesta sworn to live a virgin all her life. Soon she found herself pregnant, allegedly by the God Mars, and gave birth to two boys in size and beauty more than human, suggesting divine parentage. Amulius ordered the twins to be put in a basket and thrown into the Tiber. They drifted down stream and were washed ashore, where according to legend they were found and suckled by a she-wolf. The Latin *lupa* also meant prostitute; so the she-wolf probably referred to Larentia, wife of the shepherd, Faustulus, who adopted the infants.[163]

On attaining manhood Romulus and Remus returned to Alba Longa, killed Amulius and restored the city to their grandfather, Numitor. Then, with their companions, they decided to build a city of their own beside the Tiber. Like the Etruscans the twins believed in divination by the flight of birds. Remus on the Aventine Hill first saw six vultures, then Romulus on the Palatine Hill saw twelve, although some swore he had cheated. Remus taunted his elder brother, so Romulus killed him though the murder was sometimes attributed to his companion, Celer.

On 21st April 735 BC Romulus founded Rome!

Romulus became greatly beloved by his people and won vast honour. In 737 BC Roman morale was gravely shaken by a rain of blood which the augurs interpreted as presaging disaster, but apparently they had to wait twenty-one years. In 716BC when Romulus was delivering judgement on the Palatine Hill thunder and lightning rent the heavens, a black cloud blotted out the sun, when the storm ceased the assembly were astonished to discover their King had vanished from their midst like Enoch, Elijah, Hercules and Asclepius before him. Romulus was miraculously transported to the skies.

Soon afterwards Julius Proculus swore by the most solemn oath that he had seen Romulus suddenly descend from the sky radiantly transfigured. The hero told Proculus that it was the Will of the Gods that after founding a city destined to be the greatest on Earth he should dwell in heaven. The Romans fervently believed this miracle and honoured Romulus as their God, Quirinus.

Born to a Virgin, Fathered by a God. Guided by divine omens. Translated to heaven. Resurrection to inspire his followers. Worshipped for centuries as a God. Does the story of Romulus not startle us by its similarity to that of another Saviour seven centuries later?

Christian writers ridicule the translation of Romulus as ignorant pagan superstition but piously accept the disappearance of the body of Jesus as the very basis of Christianity, although the dispassionate Seeker of Truth might judge the evidence, slight as it is, as good for one as for the other. Commonsense swears that men do not suddenly vanish into thin air, unfortunately there are many bizarre disappearances of people apparently only explained by teleportation or kidnapping by Spacemen.

For a year the various factions in Rome could not agree on any Roman as King. Finally they chose a Sabine from neighbouring Cures, Numa Pompilius. Only when he was firmly convinced by a flight of birds over his veiled head as he prayed aloud before a silent multitude did Numa agree it was the Will of the Gods that he should rule Rome. He disbanded the King's bodyguard, reorganised the worship of Jupiter, and built the famous temple of Janus whose doors were closed in peace, open in war. Numa divided the year into twelve months instead of ten, and during the mid-winter festival in honour of Saturn he allowed the slaves to be waited upon by their Masters.[162]

Exasperated at the frivolity of the Fair Sex Numa directed that women should be seen but not heard, neither must they meddle or gossip. Unfortunately for centuries of long-suffering husbands Numa failed to silence women, so he turned with more success to the easier task of controlling lightning, a psycho-science known to the ancient Initiates still lost to us. Numa followed the doctrines later developed by Pythagoras, possibly learned from British Druids visiting Rome; the Romans believed he could call down Jupiter from the skies, snare demi-Gods with spring-water drugged with wine and honey and converse with nymphs. Could he have been taught by Spacemen?

In 708 BC an ancile or bronze shield is said to have fallen from heaven. Numa promptly told the people who were stricken by plague that the marvel was sent by the Gods, an omen signifying their protection of the City. To lessen the chances of theft the King ordered expert craftsmen to furnish eleven exact replicas entrusted to the Salii, Priests of Mars, who carried them in religious processions around the city. Bronze plates do not fall from the sky unless someone drops them. The Romans never doubted the shield's celestial origin, they must have acknowledged Supermen flying over the city in solid aircraft.

The Indo-European Sky-Father, Dyaus-Pitar or Zeus-Pater, latinised to Jupiter, symbolised the Spacemen, dominating the Roman heavens, the stars, the Sun, thunder and lightning, Ruler of Gods and Man. Apollo, Minerva, Juno, Ceres, Venus and Neptune were assimilated from the Greeks; Saturn, Vesta and many others from local cults; towering above them all presided Jupiter aided by Mars, God of War, Patron of Rome, and Quirinus, identified with Romulus. Celestial prodigies were interpreted by augurs revealing the Will of the Gods.

Numa Pompilius reigned forty-three years during which there were no wars or political strife. When he died in 672 BC his funeral rites called forth public lamentation by all, mourning not a King but rather a dear friend. He wrote twelve books on natural wisdom, but convinced such mysteries should not be published, he directed that all his writings should be buried in one stone coffin, himself in another. Four hundred years later heavy rains washed away the earth disclosing both coffins. The Senate decided that publication of the writings would reveal most sacred secrets, and they ordered all to be publicly burned. Revelations of Numa's wisdom might have revolutionised our concept of history and disclosed that ancient electrical Science.

Numa's own coffin was found to be empty. Was he resurrected or translated?

Tullus Hostilius scorned Numa's pacificism and launched fierce wars. At the height of his glory the King's superstitious soul was disturbed by a rain of stones on the Alban Mount. A mighty voice was heard issuing from the grove on the mountain-top which commanded the Albans to return to the Gods of their fathers, recalling the Voice of the Lord admonishing Abraham and Moses. He aspired to emulate Numa by using that potent electricity conjured from the atmosphere but called down a thunderbolt destroying himself and all his house.

Under Tarquin the Proud Rome dominated the Latin Federation. An old woman came to him offering twelve books prophesying the future of Rome for three hundred pieces of gold. Tarquin refused. She returned with nine declaring she had destroyed three. Again the King refused. The woman destroyed another three and returned once more with six which she threatened to sell to the King's enemies. Tarquin bought the six at the original price; they were consulted by the Senate in times of crisis. The Sibylline Books probably resembled those celebrated couplets of Nostradamus inspired by some extraterrestrial source.

CHAPTER EIGHTEEN
Ancient Rome

Livy, Dio Cassius, Plutarch, Pliny and other writers seemed acutely conscious of Divinities guiding affairs on Earth, they really believed that omens in the heavens were written by the Gods to presage great events.

Pliny in 'Historia Naturalis', comments

> 'Besides these events in the lower sky, it is entered in the records that in the consulship of Manius Acilus and Gaius Porcius (114 BC) it rained milk and blood and that frequently on other occasions there it has rained flesh, for instance in the consulship of Publius Volumnius and Servius Sulpicius (416 BC) and that none of the flesh left unplundered by birds of prey went bad, similarly that it rained iron in the district of Lucania, the year before Marcus Crassus (in the battle of Carrhae 53 BC) was killed by the Parthians and with him all the Lucanian soldiers, of whom there was a large contingent in his army; the shape of the iron that fell resembled sponges; the augurs prophesied wounds from above. But in the consulship (49 BC) of Lucius Paulus and Gaius Marcellus, it rained wool in the vicinity of Compsa Castle (now Conza in Samnium) near which Titus Annius was killed a year later. It is recorded in the annals of that year that while Milo was pleading a case in Court it rained bricks.'[161]

In 461 BC the heavens were seen to glow and people saw strange phantoms which terrified them, the forms and voices of the apparitions were dreadful to the eyes and ears of men, reminiscent of those startling tales of humanoids said to be terrorising the peasants of South America today. Those Visitants were accompanied by a rain of flesh like the appearance of snow from the sky. Such rains of flesh apparently originate from animals caught up by the gravitational-field[52] of a Spaceship confirming perhaps that those dreadful apparitions were Spacemen.

Priests, poets and mythologists prove the wide-spread deep-rooted influence of the Sky Father with his pantheon of Gods on all the peoples of Antiquity. Everyone regarded the Gods as Supermen living just out of sight and welcomed their descent from the skies to educate or entertain the mortals on Earth. Our own theologians dismiss the ancient Gods as anthropomorphisms of natural forces, as if entire races for hundreds of years would base their daily lives on lightning or thunderbolts!

Julius Obsequens recorded 64 celestial phenomena. Livy 30. Pliny the Elder 26, Dio Cassius 14. Cicero 9, confirming their psychological impact on the educated Roman mind.

Lack of scientific data makes evaluation of celestial phenomena somewhat doubtful; sceptics will probably explain most of them as meteors, sun-glare, clouds, birds, even the planet Venus. The Roman augurs with many centuries of experience scanning the skies would hardly trouble to stress natural occurrences; the sightings they recorded would surely be strange and significant apparently denoting the Will of the Sky Gods.

In 344 BC as Timoleon sailed to free Sicily from the Carthaginians the heavens burst open and a torch appeared, it accompanied his ships to Italy.[165]

In 234 BC when the Gauls invaded Italy three moons were seen at Rimini; in 223 BC in Ariminium a light like the day blazed out at night, in many parts of Italy three moons became visible in the night-time. In 221 BC at Rimini three moons were seen approaching from the distant regions of the heavens.

The century-long conflict between Rome and Carthage with such tremendous consequences for future civilisation would inevitably intrigue any Spacemen surveilling Earth. In 218BC young Hannibal crossed the Alps. For the next sixteen years this great General ravaged Italy yet never set foot in Rome.

Livy tells us

218 BC 'Phantom ships had been seen gleaming in the sky. In the district of Amiternum in many places apparitions of men in shining raiment had appeared in the distance but had not drawn near to anyone.'

214 BC　'At Hadria an altar was seen in the sky and about it the forms of men in white garments.'

This seems to us one of the great sightings of antiquity.

173 BC　At Lanuvium the appearance of a great fleet was beheld in the sky. At Priverno grey wool covered the ground.
　　　　　(Obsequens.)

A similar fall of wool in Central Italy in 49 BC is reported by Pliny.

Associated with UFO activity is a gossamer-like substance known throughout history as Angel's Hair or Threads of the Virgin, silvery filaments appearently synthesised in extremely high-voltage discharges. These strands like nylon drape the ground only to vanish when the temperature rises. Thus Obsequens suggests the manifestation of many Spaceships.

87 BC　Sulla had assembled an army in Greece to invade Italy. On route to Patrae for the crossing to Brundusium the Romans found a strange humanoid at Apollonia near Dyrrachium in Ittyria.

Here they say, a Satyr was caught asleep, such an one as sculptors and painters represent, and brought to Sulla, where he was asked through many interpreters who he was. And when at last he uttered nothing intelligible but with difficulty emitted a hoarse cry that was something between the neighing of a hoarse and the bleating of a goat, Sulla was horrified and ordered him out of his sight.'
　　　　　(Plutarch)

This recalls the God Pan worshipped by the Greeks and even that strange boy, Kaspar Hauser, found at Nuremberg on May 28th 1828, who appeared so alien. William de Newburgh in the 12th century in his 'Historia Anglicana' writes of a boy and a girl, green all over their bodies, clad in garments of unusual colour and material, who appeared from the ground at Alfpittes near Bury St. Edmunds in England. The pair said they were from St. Martin's Land, apparently a subterranean twilight world where the sun never shone. Was this Agharta? A little green man was seen in a forest in Finland at Luumaki as recently as 1965 by two well-known people. It is fascinating to speculate whether the humanoids belonged to some secret green race which were known to the Greeks and Romans as Satyrs. These quaint beings were reported by German foresters in the Middle Ages.

83 BC　During the era of Sulla a great clash of standards and of arms with dreadful shouting was heard between Capua and Volturnus, so that two great armies seemed to be locked in combat for several days. When men investigated this marvel more closely, the tracks of horses and of men and the freshly trampled grass and shrubs seemed to foretell the burden of a large war.
　　　　(Obsequens)

66 BC　In the consulship of Gnaeus Octavius and Gaius Scribonius a spark was seen to fall from a star and increase in size as it approached the earth, and after becoming as large as the moon it diffused a sort of cloudy daylight, and then returning to the sky changed into a torch; this is the only record of this occurring. It was seen by the Proconsul, Silenis, and his suite.
　　　　(Pliny)

An excellent sighting carefully observed by people of repute. Certainly Pliny thought so.

63 BC　A blazing beam from the west swept across the sky. All Spoletium was shaken by earthquakes.
　　　　(Obsequens)

UFOs today are believed to pay particular attention to Earth's fault-zones, lights in the sky frequently coincide with earthquakes.

In 44 BC the memorable year of Caesar's murder, Rome was haunted by wonderful prodigies. Plutarch records

'Now as for lights in the heavens, crashing sounds, all about by night, and birds of omen coming down into the Forum, it is perhaps not worth while to mention these precursors of so great an event but Strabo, the philosopher, says that multitudes of men on fire were seen rushing up.'

Julius Obsequens mentions a torch in the west and three suns which may have been celestial phenomena or Spaceships watching Rome during these critical times.

The description 'men on fire' approximates Biblical accounts of Angels glowing with light, the apparitions of men in shining garments seen in the Amiternum district in 218 BC, flaming phantoms witnessed in the Middle Ages and those luminous humanoids haunting the Americas today.

The Priests of Rome had inherited the lore of the Etruscans and were probably conversant with the wisdom of the Babylonians. The Romans were accomplished glass-makers, stained glass was found at Pompeii; in the reign of Tiberius an artisan brought to Rome a cup 'which he dashed upon the marble pavement and it was not crushed or broken by the fall',[16] unfortunately the secret of unbreakable glass was lost.

In 41 BC Mark Antony met Cleopatra on the river Cydnus and in the blue sky above, three suns merged into one, suggesting this brilliant encounter was witnessed by Spacemen.[41]

Ten years later in 31 BC after shattering defeat by Octavian, in the great sea-battle at Actium, Antony in theatrical climax stabbed himself; later Cleopatra cheated a Roman triumph by applying to her breast a poisonous asp. The comments of **Diodorus Siculus** for 30 BC, possibly months earlier, run thus

'In Egypt it rained not only water, where no drop had ever fallen previously, but also blood, there were flashes of armour from the clouds as this bloody rain fell from them. Meanwhile comets were seen and dead men's ghosts appeared.'

In 16 BC a torch spread across the sky from south to north making an expanse of the night like daylight. 12 BC a comet hung for several days over Rome, then dissolved into flashes resembling torches, and three years later nine suns over Kyushu baffled the Japanese.[9] Were Spacemen visiting East and West?

About 4 BC there is said to have shone in the Middle East a new star not recorded by any astronomer, completely ignored by Pliny, Seneca, Ptolemy, Plutarch, Josephus, Julius Obsequens, prolific Writers concerning this period. The only reference to this mysterious star was written about eighty years later by St. Matthew, who almost certainly never saw it.

The only celestial object to appear suddenly close enough to the Earth to be visible within only a small radius, which moves guiding followers, then stands still, is an intelligently controlled Spaceship.

In a stable in Bethlehem Jesus was born.

CHAPTER NINETEEN
Scandinavia

The rugged grandeur of the North, land of mountains and fjords, evokes the wonder of a magic world, a titanic past, when God and Giants, Heroes and Wizards, waged Superhuman war in sea and sky until their fantastic conflict shattered fair Earth to desolation. Cataclysms convulsed the northern countries, the climate grew suddenly cold, the few survivors fled from the Arctic ice to storm the warm Mediterranean. The Gods in defeat returned to the stars. This mighty epic haunts folk-memory in the myths of most countries but in Scandinavia the wild landscape still shows gaunt ruins, colossal devastation of long ago.

For dark ages the old Sky Gods dominated men's primitive minds with a power Christianity has not eclipsed. Who were these Cosmic Personalities who across the chasms of the past could force men to pagan sacrifice, whose stern traditions inspired the Vikings to scourge Europe and a thousand years later in grandiose resurrection drove's Hitler's Third Reich to Götterdämmerung? The ancient legends were told by the scalds, wandering minstrels at Court and camp-fire in the Eddas, a word meaning great-grandmother. The Elder Edda containing Norse myths is attributed to Saemund, an Icelandic nobleman about 1100 AD; a century later a picturesque character, Snorri Sturlason, Court Poet, libertine, Prime Ministrer, found time between his marriages to wealthy women to retell the legends in his delightful Younger Edda.

All peoples personified the Gods in terms of their own national character. The Scandinavian Creation legends share the same cosmic wisdom of the Rig Veda and Genesis suggesting some common source from a remote civilisation or teaching by Spacemen. For ages before earth was formed fierce war was waged between the Gods (Aesir) and the Giants (Vanir) echoing those Sanskrit tales of conflict between the Celestials and the Asuras, evoking some ancient Space War. Finally the Sons of Bor prevailed destroying Ymir. In a deluge of blood from his body was made the Earth. Odin regulated the course of the Sun, Moon and stars and decided the climate; such celestial disorder recalls those cataclysms mentioned in all mythologies confirming some cosmic catastrophe.

The Aesir built Asgard, a wonderful celestial city of golden and silver palaces surrounded by a lofty wall with only one great gate entered by the bridge Bifrost (rainbow). In the resplendent centre-hall, Valhalla, sat Odin on a golden throne. To Valhalla the Valkyries translated heroes slain in battle where they caroused and made love like the Faithful of Mohammed feasting with the houris in Paradise. Below Asgard lay Midgard, the Earth, peopled by the Son of Bor, a parallel to the Golden Age of the Gods in Greek legend.

The twelve Norse Gods lacked the geniality of those twelve Olympians of the Greeks. All seemed obsessed with Fate, defeat and death. Such Teutonic tragedy possibly originated from that cataclysm which once blasted the sunny Northern lands to twilight wilderness. Odin brooded in gloomy loneliness over the follies of men, his sombre thoughts fed by the two ravens perched on his shoulders, who flew down to the world to gather news. In his youth Odin surrendered an eye to drink from the Well of Wisdom; like the Egyptian God, Thoth, he was deeply versed in magic lore and invented the ancient writing called runes, teaching civilisation to mankind. Odin travelled on the wind sometimes winging to Earth as a falcon. He often rode Sleipner, a mare with eight legs, evoking the twelve-legged horse of Huschenk whom the peoples of the Caucasus regarded as a wondrous Teacher who built Babylon and Ispahan and then flew northwards across the Arctic to a wonderful Continent. Odin's wonderful spear resembled the staffs of power wielded by magicians. His wife, Holda, was noted for racing her chariot through the sky.

Odin was popularly visualised as a venerable figure with a

long white beard and a broad-brimmed hat shading his face, symbolism for ancient wisdom. Like Zeus he often descended to Earth in disguise bringing aid to men; when recognised he might change his shape or become invisible. The Swedes sacrificed prisoners-of-war to Odin; to prolong his own life King Aun of Upsala sacrificed his nine sons one after another.[190] The Eddas venerate this All-Wise Father of the Gods giving him attributes like those of Jehovah, Indra, Zeus and Jupiter and even Mercury, suggesting that all were actually similar Spacemen.

Odin's eldest son, Thor, was renowned as the strongest, most warlike of the Gods, hero of the Vikings. Around Thor's head was often depicted a circle of stars which may have been symbolism for a Spaceman. His chariot had a pointed iron pole and its spark-scattering wheels drawn by rams with silver bridles rolled over rumbling thunder-clouds suggesting some primitive conception of a Spaceship motivated by atmospheric electricity, the lightning controlled by the ancient magicians. More than any other God Thor was identified with thunder and lightning. His mighty hammer, which returned to his hand each time he threw it, was manufactured by the Elves underground, as the wonder-weapons of Zeus were devised by the Cyclops.

Before wielding his hammer or thunderbolt Thor was obliged to put on his iron gauntlets. He wore a magical belt which greatly increased his strength, suggesting the use of some mechanical device. Thor gloried in continuous battles against the Giants; his most terrible conflict was waged fighting the World Serpent coiled around the Earth, like Indra, Zeus and Marduk who fought Sky Dragons suggesting War in the Heavens between Spacemen. This powerful God associated with war was also honoured for peaceful pursuits. He presided over agriculture, protected seamen, acted as a leech, and gave his name to Thursday, the peasants' rest day.

Freyr was associated with light, and had a wonderful ship built by the Elves which could fly in any direction. Freyr was much loved by the Swedes. With his sister, Freyja, the pair resembled the Twin Aswins of India, Castor and Pollux of Greece and Rome; they were always ready to descend to benefit mankind. Freyr was honoured as God of agriculture, beneficence and plenty; he loved to carouse and feast with men.

Tyr, God of War, like Mars, gave his name to Tuesday, but his other title Tiwas suggests derivation from Dyaus or Zeus. This God was renowned for chaining the fearsome wolf, Fenrir, which bit off his right hand; sometimes he travelled in Thor's thunder-chariot. The evil genius of the Gods, Loki, wore shoes with wings bearing him swiftly through the air, often he appeared as a bird. Loki treacherously misused his magic powers to plot the downfall of the Gods. He caused the death of Baldur, the beloved Sun God, his heart pierced by a sprig of mistletoe. In punishment Loki, like Prometheus, was chained to a rock, a serpent suspended there dripped venom on his head.

Freyja, the Scandinavian Venus, is remembered in Friday. She was worshipped as a fertility Goddess and feared for her occult feminine arts of prophecy and witchcraft. The Valkyries, winged Maidens, resembled the Angels associated with the dead in Semitic theology and may be a race-memory of Space Beings.

The Elves with wondrous powers were inferior to the Gods. The Light Elves were associated with the Sun; they wore delicate and transparent garments and lived beyond the clouds in Alfheim. The Night Elves, Trolls and Swarfs dwelt in solitude underground. Ugly and ill-formed they fashioned wonderful weapons for Gods and heroes.

The forests and lakes of Finland were haunted by Spirits who influenced men's lives by subtle spells. The national epic, the Kalevala,[114] sings of Väinamöinen, the hero of ancient Suomi, who after fantastic adventures in an enchanted world with beautiful witches sails off in a copper boat to a land between Earth and Heaven like Quetzalcoatl of old Mexico. In Lithuania the God Pranzimas observing from heaven the folly of men sent down two Giants, Wandhui and Weyas, to lay the Earth waste.

In Teutonic mythology Woden was depicted as a one-eyed Giant wearing a sky-dome hat and a sky-cloak flecked by clouds, sometimes he drove a star-chariot or the stars themselves. In folk-lore he was feared as the Wild Huntsman, the Headless Hunter or the Erl Konig, dreaded in England as

Herne the Hunter. Associated with the Wild Huntsman was the Schimmelreiter or Headless Rider mounted on a white horse, who wore a strange, broad-brimmed hat. The hat-shape, pack of celestial hounds, aerial speeding through the night, resemble present-day descriptions of UFOs.

CHAPTER TWENTY

Britain

Classical writers were fascinated by mysterious Britain. Diodorus Siculus[58] wrote 'Of those who have written about the ancient myths Hecateus and certain others say that in the regions beyond the land of the Celts (Gaul) there lies in the ocean an island no smaller than Sicily. This island, the account continues, is situated in the north and is inhabited by the Hyperboreans. They have a language, we are informed, which is peculiar to them and are most friendly disposed towards the Greeks ... Certain Greeks visited the Hyperboreans and left behind them there costly votive offerings, bearing inscriptions in Greek letters. And in the same way, Abaris, a Hyperborean, came to Greece in ancient times and renewed the goodwill and kinship of his people to the Delians ... The account is also given that the God visits the island every nineteen years ... at the time of this appearance of the God he both plays on the cithara and dances continuously.'

The priest, Abaris, was said to fly on the Arrow of Apollo through the air and to take no earthly food. This description seems to fit an Extraterrestrial in a Spaceship. The periodic visit of the God every nineteen years suggests regular intercourse between the Space Beings and Britain. Perhaps in those distant days Saturn rotated much nearer to Earth.

Julius Caesar commented that the Druids claimed descent from the God, Dis or Jupiter and worshipped Mercury, Apollo, Jupiter and Minerva, probably Space Beings, identical to the deities of Greece and Rome. Dionysius of Halicarnassus revealed that Hercules stormed Europe with a great army from Erytheia, Red Island, in the West; Hercules was believed to be represented by the Cerne Giant, a colossal human shape cut in the turf on the hillside above Cerne Abbas in Dorset.[199]

Few records now remain of the past save a few weather-eroded petroglyphs which no man can read. Legends assert that Britain was a colony of Atlantis and after the submergence of the Motherland preserved the ancient wisdom in sacred sites like Glastonbury and the great Earth Zodiac in Somerset. Occult teachings and folk-lore recalling Giants are confirmed by huge skeletons and great tools found all over the world. Traditions said that two hundred years after the Flood, Noah's son, Japhet, planted a colony in Britain, which he named Samothea. Japhet was succeeded by Mahus, Daron, Druis and Bardus, who was slain by Albion, a giant. He called the island after his own name and ruled for forty years until killed by Hercules.

A Scottish myth states that the terrible race of Giants sprang from thirty-three daughters of Diocletian, a King of Syria or Tyria, who drifted to Britain, then uninhabited, and became enamoured of a powerful order of demons begetting giant offspring. Irish manuscripts describe the giant race of the Formori, a great maritime nation who lived before the Flood. Were they the sons of Space Beings and the daughters of men?

Mountains in Ireland and Scotland are pitted with the remains of prehistoric fortresses vitrified by titanic electric-blasts, fusing the solid rock. In 1778 John Williams, a mining-engineer, described grandiose mountain-forts in the Scottish Highlands vitrified into glass, not transparent glass but fused rock, its surface like shining enamel. Charles Fort notes sagely that 'Once upon a time something melted in streaks, the stones of forts on the tops of hills in Scotland, Ireland, Brittany and Bohemia. Lightning selects the isolated and conspicuous. But some of the vitrified forts are not upon the tops of hills, some are very inconspicuous, their walls too are vitrified in streaks.'[74] Italo Sordi suggests that Extraterrestrials once landed on Scottish mountains and persuaded the natives to build walls of stone for their base, then the cosmonauts switched on the motors of their

spaceships and directed their discharge on to the stonework
instantly fusing the boulders into a block of glass.[186]

> 'Not of the Seed of Adam are we,
> Nor is Abraham our Father.
> But of the Seed of the Proud Angel
>   Driven forth from Heaven.'[76]

This Gaelic chant from the Hebridean island of Barra may
be the only reference now extant linking the earliest
inhabitants of Britain with Extraterrestrials. At New Grange
in Ireland and elsewhere there are frequently seen carvings of
a ship or solar bark on prehistoric tombs resembling the solar
ships painted in ancient Egypt. The worl-knots or cup-and-
ring markings on cromlechs and mehirs are similar to
concentric circles and spirals found in many countries
postulating a common world-wide civilisation in prehistoric
times.

The erection of the great temples at Avebury, Woodhenge
and Stonehenge compare in achievement and significance
with the building of the Pyramids. The intriguing trace of a
double-headed axe on a trilithon at Stonehenge forms a link
with Minoan Crete showing that the early Britons
communicated with peoples of the Middle East. Sir John
Morris-Jones noted remarkable identities between the syntax
of the Welsh language and that of early Egyptian. Gerald
Massey gives a list of 3,000 close similarities between English
and Egyptian words. The astronomer, Sir Norman Lockyer,
concluded that about 4,000 years ago the Britons were
completely familiar with Egyptian culture. In the Secret
Doctrine Madame Blavatsky claimed that three thousand
years ago Egyptian Priests travelled to Gaul, perhaps to
Britain.

It seems probable that Stonehenge was associated in some
way with Spacemen, whose visitations would oblige the
Britons to take special cognisance of the stars dreading
perhaps some cataclysm or maleficent invaders from other
planets. Traditions assert that Britons of the pre-Druid era
worshipped a Being living inside the Sun. This may have
meant a Celestial on another planet or an Extraterrestrial in a
Sun Disk depicted all over Britain by circular tumuli or golden
discoid[100] adornments like those of Ancient Egypt. A Druidic

fairy-tale told of a young Prince in his astral body borne aloft into the air towards the Sun which consisted of an assemblage of pure souls swimming in an ocean of bliss.

During the second millennium BC a cosmic cataclysm shattered the West. The British priests plotting the motions of the planets probably prophesied this, which may be the reason they built their stone observatories just as we today are erecting radio-telescopes all over the Earth. Though the precise date can only be guessed, it is obvious that Britain suffered immense damage, its solar culture almost destroyed.

Legend avers that Brut, great-grandson of Aeneas, quarrelled with his family in Northern Italy and fled to the island of Albion, to which he gave his own name calling it Britain. On the Thames the Trojans built Trinovantum, New Troy, centuries afterwards renamed London. Edward the Confessor considered London was built in the likeness of Troy. According to Dio of Sicily the arms and chariots of the Britons were Trojan in design. In the 16th century Polydore Virgil, sent by the Pope to collect St. Peter's pence, wrote a popular history proving that Britain's Bronze Age Kings originated from Troy.

Geoffrey of Monmouth[84] recorded that about the time of Elijah, 850 BC, King Bladud built Kaerladon, now Bath, and fashioned hot baths for the temple of Minerva. There he placed fires that could not be quenched and never turned to ash, but as they began to fail became, as it were, round balls of stone. This fanciful description suggests some nuclear-reactor device.

Bladud also fashioned wings and actually flew, but he crashed on the Temple of Apollo on Lud's hill in the city of Trinovantum, (London) leaving the throne of Britain to King Lear. King Belinus made himself immortal with a gate of marvellous workmanship later called Billingsgate and nearby built a great tower beside the Thames, now known as the Monument.

The earliest known religion is a belief in the divinity of Kings in Egypt, Sumeria, early Greece and Rome, whose symbol was the solar wheel, probably meaning a Celestial in a Spaceship, who descended to rule the countries of Earth. The Spaceships visiting Greece, Rome and Israel during the first millennium BC would surely survey Britain, where the popular cult of the Dragon like the Dragon-worship in China proved the influence of the Sky Gods. Julius Caesar wrote that the Britons worshipped deities identified with Mercury, Apollo, Mars, Jupiter and Minerva. The British God, Bel or Alan, was identified with the Semitic El, the Hebrew Yahweh.[28]

The Druids taught reincarnation and immortality of the soul, the worship of the Sky-Father and Earth-Mother and many elements of the Egyptian religion. Centuries later St. Patrick is said to have burned three hundred volumes of Druid lore, not before studying their secrets, for he once destroyed nine Druids with fire from the skies.

The Irish Druids claimed to be descendants of the Tuatha De Danaan, God-like Beings, who taught them the secrets of heaven; they possessed the Slat-na-devithta or magic wand, and fought the Fir bolgs, a race of Giants who defended Ireland from the Vikings. Irish chroniclers tell of the Roth Ramrach, a huge Wheel with a thousand beds, a man for every bed, carrying a thousand warriors over land and sea. Seemingly sheer fantasy until we recall the immense motherships seen today.

CHAPTER TWENTY ONE
Saxon Times

For nearly two thousand years theologians have considered the light which shone down from heaven and blinded Saul on the road to Damascus in 35 AD as a spiritual illumination. Could a beam of light under intelligent control from the skies, from a Spaceship, have shone on Saul and a voice auditorily or telepathically directed him to evangelise for Christ, as centuries earlier similar lights and voices had inspired Abraham and Moses and as today the very same lights and voices are alleged to prompt Sensitives and Flying Saucer Contacts all over the world?

Lights in the sky in antiquity are chronicled by many writers, the various quotations from Livy, Cicero, Pliny, Josephus, Dio Cassius and Julius Obsequens should haunt the most cynical sceptic.

The Venerable Bede, 673-738 AD, the Father of English History, was the most learned Englishman of his age; the forty books which he wrote are particularly noted for the care with which he sought out and selected reliable information.

AD 664 'In a monastery at Barking near the Thames in the burial-ground at night as the nuns were singing at the graves, behold suddenly a light sent from heaven like a great sheet came upon them, and the light lifted up, moved to the other side of the monastery, then withdrew to the heights of heaven. The self-same brightness of the light made the sun at midday seem but dark, in the morning young men in the Church reported that the beams of light entering the chinks of the door and windows did seem to pass all brightness of the day before.'
(Bede. 'Ecclesiastical History', Book 4. Chap. vii)

Visitants from Space?

In the same year shortly after the beam of light investigated the monastery at Barking another apparition there intrigued Bede who reported

> AD 664   'Tortygath, a sister at Barking monastery on a certain night when the daylight began to appear, as she went out of her chamber that she abode in, so plainly as it were, a corpse brighter than the sun wound up in muslin and carried upward being taken indeed from the house in which the sisters were wont to rest. And as she diligently marked what it should be that drew upwards, this vision of the glorious body which she beheld, she saw that it was lifted up on high as it were by cords brighter than gold, until it was taken into the open heavens and could be seen by her no longer.'

(Bede 'Ecclesiastical History, Book 4, Chap. IX)

This reverent nun describes the sighting in the terms she knew best. We may feel disposed to view the manifestation as extraterrestrial.

Sightings in Britain and Japan suggest world-wide surveillance during the seventh century.

> AD 600   'About 600 AD Peter, Abbot of St Augustine Monastery near Canterbury, was sent as a legate to Gaul and was drowned near Ambleteuse. For several nights a light from heaven played over his body ...
> (Bede. 'Ecclesiastical History', Book II, Chap. XXXIII)

> AD 634   'In AD 634 the body of Oswald, King of Northumbria, killed in battle, lay in a chariot outside the Monastery of Bardney in Lincolnshire. For all that night long a pillar of light reaching from that chariot unto heaven stood, so that it was plainly visible in all places almost of the same province of Lindsay.'
> (Bede. 'Ecclesiastical History', Book III, Chap. XI)

> AD 634   'A long star seen in the south ... which the people called a besom-star ...'
> ('Nihongi', Book Two.)

> AD 637   'A great star floated from East to West and there was a noise like that of thunder.'
> ('Nihongi', Book Two.)

> AD 640   'On the 7th day of the second month of Spring a star entered the Moon.'
> ('Nihongi', Book Two.)

> AD 642   'In Autumn, 9th day, 7th month ... a guest-star entered the moon.'
> ('Nihongi', Book Two.)

> AD 661   'In Autumn, 1st day, 8th month. The Prince Imperial in

attendance on the Empress's remains returned as far as the Palace of Ihase. That evening on the top of Mount Asakura there was a Demon (or Spirit) wearing a great hat, who looked down on the funeral proceedings. All the people uttered exclamations of wonder.'
('Nihongi', Book Two.)

This sighting evokes the amazing incident on June 26th 1959 in New Guinea when the Rev. William Booth Gill, an Anglican Missionary, beheld a huge disc with two pairs of legs pointing diagonally downwards. Four men on the 'deck' waved back to him.

AD 680   'At that time Coldingham was burnt. Fire from heaven lighted it. As it pleased God it fell there.'
(Gaimar 'Le Storie des Engles'. – 'Anglo-Saxon Chronicle'.)

AD 680   '11th month 1st day. There was an eclipse of the Sun. On the 3rd day there was a brightness in the East from the hour of the Dog to the hour of the Rat.' (8pm to midnight.)
('Nihongi', Book Two.)

AD 680   'The Abbess of the Monastery at Whitby was ill. In the neighbouring monastery of Hackness, a nun named Begu saw the roof of the house uncovered and all poured with light and she saw the soul of Hilda in that very light carried toward heaven accompanied and led by Angels. At the same time 13 miles away as Hilda died, a nun in the monastery at Whitby saw Hilda's soul go to heaven with Angels.'

AD 681   A young Saxon boy in the monastery at Basham near Chichester who was ill, described a visitation by 'two men altogether notable in their array and countenance, one shaven like a clerk, the other had a long beard ... sent from heaven itself.' Thirteen years later in 696 the devout and godly Sebbi, King of the East Saxons, reported that three men arrayed in bright apparel appeared to him as he lay sick. Three days later he died. These apparitions might be dismissed as hallucinations, were it not for their similarity to that startling incident which occurred to the father of the famous philosopher, Jerome Cardan, who in his book *De Subtilitate* recorded that on August 31 1491, in Milan, his father was visited by seven men clothed in colourful silken garments.[211]

AD 690   'Two English priests were murdered by heathens in Saxony and their bodies thrown into the Rhine. A very great beam of light reaching up to heaven followed their bodies as they floated in the river.
(Bede 'Ecclesiastical History', Book V, Chap. X.)

AD 692   'Autumn, 7th month. 28th day ... On this night Mars and Jupiter approached and receded from one another four times in

the room of one pace, alternately shining and disappearing.'
('Nihongi', Book Two.)

Many are the signs and sightings recorded from this time on.

CHAPTER TWENTY-TWO
Norman Times

Invasion of England by William the Conqueror was soon marked by prodigies in the skies. Geoffrey Gaimer marvelled

> 1067 'This year truly many folk saw a sign in the likeness of fire it was. In the year it fiercely flamed and burned, it came near the earth and for a time brilliantly lit it up. Afterwards then it revolved ascending on high, then descended deep into the sea. In many places it burned woods and plains. There was no man certain, nor who knew what this meant nor what this sign portended. In the county of Northumberland this fire went about showing itself and for one year in two seasons were these displays.'

Wild fire burned many towns and crops in 1032 AD, 1048 and 1078. These conflagrations could have been heath-fires caused by abnormally hot summers although the reference to the fiery sign in the sky in 1067 suggests a Spaceship under intelligent control. Many UFOs today are said to have signed people with heat-rays.

The Benedictine Monk, Matthew of Paris, writing in the monastery of St Albans until his death in 1259 chronicled from State Papers in his Historia Anglorum about sixty intriguing phenomena; he followed the tradition of William of Malmesbury, William of Newbury and Ralph Coggeshall. These works form our main sources regarding the twelfth century.

> 1077 9th April 'Now in this year on Palm Sunday about six o'clock in a sky quite serene an immense star appeared near the sun.
> (Matthew of Paris 'Historia Anglorum'.)

Intriguing eleventh century aerial hosts occurred in

1096   'Battalions sweeping through the air.'
       (Perts 8-2.)
1098   'Cavalry forces in the sky near Worms.'
       (Meland 2No8.)

An astonishing manifestation appeared to the Crusaders besieging Jerusalem.

1099   'Now on the Mount of Olives a certain soldier shining and quite splendid waving a shield made a sign to our forces to resume the conflict and to march for a meeting. Encouraged by this sign Duke Godfrey with great shouts recalled the whole throng swiftly and confidently and the returned to fight with such fervour that the recent battle seemed to start again.'
       (Historia Anglorum.)
1100   'In the thirteenth years (of William Rufus) here and abroad life was very adverse, also there was great horror as the Devil appeared visible to men in forest glades and out-of-the-way places. He spoke out to passers-by.'
1105   'In the first week of Lent on Friday, 16th February, a strange star appeared in the evening and for a long time afterwards was seen shining for a while each evening. The star made its appearance in the south-west and seemed to be small and dark but the light that shone from it was very bright and appeared like an enormous beam of light shining north-east and one evening it seemed as if the beam were flashing in the opposite direction toward the star. Some said they had seen other unknown stars about this time but we cannot speak about these without reservation because we did not ourselves see them. On the Eve of Cena Domini (The Last Supper), the Thursday before Easter, two Moons were seen in the sky before day, one to the east and the other in the west, and both at the full, and that same day the moon was a fortnight old.'
       (William of Malmesbury.)
       Were these Moons UFOs?
1110   'Now in this year a comet in an unusual manner appeared rushing from the east it ascended to the heavens, it was seen to go not forwards but backwards.'
       (Historia Anglorum.)
1120   'Now in this year on the 13th May a celestial light came over the Sepulchre of Our Lord.'
       (Historia Anglorum.)

But all Spacemen were not benevolent, some apparitions were strange and menacing like many alleged today. The Brothers Grimm in Deutsche Sagen, quote an odd story in the Brunswick dialect 'Der Feurige Mann' in 1125 AD.

1125   'In this year a fiery Man was haunting the mountains like an apparition. It was just on midnight. The Man went from one birch-tree to another and set it ablaze. The Watchman said he was like a glowing fire. He did that for three nights then no more. George Miltenburger living in a so-called hopfield Railbach in the District of Freienstein, explained "On the first appearance Sunday night between 11 and 12 o'clock not far from my house I saw a Man burning all over with fire. One could count all the ribs on his stomach. He continued his way from one landmark to another until after midnight he suddenly vanished. Many people were struck by him with fear and terror because through his nose and mouth he belched forth fire and in dashing speed flew hither and thither in all directions." '

This fantastic incident more than eight hundred years ago recalls that fiery Space Thing which seared Scoutmaster Desvergers in[125] 1952 at West Palm Beach, Florida, and with some of those alarming 'little men' recently frightening peasants in South America.

CHAPTER TWENTY-THREE
The Middle Ages

With seventy sightings for the 12th and 13th centuries to be found in various chronicles and many other mediaeval manuscripts, it is frustrating that so few can be quoted here. Mention must be made of the celestial crosses which inspired pious Christians but baffled the Church.

1189 'Above the public road, which continued to London, a village by no means wretched, called Dunstaple, by chance, so to speak, an hour after noon, those who looked up at the sky saw in the serene vault of heaven the striking shape of the Emblem of Our Lord with a dazzling milk-white likeness and the conjoined form of a man crucified, which is painted in Church to the memory of the Passion of Our Lord and the devotion of the Faithful.'
(William of Newbury, Historia Anglicana.)

1200 'It was said that a warning letter was sent to Earth from God in heaven, which men prophesied hung in the lofty air for three days and nights, and everyone fell on the ground praying that this prodigy would forbode good to this world and descending on Jerusalem it hung above the altar of St. Simon in Golgotha where Jesus Christ was crucified.'
(Historia Anglorum.)

1227 'At the same time in Germany while Master Oliver was preaching (for the Crusades) there appeared manifest to all the people a Crucifix in the air, on account of which sealed letters were sent by several prelates under seal to the University of Paris and they were read out to the public.'
(Historia Anglorum.)

These luminous crosses recall that famous crucifix in the heavens in 312 AD beheld by Constantine and all his army, which inspired him to establish Christianity as the State religion. The mediaeval chroniclers were fortunate, they could naively report what people saw.

In the early morning, October 24th 1967, near Okehampton,[216] Devon, England, two Police-Constables on road-patrol were astonished to see in the night-sky an immense bright object in the shape of a cross, they followed it for about twelve miles then it disappeared, to be seen later elsewhere in Britain. The Ministry of Defence Spokesman, who was in bed at the time, said everyone had seen an American airplane refuelling at night; this was news to the American Air Command who issued a prompt denial. Ignorant of airplanes the old chroniclers thought the fiery crosses just descended from heaven.

1236　'Also about this time in the month of May along the boundaries of England and Wales portents appeared in the sky of armed soldiers superbly though hostilely congregated. This is seen to be incredible to all who hear this unless the same thing is read in the beginning of Maccabees. The same thing was seen however assembled in Ireland of which apparition we are taught by a certain close relative of the Duke of Gloucester.'
　　　　(Historia Anglorum.)

This sighting evokes the troops of horsemen seen in the skies of Palestine in 168 BC. Identical portents were reported by Josephus to have preceded the destruction of Jerusalem in 70 AD by the Romans.

The scholar, Harold Wilkins, resurrected from Historia Anglorum by Matthew of Paris a fabulous apparition oft quoted by other notable writers.

1254　'On the night of the Lord's Circumcision (Jan 1), at midnight, in serene sky and clear air, with stars shining and the moon eight days old, there suddenly appeared in the sky a kind of large ship elegantly shaped and well-equipped and of marvellous colour. Certain monks at St Albans saw it ... for a long time, as if it were painted, and a ship made of planks but finally it began to disappear.'

Also from the Historia Anglorum comes

1254　'On the seventieth day indeed there steered towards land certain foreign ships driven by the fury of the winds, they were certainly great and elegant with naval equipment and military stores which entirely are not seen in communities like ours. They landed not far from Berwick. And when they were questioned as to who they were, they refused or really did not know how to intimate intelligently who they were or whence they come. No one from

the wars understood their language, so they were permitted to
return in peace. Even other ships like these were seen upon the
sea.'

Whose ships these were, Matthew of Paris never discovered,
had they really descended from Space we feel he would have
said so!

In 1260 St Thomas Aquinas published his Summa
Theologica expounding Angelology; odd though it seems his
descriptions of Angels translated into modern terminology are
very similar to present-day accounts of alleged Spacemen.

Most Students of Flying Saucers must now expect mention
of that notorious 'large, round, silver thing like a disc' alleged
in 1290 to have flown slowly over the brethren at Byland
Abbey in Yorkshire 'and excited the greatest terror. Whereat
Henry the Abbot immediately cried that Wilfred was an
adulterer, wherefore it was impious to. ...' A noted Authority
shows the source of this exhilarating sighting as William de
Newburgh's Historia Anglicana. No reference is therein to
AD 1290. Not surprising since William would then have been
154 years old, (and he died in 1198). One eminent expert
claimed that this much lauded sighting came from an old
manuscript conveniently discovered at Ampleforth Abbey in
January 1953 and unfortunately lost before verification, a
rumour avers that the story was concocted in dog-Latin with
diverting detail by a couple of students with a warped sense of
humour!

The Chronicon de Lanercost written in the reign of Edward
III by one of the Franciscan Minorities at Carlisle contains a
general history of the affairs of England and Scotland with
incidental allusions to Continental proceedings extending
from the year 1201 to 1346. An interesting tale alleges

1289   'John Fraunceis, an elderly shepherd, instead of attending
Church, was guarding his flock amid the forest at Dalton near
Richmond in England, when suddenly Spirits of the Air
appeared, these deformed dwarfs beat him with blows until his
whole body ached. As they tried to lift him aloft, he clung grimly
to the earth and thought with fervour of the Passion of Christ
until the frustrated Spirits finally flew off. He stumbled home,
spent a week in bed and told the event to all his friends.'

Startling though it may seem, in our context of Spacemen
such bizarre attack by Extraterrestrials could possibly occur.

1295   'On July 27 in the Scottish skies were seen red shields bearing the arms of the King of England, all combined, heads joined together with thick sides. A multitude occupied the whole surface of the heavens.'[44]

Of the many sightings in Western Europe during the fourteenth century mention must be made of

1314   'Three moons appeared in the sky. In this year Philip of France passed away.'

1320   'The Abbot (of the Abbey of Durham) died on the feast of St Gregory – and was buried in the choir of St Leonard before the great altar, and after his death there appeared in the sky a light like the rays of the sun. It seemed to shine over the burial place. Anon, it descended in the night and moved from that pace to another, as if passing quickly from place to place ... Many saw this, and it was harmless, but they fell on the ground in terror.'

   (Roberti de Greystones 'Historia de Statu Ecclesiae Dunelmensis'.)

1322   'Germany. On June 5th a reddish circle surrounded the sun and nearby appared two conspicuous crosses.'

   (Lycosthenes.)

1345   'The people of Manresa in the District of Barcelona still celebrate the "Festival of the Mysterious Light." In 1345 the land was parched with drought, the people continued the construction of a canal which crossed the lands of the Bishop of Vic who excommunicated the townsfolk. "The Divinity One and Three" was shown magnificently to the people of Manresa on the 21st of February when a light coming from the Mountain of Montserrat blotting out the illumination of the Sun penetrated into this church shining like sunlight in the corner on a stone of the temple, in the church which by celestial inspiration was dedicated to the Most High Trinity and at the same time in the other Chapel of Santo Salvador, still with the same magnitude and splendour for first, second and third times, repeating it alternately and shining like one sunlight then like three together. Finally the Bishop authorised the completion of the canal. Manresa was saved.'[191]

1350   An anonymous artist painted the now celebrated fresco of the Crucifixion at the monastery of Visoki-Decani, Yugoslavia, showing Saints apparently piloting Spaceships.

1352   'A celestial torch glided through the sky.'
   (Lycosthenes.)

1372   'Basle. Switzerland. On June 5th or 6th. An unusual circle was seen around the Sun above which shone two red-coloured crosses.'
   (Lycosthenes.)

In the early 15th century inspiration from Celestials

prompted a young peasant-girl from Domremy in Lorraine to free most of France from the English, to meet the death of a martyr and later to be canonised as a Saint.

At the Ecclesiastical Court in Rouen in 1431, Joan of Arc, a maid of twenty, explained to the judges

> 'When I was thirteen years old, I had a voice from God to help me govern my conduct. And the first time, I was very fearful. And came this voice about the hour of noon, in the summer-time, in my father's garden. I had not fasted on the eve preceding that day. I heard the voice on the right-hand side towards the church; and rarely do I hear it without a brightness. The brightness comes from the same side as the voice is heard. It is usually a great light. When I came to France, often I heard this voice ... The voice was sent to me by God, and after I had thrice heard this voice, I knew it was the voice of an angel. This voice has always guarded me well and I have always understood.'[150]

The voices gave Joan three specific commands. Relieve the besieged city of Orleans, crown a new French King at Rheims and drive the English army out of the country.[220] This simple girl became an inspired leader; Joan imbued her soldiers with spiritual strength and martial resolve. She defeated the invaders and restored Charles VII to his throne. On May 23rd Joan was captured by the Burgundians and later handed to the English, then tried by the Church.

Pierre Cauchon, Bishop of Beauvais, President of the Court, had developed a personal hatred and fear of Joan. In 1452 Cardinal Guillaume d'Estouteville declared the trial procedure had been invalid.

The celestial phenomena of earlier centuries continued during Joan's lifetime in her beloved France. A remarkable miniature painted in the 15th century represents Fortune.[155] A wooded hill, in the foreground an elegantly-gowned young lady greets three men, and above them in the air accompanied by 'stars' in the blue sky is an enormous light-brown sphere like those Montgolfier balloons three hundred years later. It must have appeared swiftly for the group below seem unaware of its presence, to the right high on a rock an elderly man stares with evident surprise. If this Saucer is merely artistic licence, what prompted its astounding shape not shown on any other mediaeval landscape, to our knowledge. Why did the unknown artist not paint the conventional Angels beloved by the Renaissance?

The French review 'Planète', mai/juin 1964 published a fascinating feature, the Madonna and the helicopter, saying 'There exists at Le Mans a mediaeval panel which dates from 1460, and which represents the Child, Jesus, holding in his hand a kind of helicopter manipulated by a cord. This helicopter which inspired Leonardo da Vinci and which constitutes one of the most astonishing anachronisms of history ... There exists a stained glass window with helicopter and Christ of Norman origin made about 1525. It is found in the Victoris and Albert Museum in London.' A helicopter in the Middle Ages!

Who gave the divine Leonardo his marvellous ideas?

'Occasionally' says the Italian historian Vasari 'Heaven bestows upon a single individual beauty, grace and ability, so that, whatever he does, every action is so divine that he distances all other men, and clearly displays how his genius is the gift of God and not an acquirement of human art. Men saw this in Leonardo da Vinci, whose personal beauty and grace cannot be exaggerated, whose abilities were so extraordinary that he could readily solve every difficulty that presented itself.'[203] Was Leonardo inspired by Spacemen?

In his Catalogus Prodigiorum Miraculum' printed in Latin in Nuremberg, 1563, Marcus Frytsche like his contemporary, Konrad Wolffhart, better known as Lycosthenes, collated scores of celestial phenomena. In 1453 while the Turks were storming Constantinople the skies above Como in the Italian Alps, appeared filled with a panoramic vision of animals, soldiers in armour with lances and shields, ranks of cavalry in battle order, marching for three hours until joined by their great and terrifying leader on horseback. At nightfall the phantasmagoria slowly vanished.[51]

Holinshed in his 'Chronicles' published in 1578 mentions an intriguing sighting during the Wars of the Roses between the future Kings, Edward IV and Richard III at the Battle of Mortimers Cross in 1461.

'Newes was brought to Edward that Jasper, earle of Pembroke, halfe-brother to king Henrie and James Butler, earle of Ormund and Wiltshire, had assembled a great number of Welsh and Irish people to take him, he herewith quickened, retired backe and mete with his enemies in a faire plaine neer to Mortimer's Cross and not far from Hereford east, on Candle-masse daie in the morning. At which time the sunne (as some write) appeared to the earle of March like three sonnes, and suddenly ioined altogither in one. Upon which sight he tooke such courage, that he, fiercelie setting on his enimies, put them to flight, and for this cause men imagined that he gave the sunne in his full brightness for his badge or cognisance.'[99]

Leone Cabelli in his Cronache Forlinesi, 1874, quotes an intriguing sighting at Forli in March 1485.

'In 1485 on the 14th March in the sky at Forlivio a sign of a circle with three suns, that is one large, resplendent sun, the other two not so bright, then came a rainbow and a star.'[143]

1492 'After the middle of December in Poland three suns were seen in the south.'
(Lyscosthenes.)

Christopher Columbus sailing towards the New World recorded in his log that as he stood on the deck of the tiny 'Santa Maria' three stars appeared high in the West inspiring him on.

On August 13th 1491 a marvellous incident occurred in Milan. In his De Subtilitate Rerum, Nuremberg, 1550, the famous eccentric, Gerolamo Cardano (1501-1570), noted as a mathematician, related how his father, Fazio Cardano, had completed his evening devotions when seven men appeared in his room. They were clad in silken garments of antique fashion, with shining boots and armour, beneath appeared purple attire of extraordinary splendour. Two seemed superior to the others and a third, ruddy-complexioned, was leader of the group. The Apparitions said they were forty but looked no more than thirty and revealed that they were like humans but came from the ether. The Visitants remained with Fazio Cardano for three hours then suddenly vanished. Gerolamo Cardano like his contemporary Leonardo da Vinci (1452-1519) was a genius in many fields; he studied medicine, mathematics, astronomy, philosophy, physics, chemistry, and learned Latin in three days. In his Autobiography Cardano describes visions throughout his whole life, telepathic communications, presentiments, extra-sensory perceptions, psycho-kinesis and paranormal phenomena.

In De propria Vita, Cardano wrote

' ... I have been able to observe also many extraordinary facts, which re-enter within the ambit of natural phenomena, for example, that star which shone in the sky like Venus, about 22 hours. (I was then a child), so refulgent that it was seen over all our city.'

'In April 1531 at Venice where by chance I found myself, I saw shine three suns, all in the East, with their rays. This spectacle lasted almost three hours.'

' ... about 1512, in Bergamo, near the Adda, there fell in one night alone more than a thousand stones, (at least so they said) the evening before, there has crossed an enormous flame which seemed like a beam which had crossed the sky.'

In 1519 across the world in far-off Mexico Montezuma watched an ominous light illumine the eastern sky.

'It spread broad at its base on the horizon and rising in a pyramidal form tapered off as it approached the zenith. It resembled a vast sheet, or flood of fire, emitting sparkles, or as an old writer expresses it, seemed thickly powdered with stars. At the same time low voices were heard in the air, and doleful wailings, as if it announce some strange mysterious calamity.'[166]

Shortly afterwards Cortés and the Spanish Conquistadores landed. The White Gods had returned, soon the great empire of the Aztecs sprawled shattered, its people enslaved.

Lycosthenes chronicled several sightings in his own century.

1523   'In Switzerland during May three suns and various circles were seen at the same time in the sky.

1527   'Not far from Kaufbunna, a fine town in Swabia, were seen three suns with various celestial circles.

1528   'In Switzerland during the month of June various suns and three haloes were observed.

These suns might have been parahelia, atmospheric phenomena, they could have been UFOs.

Benvenuto Cellini, 1501-1570 born the first year of the Cinquecento, was soldier, artist, libertine, writer, a colourful genius of the Renaissance, probably the greatest goldsmith who ever lived. In his fascinating Autobiography Cellini tells how in 1537 he returned to Rome to make a medal for Duke Alexander and was reproached by exiles, then one day he went off to hunt wild geese with his apprentice, Felice. After bagging a brace of birds, it became so cold, they hurried home. We now render inadequately his actual words.

'We mounted our horses and returned hastily to Rome. We happened to be on a certain low embankment (night had already fallen). Looking towards Florence both of us with one accord exclaimed in marvelling voice saying "O God in heaven, what huge thing is that seen above Florence?" This was like a great beam of fire which sparkled and shone with the greatest splendour. I said to Felice "I am certain we shall hear tomorrow that some great thing has happened in Florence!" "[33]

Theophrastus Aureolus Bombast, (1493-1541) known to the World of Magic as Paracelsus, an alchemist and physician, born near Zurich, travelled throughout Europe, even visiting the Near East, Finland and the Arctic, so he said, dispensing wisdom centuries ahead of his time, which makes us wonder whether he was inspired by Spacemen. People alleged he kept a familiar demon hidden in the pommel of his sword and boasted he could summon a million devils to demonstrate transcendental powers. Despite his grandiose boasts Paracelsus did much to free science from superstition and was the first to recognise the importance of cleanliness in medical practice. His claims to have manufactured portable gold conferring prolonged youth may have been symbolism for the esoteric doctrine of a Universal Medicine based upon Light, the creative agent, the vibrations of which are the movement and life of all things; his sixteen volumes of theosophic and hermetic speculation are said to have greatly influenced the early Rosicrucians, some of his ideas are startling even today. For centuries scientists considered Paracelsus a charlatan seeking to find the elusive Philosopher's Stone. A close study of his works in the light of our new Space-knowledge may give insight into a truly remarkable mind nearer perhaps to the science of next century than to our own.[147]

Today in our troubled times the most fascinating character of the 16th century is surely Michele de Nostredame (1503-1566) known to all as Nostradums, born at Saint-Remy in Provence. He became a Doctor and worked remarkable cures during the plagues. In 1547 he dabbled in astrology then turned seriously to prophecy. From 1555 he began his famous Centuries and Prophecies couched in obscure quatrains, a fantastic kaleideoscope of the future, which to date has apparently come true. In retrospect it is easy to read into his quaint verse events which have happened yet it does seem as if

Nostradamus did really prophesy the French Revolution, Napoleon, Hitler and Hiroshima. For the end of our twentieth-century Nostradamus foresees frightful wars, earthquakes, shattered cities then a new rebirth for all mankind. True prophecy is most profound. Whence did Nostradamus obtain such insight?[40] From Extraterrestrials? Lycosthenes reported

1551 'On 25th February three suns were seen at Antwerp. On the 21st March at Madgeburg seven irises and three suns were seen. On 12th April three suns and various circles were seen at Wittemberg, Saxony.

1554 'On the 19th February the images of two crosses coloured purple were seen in the sky at Nebra. They were seen at the town of Grussem in Thuringia and shone most resplendently, the first cross covered the whole sun. And both sideways looked like immense beams with celestial circles.'
(Reported by John Fincellus at Jena.)

1554 'Different kinds of suns were seen in Bavaria. In March at five o'clock in the afternoon appeared over many German cities different kinds of crosses, so me like the Burgundian crosses, white in colour, they appeared joined somehow in the sky.'

1556 'In Switzerland near Basle on two different days in August three suns were observed. On the 23rd of this month three suns were observed in the southern sky.'

1566 'A well-known woodcut printed in the Gazzetta di Basilea represents an astonishing event on 7th April. A group of people stand marvelling at more than a score of globes and disks hovering over the cathedral and roof-tops.'

1571 'On 7th October took place a battle decisive in the history of Europe and of the world. In the waters of Lepanto in fact occurred the naval encounter which crippled the power of the Turks and signified the beginning of its decline. What is generally ignored however, is that "the night before 21st September appeared high in the sky, a sign which all men believed prodigious. The night was quite serene, the north-wind very fresh, the stars clear and scintillating, and behold in the middle of the air, a fiery flame, so shining and so great in the form of a column for a long time was seen by all in wonder. And although nowadays it is demonstrated that among electrical and pneumatic phenomena in the atmosphere the most vigorous appear at the fall of summer, there must be enumerated not only Will-o-the-wisps, and St Elmo's light but also fiery globes and burning beams like this, nevertheless the spectators from this prodigious apparition, divined most felicitous augury of great victory." So narrated Father Albero Guglielmotti, adding "They

believed the column of fire must guide the Christian armada on
the sea as it guided the people of Israel in the dessert".'15,1

The great Danish astronomer, Tycho Brahe (1546-1601)
recalled

'One evening as according to my usual habit I was considering the
celestial vault, to my indescribable amazement I saw close to the zenith
in Cassiopeia, a radiant star of extraordinary size, struck with
astonishment I knew not whether I could believe my own eyes. Some
time after that I learned that in Germany cartmen and other persons of
the lower classes had repeatedly warned the scientists that a great
apparition could be seen in the sky.'16

For many centuries the Church waged a ruthless and
savage war against witchcraft inhibiting free study of natural
phenomena and the beginning of modern Science. We today
are inclined to dismiss such persecution as fanatical hysteria
and bigoted intolerance and to discredit the confessions
blurted out under such fearful torture; yet when we read with
nauseating frequency of Satanic apparitions reeking with
brimstone we think of those three mysterious Men in Black
smelling of sulphur who menaced Al Bender, the American
UFO investigator. Again we wonder!

Sightings of celestial objects were not restricted to Europe
but occurred with equal frequency across the world. Yusuke J.
Matsumura of Yokohama, Japan, reports in Flying Saucers
over Nippon printed in Brothers Vol 3 No. 1

1213   'Mar. 10. Luminous object about 1 ft. in length appeared from
       behind the mountain of the late General's Hokkedo Temple,
       lighted up far and near for some time.'
1256   'June 14. Shining object 5 ft. in length looking like a white eagle
       at first, then like a red fire as if leaving a white cloth trail.'
1271   'September 12. Famous priest, Nichiren, was about to be
       beheaded at Tatsunokuchi, Kamakura, when shiny object like the
       moon came from the heavens and prevented him from being
       executed by Government officials. Also according to his
       statement "Residents of Sado Is. reported 'two suns' in the west
       around 5 in the evening. Jan. 23 the same year 'three suns'
       claimed spotted, again 'two Venuses' in the east".'
1305   'January 26. Blue object about 5 ft. in length flew across the sky N
       to S early morning. The head looked like a lantern!'
1422   'October 12. "People were amazed by two brilliant round objects
       just like two suns in the sky." '
1468   'March 17. During a big war object like a big umbrella flew

slowly N to S at the dawn, the light was like the moon."

1574 'January 29. A bright object as big as a large parasol flew about in the evening, illuminating heaven and earth, and was seen flying later again.'

1576 'December 21. "A wheel-like luminous object flew over the castle on Mt. Kasagu about 12 o'clock midnight, was seen for one hour." '

The old chronicles East and West continue the familiar pattern of sightings and materialisations. The wonders enchanting mediaeval literature anticipate in startling parallel the Flying Saucer phenomena reported today.

CHAPTER TWENTY-FOUR
The Age of Reason

'Thus I have declared that there are infinite particular worlds similar to this of the earth, which with Pythagoras I understand to be a star similar in nature with the Moon, the other planets and the other stars which are infinite, and that all these bodies are worlds and without number, which thus constitute the infinite invisibility in an infinite Space and this is called the infinite Universe in which are innumerable worlds.'[16]

After eight long years imprisonment by the Inquisition Giordano Bruno, who proclaimed such cosmic truth, on the seventh of February 1600 was burned at the stake. A martyr to Science, his ashes like his words were blown away on the winds.

Ten years later Galileo with his newly-invented telescope discovered the four largest moons of Jupiter, thus supporting the heliocentric theories of Copernicus and Kepler to refute the Earth-centred teachings of the Church. His fellow-Professors at Padua refused to look through the telescope lest they saw the moons proving the Scriptures to be wrong. In 1635 Galileo, an old man, was tried in Rome by the Inquisition and forced to recant that the Earth orbits the Sun, although he is said to have whispered defiantly 'Eppure, si muove!' 'And yet it does move!'

In the 17th century heresy was considered a grievous sin imperilling a man's immortal soul; the Inquisition abetted by countless informers, with its dungeons and tortures strove ceaselessly to ensure that no dangerous doctrines infected the community. The solitary freethinkers banded in secret societies or kept their thoughts to their trusted friends like dissenters in totalitarian States today. The Catholic Church found its authority gravely challenged by the new learning after the Renaissance. The discoveries of Columbus, the voyages of Magellan brought a new vision of the world extending men's horizon far from a Europe torn by the religious strife of the Thirty Years War.

The liberating movements in the Arts and Sciences, the political struggles between Kings and People from the 17th century constitute the glory of our European culture, we forget that in the shadows the arcane wisdom of the ancients, the mystic lore of the alchemists, was still preserved by adepts in Masonic Brotherhoods. Masters of the occult arts faced not only the hostility of the Church, the ignorance of the populace but met scorn from the scientists who based their researches on reason and experiment with remarkable results; charlatans brought much discredit, the true Initiates shrouded their works in secrecy. Only today in our studies of the occult and the paranormal do we realise that those practitioners of astrology, diviners of the Tarot, mediums and mesmerists, had explored the phenomena of Inner Space.

The Jesuit Father, Albert d'Orville, a Belgian, wrote about a fascinating sighting at Lhasa, Tibet.

1661 'November. My attention was attracted by something moving about in the heavens. I thought it was some unknown species of bird which lived in that country, when the thing on approaching took an aspect of a double Chinese-hat (the classical conical straw-hats) and flew rotating silently as if borne on invisible wings of the wind. It was surely a prodigy, an enchantment. That thing passed above the city, and as if it wished to be admired, it completed two circles, then surrounded by mist it vanished, and no matter how one strained one's eyes it could no longer be seen. I asked myself whether the altitude where I was had not played some trick, however perceiving a lama not far away I asked whether he had seen it. After assenting by nodding his head, he said to me "My Son, what you have seen is not magic, Beings from other worlds have centuries sailed the seas of Space, they brought intellectual illumination to the first people populating Earth, they banished all violence and taught men to love one another, but however these teachings are like seed scattered on stone, which does not germinate. These Beings, all light, are well received by us and often descend near our monasteries teaching us and revealing things lost for centuries during the cataclysms which have changed the aspect of the world".[71]

A shining disk was seen high over the Himalayas by the

explorer Nicholas Roerich in 1921.
UFOs haunted 17th century Japan.

1665   'Mar 12. A huge "shooting star" was seen travelling from north-
       east to south-west. It was about 50 feet long, sounded like
       thunder and lit up the sky, turning night into day.'
1666   'May 26. People in Edo (Tokio) were amazed to see a luminous
       object flying toward the east in the shape of a human figure, 20
       feet in length.'
1680   'October. A strange star like a half-opened fan appeared over Edo
       (Tokio) and caused all people to wonder seriously.'
1680s 'There appeared a "big star' from which a fan-shaped beam was
       projected. A witness claimed it was staying over Echigo Prov.,
       Northern Japan, and soon the Lord of Echigo was destroyed.'

Aimé Michel[136] recalls that one of the greatest religious
figures of the 17th century, Saint Vincent de Paul (1579-1666)
was said, both at Avignon and in Rome before the Vice-
Legate and the Pope and Cardinals, to have displayed
machines that were incomprehensible, one of them being in
the form of a head with a bust which talked. For two years,
when about twenty-six and twenty-seven St Vincent de Paul
apparently disappeared from the haunts of man, then
returned with phenomenal powers. He claimed to have been
captured by the Turks like Cervantes decades earlier; modern
scholars have their doubts and suspect abduction and
education by Extraterrestrials. Mediaeval legends credited the
poet, Virgil, with a castle near Naples; he apparently
possessed a brazen head like a talking-computer, which
evaluated dangers and gave warning.

Montfaucon de Villars born about 1638 came from
Toulouse to Paris to make his fortune by teaching; he strongly
reacted against the theological dogma of his day and sought
inspiration from the works of Paracelsus, particularly in his
resurrection of Pythagorean doctrines concerning Spirits and
Elementals. The 17th century Jesuit, Athanasius Kircher, in
his Mundus Subterannus wrote of Subterranean Spirits in
terms which suggest to us the fantasies of our modern
believers in Agharta. In Le Comte de Gabalis,[211] first
published on 28 November 1670, de Villars expounded on
those Realms peopled by Sylphs in human form, great lovers
of Science, whose wives and children bloomed in wondrous
beauty. Our modern minds instinctively ridicule such

pretensions of invisible Spirits co-existing in parallel dimensions as nonsense, until advanced researchers tell us that from this Inner Space materialise the UFOs and the Spacemen.

On 2nd December 1669 the Parlement of Toulouse condemned Montfaucon, Abbot of Villars, for writing Le Comte de Gabalis, to be broken alive on the Wheel. Montfaucon was spared this barbarous death; he was murdered in 1673 on the road from Lyons by persons unknown. Rumour whispered that he had been assassinated by Sylphs for revealing their secrets. Today we remember the mysterious deaths of Dr M.K. Jessup, Dr J.E. Mcdonald and other noted UFO investigators; we recall those sinister Men in Black, who silence researchers stumbling too close to truth. Was Montfaucon de Villars murdered by Spacemen for knowing too much?

A great light suddenly appeared in the western sky in

1718 'It shone with a brightness much greater than the Moon which was then shining brightly. At first I thought it was only a rocket but it moved more slowly than a falling star in direct line. It seemed to descend below the stars in the constellation of Orion. A long stream was branched in the middle and the meteor (?) turned pear-shape or tapered upwards. At the lower end it became spherical not so big as the full Moon. The colour of it was white and blue, and the lustre was dazzling like the Sun on a clear day. It seemed to sparkle but kept place without falling. I hear it was also seen at Oxford and Worcester.'

Harold Wilkins[218] reporting this sighting by Sir Hans Sloan comments 'This slow-moving body, so bright and dazzling, had all the appearance of what we should today call a spaceship. But one does not dogmatize.'

The revelation that the native Dogon of Mali knew that Sirius had two satellites with known periodicity, the smaller of a substance fantastically heavy, astounded our astronomers who have only lately rediscovered this tiny neutron-star. Instead of admiring primitive people for such startling knowledge, we feel mortified, even resentful that somehow they knew this ages before we did. Our ancestors were long aware of the two moons of Mars before Asaph Hall of Washington Naval Observatory stared at the red planet in 1877 and suddenly saw them.

Homer mentioned the War God's twin steeds in the Iliad Virgil in his Georgics poeticised the 'coursers bearing the God of Thrace'; scholars thought this poetical fancy, for Galileo who saw four moons of distant Jupiter failed to see the satellites of Mars.

In 1726 Jonathan Swift in Gulliver's Travels[193] discoursed with surprising erudition about the learned astronomers on the Flying Island of Laputa.

> 'They have likewise discovered two lesser stars, or satellites, which revolve about Mars, whereof the innermost is distant from the centre of the primary planet exactly three of his diameters, and the outermost five, the former revolves in the space of ten hours, and the latter in twenty-one and an half; so that the squares of their periodical times are very near in the same proportions with the cubes of their distance from the centre of Mars, which evidently shows them to be governed by the same law of gravitation, that influences the other heavenly bodies.'

Astronomical data a hundred and fifty years before the rediscovery of Deimos and Phobos by Asaph Hall!

Knowledge of the Moons of Mars, then unknown to Science, has prompted the curious theory that Jonathan Swift was a Martian! Probably the greatest satirist in the English language Jonathan Swift seemed strangely alien in 18th century society. The celebrated Dr Johnson described his complexion as 'muddy', some said 'olive-coloured, bronze or brown';[142] he was 'wall-eyed', his much-publicised relations with Stella and Vanessa were frigid. Swift became increasingly morose and misanthropic and died on October 19th 1745, almost insane.

Swift probably took the two moons of Mars from Homer and quoted Kepler's Law for scientific verisimilitude, he does not state the planet's diameter; based on modern measurements his calculations differ from those today. After two hundred years the braking-effect of the tenuous atmosphere on both moons inevitably falling towards Mars would alter Swift's original concept, he might have been right, few now think so.

Some noted astronomers[184] suggested that Deimos and Phobos were artificial satellites launched by Martians long ago, photographs from Mariner 9 disappointingly show them to be rocks.

Emmanuel Swedenborg, philosopher, man of science and mystic, was born on 29th January 1688 at Stockholm; from his fourth to his twelfth year, his thoughts were constantly occupied by God, so he said. Many times he discovered things which astonished his father and mother, and made them declare that Angels spoke through his mouth. After education at Upsala University he travelled throughout Europe meeting prominent scientists and became Assessor in the Department of Mines. In 1734 appeared his great work Opera Philosophica et Mineralia wherein he astonished his contemporaries by elaborating our modern theory of the atom, the solar origin of the Earth and other planets, the undulatory theory of light, the nebular theory of the origin of the Solar System, the kinetic theory of heat, etc. The next fifteen years Swedenborg studied all the Sciences, made fundamental discoveries and when nearly sixty became engrossed in theology and mystical visions inspiring him to found a new spiritual society. The philosopher, Immanuel Kant, reported that in July 1759 arriving at Gothenburg from London Swedenborg was suddenly astounded by the vision of a terrible fire in distant Stockholm. He startled his friends by giving a vivid commentary on the conflagration naming the flaming streets and actual houses being burned down. Two days later a courier from Stockholm proved his clairvoyance completely correct.

Swedenborg claimed to have spoken with Spirits from the planet Mercury.[192] He told of the marvels of the spiritual world with child-like wonder as though like Enoch and Mahomet he had been translated to the heavens. Before his death at the age of eighty-five on 29th March 1772 he said to Dr Hartley 'I have written nothing which is not true, as you will find out more and more.' Today thousands of people follow his inspired teachings proclaiming inhabited planets peopled by Spirits, other worlds with Spacemen.

Yusuke J. Matsumura and devoted researchers of the Cosmic Brotherhood Association, Yokohama, have collated many sightings in Japan during the 18th century;[134] together with similar phenomena seen over Europe they present an intriguing panorama of possible Spaceships surveilling the whole world.

1704   'January 8th. Strange lights over England. November 4th, Switzerland, Luminous cloud moving at high velocity disappearing behind horizon.'

1714   'November 1st. Mysterious light travelled over Central Japan from south to north-west with rumblings. Ten days later, a luminous object flew from north to west again.'

1719   'September 24th. Fireball as big as a hand-ball flew over Kanto, Japan, towards north-east.'

1731   'December 9th. Florence, Italy. Strange globes of light in sky.'

1742   'May 2nd. Three rising suns could be seen over northern Japan one day after a solar eclipse which amazed people almost to death. December 16th. "C.M.", a Fellow of the Royal Society, saw a light arise behind trees and houses near St James's Park in London; he watched it soar like a sky-rocket beyond the Haymarket.'

1749   'January 2nd. Chaos spread all over Japan when three round objects like the Moon appeared and were seen until 6th.'

1751   'January 1st. In Japan rioters were executed as confusion prevailed over the land when people were surprised seeing three moons lined up in the sky, also "two suns" appeared on January 6th.'

1755   'October 15, Lisbon, Portugal. Immense bright flying-globes seen many times.'

1777   'June 17th. The French astronomer, Charles Messier, observed a large number of dark, round disks in the sky. This was before the ascent of the balloons by the Montgolfier brothers first made in 1783.'

1783   'March. Luminous bodies flew over Japan. On 15th March a great flood struck Edo (Tokio) when an object as big as a wheel flew from north-west to east.'

1792   'June 18th. A luminous object as big as a bamboo-hut travelled over Edo, south-west to north-east around 11 o'clock at night, the light illuminated the whole country.'

Falls of 'Angels' hair' associated with Flying Saucers occurred in Japan in 1650, 1702, 1729, 1768, 1779 and 1793.

Many luminous objects may have been atmospheric lights easily explained, a residue do seem to be UFOs like those seen today.

These ancient records suggesting that Flying Saucers have had our Earth under surveillance for many millennia evoke speculation as to whether any Spacemen have ever landed to live among us. We think of Moses, Apollonius of Tyana, possibly Roger Bacon, then we stop in 18th century France and marvel at the mysterious, grandiose, glittering Count St. Germain. Voltaire extolled this Wonder Man to Frederick the

Great as 'A man who never dies and who knows everything.'

St. Germain's origin was esteemed as of the very highest rank. He was said to have been a son of the King of Portugal, some thought him son of a Queen of Spain, Viennese records credit him with being the younger son of Prince Francis Leopold Rococzi and born about 1696. Whatever the truth, he was welcomed in all the most exclusive Court circles of Europe being received with deference by Louis XV and the nobility of France. The Count himself made no positive assertions blandly hinting that he might be older than Methusaleh.

Many contemporaries from Madame de Pompadour to the German philosopher, Grimm, in letters and diaries all stress the Count's extraordinary talent for story-telling, his command of all languages ancient and modern, his amazing knowledge of historical details so that his enthralling ancedotes of Cleopatra, Pontius Pilate, Henry VIII and Francis I recounted with all the colourful detail of an actual eyewitness really convinced his entranced listeners that he was actually describing his own experiences.

This man of mystery, fabulously rich, handsome and fantastically accomplished, appeared among the Courts of Europe towards the middle of the 18th century, bedazzling even that glittering Society with his bejewelled magnificence and amazing knowledge. In 1760 Madame du Hausset described St. Germain as looking about fifty, he was neither thin nor stout, had polished manners, seemed clever and dressed simply but in good taste. On his fingers as well as on his snuff-box and watch he had brilliants of the first water, the diamonds on his knee and shoe-buckles alone were valued at 200,000 francs; in his ruffles glistened rubies of extraordinary beauty. Countess d'Adhemar recalled that his figure was graceful, his hair black, his glance soft and penetrating, his eyes beyond description. Countess de Gengy remembered meeting him in Venice fifty years before in 1710, when he called himself the Marquis Balletti.

The writer, Horace Walpole, wrote that in 1745 St Germain was arrested in London as a Jacobite spy but soon released. He commented that the Count sang, played the violin wonderfully, composed, was mad and was believed to have married an heiress in Mexico and run away with her jewels to

Constantinople. All stressed his chief talent was storytelling.

Count St. Germain's inexhaustible wealth aroused particular intrigue. He was generally credited with powers of washing diamonds to enhance their value, melting diamonds or fusing several into one large stone, of even making excellent diamonds, feats which would tax our own nuclear scientists. One day Louis XV showed him a stone with a flaw valued at 6,000 francs, a month later the Count returned the diamond, the flaw removed, its value increased to 9,600 francs. St Germain perfected a striking alloy of copper and zinc, dyeing stuffs, many beautifying preparations and a pomade for Madame de Pompadour, which maintained her hair beautiful until she died. The Count also had a remarkable flair for international finance, unusual in that age, and was known to have advised Governments and cities on financial operations.

Such a cosmopolitan personality moving among the Courts of Europe inevitably played a mysterious role in international politics. From Venice in 1710 he disappeared, perhaps to the East, the Countess d'Adhemar records his materialisation at the French Court in 1743 apparently from nowhere, when his magnificence bedazzled even the Parisian aristocracy; in 1745 he was in London and from 1746 to 1755 he was a privileged figure at the glittering Court in Austria, where he called himself Prince Rococzi; in 1755 he is said to have met Clive in India. St Germain appeared at Versailles about 1757 and there enjoyed extraordinary influence; his ready access at all times to Louis XV scandalised officials of the French Court. His affairs with the Ladies of the Court seem to have been quite platonic for that licentious age, foreseeing the imminent Revolution he comforted them with vistas of the spirit-world to come. St Germain prophesied to Marie Antoinette the day and hour of her death; the Queen herself testified that he appeared to her in her prison cell in his astral body and uplifted her soul with the certainty of the glorious life hereafter, which inspired her noble dignity on the guillotine.

Unknown to his Ministers Louis employed St Germain as a secret-agent, sending him in March 1760 to the Hague, where he caused a great sensation, to arrange peace with Prussia at the expense of Austria. The Duc de Choiseul, Minister for Foreign Affairs, was so incensed that he insisted the Count be arrested, bound hand and foot, and thrown into the Bastille. The Dutch authorities evidently charmed by St Germain refused to extradite him, and he proceeded to England.

After a year in London, St. Germain is said to have gone to Russia and he played an important part in the conspiracy against Emperor Peter III in July 1762, a plot which placed on the Russian throne the formidable Catherine the Great. In 1769 he established in Venice a factory converting flax into a textile resembling silk. For several years St Germain lived in Germany with the Landgrave Charles of Hesse teaching him experiments in science. He offered Frederick the Great a list of various chemical operations, which had they been taken seriously by that Monarch, might have given Germany the lead in the Industrial Revolution making that country master of Europe.

The Count's greatest work and the secret of his friendship with so many notable personages lay in his arcane influence in the mystery, Brotherhoods, such as Freemasonry, which he founded; to the Initiate he possibly revealed his true origin and purpose on Earth. Mesmer claimed the Count instructed him about the sub-conscious mind, thus preparing the way for our present-day psychiatry.

The place and year of St Germain's death remain unknown. Madame Blavatsky a century later insisted that the death or such a celebrity would have been widely publicised, the fact it was not, proved he was still alive. The Count was reported to have had an important conference with Catharine of Russia in 1785, to have appeared to Madame du Barry on the scaffold in 1793 and to have talked to Madame de Genlis during the Treaty of Vienna in 1821. St Germain was said to be a close friend of Lord Lytton in 1842 and created the latter's great supernatural character, Zanoni; in 1867 he is credited with attending a meeting of the Great Lodge in Milan, and later with inspiring Chopin and Tchaikovsky. Dr Annie Besant, the theosophist, is quoted as having met St Germain for the first time in 1896. Andrew Lang believed him to be that Major Fraser living in Paris in the 1860s, a mysterious individual of great wealth, who claimed undying friendship with Madame de Pompador. No record existed of Fraser's death; Lang speculated whether Fraser, that is to say, St Germain, became that mysterious Muscovite, who at the turn of the century was adviser to the Dalai Lama.

The Count is said to have frequently puzzled his contemporaries by describing inventions such as the train and the steamboat unknown to the 18th century, and he once intimated that he had received cryptic instructions to proceed to England to prepare for their development.

Viewed in our context of Spacemen throughout the Ages the appearances and disappearances across the centuries of this fantastic man with phenomenal talents and inexhaustible wealth, without origin or social background, which so baffled his contemporaries, become suddenly illumined in one startling revelation. Count St Germain was a missionary from Space, perhaps an Avatar from Venus, source of his longevity, his spiritual ideals and nobility of life; periodically descending to Earth to direct Man's evolution. We wonder under what famous name he inspires Earth's destiny today?

Demons from realms invisible materialising among men fascinated writers and composers of the 18th and 19th centuries especially during the Romantic Period much more than Spacemen influence our literature today. The legend of a sorcerer who sold his soul to the Devil, like the tale of the Wandering Jew, was popular in the Middle Ages. He was first identified with Johannes Fust who graduated from Heidelberg in 1510, then with Dr Johannes Faust from Cracow, who about 1530 practised magic in Germany. In 1587 the first of numerous Faust books was printed at Frankfort by Johann Spiess entitled 'History of Dr Joann Faustus, the far-named Sorcerer and Master of the Black Art. How he sold himself to the Devil for an appointed time'.

The Faust-drama caught the imagination of genius; the great poet, Johann Wolfgang von Goethe,[87] born on 28 August 1749 at Frankfort commenced the First Part of 'Faust' in 1773 and completed the Second Part in 1831, two months before his death. What titanic theme could captivate the mind of such a gifted dramatist, versed in all the Sciences and the Arts, perhaps the greatest genius of his age, for nearly sixty years?

Goethe was initiated into the mysteries of magical philosophy, he mingled the teachings of the Greeks, the theories of Paracelsus, the discoveries of Science into a Cosmic

Wisdom later to inspire Rudolf Steiner and the Anthroposophists. Goethe's universality, his consciousness of omnipresent life on all planes of existence, exquisitely anticipate our latest conception of Spacemen. His concepts of the living Cosmos, the regeneration of Man through Love-Wisdom may inspire the union of Science with Religion in a glorious Space-Philosophy for the 21st century.

The irrational erratics, the odd phenomena irritating scientists attracted the interest of a neglected genius uncommonly endowed with that rare commodity, commonsense. Charles Hoy Fort born August 9th 1874, in Albany, New York, may be justly called the Father of Ufology. He sought to remove the halo from Science, to make human beings think and to destroy awe for dogmatic Authority. Up to the age of thirty-four, Fort, whose parents were grocers, earned a slender living from journalism and embalming butterflies; when his parents died, he sold their shop and sustained by a small income devoted his life to reading scores of miscellaneous periodicals extracting unusual data about balls of fire, rains of frogs, showers of blood, mysterious manifestations, inexplicable disappearances, sudden fires, erratic comets, and records of flying disks. Fort amassed 40,000 notes under 1,300 headings on every fascinating subject under the Sun to form the basis of his four wonderful works,[73] the Book of the Damned, New Lands, Lo and Wild Talents. It is said that Charles Fort died on May 3rd 1932 in New York; all Students of Spacemen swear he still lives, more impish than ever today.

In *The Book of the Damned* first published in 1919 long before our Space Age, Charles Fort wondered in his whimsical way

'I think we're property.
I should say we belong to something.
That once upon a time, this earth was No-Man's Land, that other worlds explored and colonised here, and fought among themselves for possession, but that now it's owned by something.
That something owns this earth – all others warned off.'

The very source of our Spacemen in History!

From the researches of Charles Fort, Harold Wilkins, Jacques Vallée and devoted Students all over Europe and Japan, many scores of sightings, even landings, during the

19th century could be quoted. Many sightings possibly were natural phenomena but sufficent inexplicable residue remains to baffle the most cautious critic. A few cases are mentioned here merely to continue the familiar pattern of previous centuries.

1808 'June 8. In Japan a mysterious light was seen towards the south about 8.30 pm. After a while there was a sound like thunder but differed from it, sounding from west to east for some time and shaking the sliding doors. The light came into view, so clearly the people could see one another's face. All people heard it within scores of miles around Mito, Kanto area.'
('Brothers', Vol. 3-1. C.B.A. Yokohama.)

1819 'June 26. Five unknown bodies were seen crossing the Sun according to Gruithuisen.
(Charles Fort, New Lands.)

1826 'Sunday. December 17. Migne, near Poitiers, France. A regular cross of vast dimensions suddenly appeared in the sky.'
(Alberto Cotogni, Giornale dei Misteri.)

1833 'November 13. A large luminous body almost stationary for a time shaped like a square table, visible at Niagara Falls.'
(Charles Fort, the Book of the Damned.)

1843 'Tuesday. October 3. A remarkable cloud passed over Warwick, England, and one Charles Cooper, reported seeing three white, human-shaped figures in the sky. Another person, six miles away, is supposed to have also seen these flying beings.'
(John Keel. Operation Trojan Horse.)

1854 'May 22. Near Mercury, an object was seen equal in size to the planet itself and behind it an elongated object, and behind that something else smaller and round.'
(Charles Fort, New Lands.)

1868 'July. Something was seen in the sky near Copiapo, Chile – a construction that carried lights and was propelled by a noisy motor or a gigantic bird, eyes wide-open and shining like burning coals; covered with immense scales which clashed together with a metallic sound.'
(Charles Fort, Lo.)

1873 'June 17. Dr Sage of Rybnik, Upper Silesia reported seeing a luminous object apparently issue from Mars, the planet quaked with shock, the thing came to Earth and exploded in the sky of Hungary, Austria and Bohemia.'
(Charles Fort, New Lands.)

1882 'November 17 ("Observatory" 39-214(E.W. Maunder saw something which he termed a strange celestial visitor. At the Royal Observatory, Greenwich, he observed "an aurora, without features of special interest. In the midst of the aurora, a great circular disk of greenish light appeared and moved smoothly

across the sky. But the circularity was evidently the effect of foreshortening. The thing passed above the Moon, and was by other observers, described as "cigar-shaped", "Like a torpedo", "a spindle", "a shuttle" ... Had "the incident occurred a third of a century later, beyond doubt everyone would have selected the same simile – it would have been just like a Zeppelin".'
(Charles Fort, the Book of the Damned.)

1897 'April 16. A great many persons around Chicago told of seeing an airship. The New York Sun stated "Reports from other towns in Texas, Fort Worth, Dallas, Marshall, Ennis and Beaumont. It was shaped like a Mexican cigar, large in the middle and small at both ends with great wings resembling those of an enormous butterfly. It was brilliantly illuminated by the rays of two great searchlights, and was sailing in a south-easterly direction with the velocity of the wind, presenting a magnificent appearance".'
(Charles Fort, New Lands.)

After studying 126 accounts 'which seemed reliable' John A. Keel, concluded[110] 'I do not doubt that someone was carefully flying over the United States in 1897 paying great attention to special isolated areas.' Meticulous research of the 1897 airship by Jerome Clark and Lucius Farish[48] reveals sightings of 'flying cigars' throughout North America. Aerial craft were also seen over Sweden and Siberia.

Amid the rapid industrialisation of the 19th century men concentrated attention on worldly affairs, heedless of bizarre events confounding contemporary Science. On the night of 23 September 1823 young Joseph Smith in Palmyra, New York, awoke to behold a Celestial robed in light; Moroni revealed to him the whereabouts of plates of gold inscribed with occult revelations, which four years later he was to unearth. With the aid of an optical instrument Joseph Smith, ignorant, unlettered, translated the arcane text, published in 1830 as the Book of Mormon, and he established the Church of the Latter Day Saints, which today has nearly 3,000,000 members.

Near the New Gate of Nuremburg on Whit Monday, May 1828, stumbled an awkward, incoherent youth about sixteen, Kaspar Hauser, knowing no German and completely unacquainted with the normal things of life like some Alien from another world. In New York during the 1840s the two young Fox sisters attracted occult rappings and poltergeist phenomena, which in an earlier century at Salem would have brought accusations of witchcraft; some open-minded scholars and scientists investigated the Occult initiating modern psychical research. A fourteen-year old girl, Bernadette Soubirous, in February 1858 on a hillside at Lourdes beheld the Vision of a beautiful Lady, from the grotto nearby trickled forth a spring of healing water; since then pilgrims have brought the sick from far and wide expecting and receiving miracles. On 5th December 1872 between the Azores and Lisbon drifted the Marie Celeste, not a soul on board, no sign of strife, the Captain, his wife, and all the crew mysteriously vanished, as if suddenly translated elsewhere.

In November 1874 John Worrell Keely exhibited in Philadelphia a fuel-less motor without any apparent source of power, now believed to have been a novel, anti-gravity device; he was said to have been mysteriously silenced, his invention destroyed. Mrs Mary Baker Eddy cured herself by reading the Bible, in 1875 she published 'Science and Health, with Key to the Scriptures' for the practice of Christian Science founding the new Church of Christ which brings healing and comfort to millions of people in many countries. Phylos the Thibetan in 1883 communicated telepathically to a simple, country-boy, Frederick S. Oliver, the wonders of lost Atlantis. The closing decades were to witness surveillance of Earth by unknown airships, grim omen for the twentieth century.

The Age of Reason from 1600 diverted men from mediaeval superstition to methodical Science transforming the world, but the same supernatural phenomena persisted.

CHAPTER TWENTY-FIVE
Today

On the lovely sunny Tuesday, June 24, 1947, Kenneth Arnold, a young businessman from Boise, Idaho, completed the installation of some fire-fighting apparatus for Central Air Service at Chehalis, Washington, and at two o'clock in the afternoon took-off in his specially-designed mountain-airplane for Yakima. A C-46 Marine transport was reported lost in the mountains, having an hour to spare and attracted perhaps by a $5,000 reward, he flew directly towards the high plateau of Mount Rainier, an elevation over nine thousand feet. Suddenly Arnold was startled by a tremendously bright flash, no aircraft were nearby; again a flash. To the north he observed a formation of very bright objects skimming the mountain-tops at fantastic speed. As they approached he thought they must be nine jets. "They were flying diagonally in an echelon formation with a larger gap in their echelon between the first four and the last five." Arnold, with perfect visibility, was astounded because the craft had no tails; he was immensely impressed by "how they fluttered and sailed, tipping their wings alternately and emitting those very bright blue-white flashes from their surfaces,'[8] highly polished, reflecting the sun. The strange aircraft covered the twenty three miles between Mount Rainier in the north and Mount Adams in the south in one minute and forty-two seconds; he felt sure they were travelling in excess of a thousand miles an hour, a speed at that time unattained. On landing Arnold told newsmen in Pendleton, Oregon, 'They flew like a saucer would, if you skipped it across the water." More precise measurement on a map increased the actual distance between the two peaks to 39.8 miles making a speed of over thirteen hundred miles an hour, convincing Arnold that the objects must have been guided missiles.

Later Arnold heard a rumour that the Harbour Patrol Staff at the Washington port of Tacoma had not only seen 'strange things' but had collected fragments of something dropped from the sky. He met a Mr Harold Dahl, who related that on June 21, 1947, while in his boat patrolling the east bay of Maury Island, about three miles off Tacoma, he looked up to see six very large doughnut-shaped aircraft about 2,000 feet directly overhead; they apparently had no motors, propellers or any visible signs of propulsion and made no sound; each, at least one hundred feet in diameter, had a hole in the centre about twenty-five feet across, their surface, a shell-like gold and silver in colour, seemed of burled metal, reflecting many brilliancies of the sun. All appeared to have large round portholes equally spaced around their perimeter and a dark, circular observation window on the inside and bottom of their doughnut-shape. The centre-craft was losing altitude. Fearing it would crash, Dahl and his companions beached their boat, then he took three or four photographs. In the silence sounded a dull thud, the centre-craft began spewing forth a white type of very light metal, then a black or darker type of metal like lava, intensely hot, which raised steam on falling into the water; thus lightened, the craft ascended to rejoin the others, then the whole formation disappeared out to sea. Some of the slag fragments from Maury Island were collected by a Lieutenant Brown from Military Intelligence and a Captain Davison; on flying back to Hamilton Field their B-25 crashed, both were killed, though the other two occupants survived. A Major Sanders of Air Intelligence, who heard Arnold's story said 'The metal's just a slag, and the story is a hoax.' The noted scientific author, Gerald Heard, comments ·tersely[92] 'But the explanation did not cover all the facts.' All the double-talk of official Spokesmen since that date must make us concur!

Kenneth Arnold's famous sighting in 1947, the beginning of a new wave, was far from being the first extraterrestrial visitation in the twentieth century. On June 30, 1908 a tremendous explosion levelled acres of forest in the Tunguska region of Siberia; the absence of a metallic core excludes a comet or meteor; latest theories propose that Earth had been hit by a bullet of anti-matter, or actually encountered a mini 'black hole' an object under intense gravitational collapse preventing the escape of light, which would cause huge shock waves on meeting terrestrial matter. Popular opinion prefers to attribute the Tunguska cataclysm to the explosion of a crashed nuclear-powered spaceship. At the village of Fatima in Portugal on 13 May 1917 Lucia de Jesus aged ten and her two young cousins minding sheep, saw a flash in the sky and beheld a 'Lady of Light', who appeared above an ever-green oak; she returned on the 13th of June, July, August and September, although many of the great crowd saw only a luminous globe crossing the sky and falling flakes of 'snow' which dissolved on touching the ground, perhaps the well-known 'Angel's Hair'. The 'Lady' confided to Lucia telepathically certain most important secrets later entrusted to the Pope. Finally on 13th October at Cova da Iria before 70,000 people appeared a bright, luminous, pearly disk like a 'living Star', which transformed into a wheel emitting rays of blue, red, violet, yellow and green, then it seemed to rebound to the lofty heavens.[196] During the 1930s mystery planes haunted America, Norway and Sweden; pilots on both sides in World War II were dogged by luminous balls which they called 'foo-fighters'; in 1946 Scandinavians were mystified by hundreds of 'ghost-rockets', 'some released fragments of metal which proved to be common slag.'[110]

Since 1947 many thousands of Unidentified Flying Objects have been seen all over the world; these UFOs have been photographed, tracked by radar, their radiation has stopped motor-cars, their heat-beams have burned men and buildings,[126] these Visitants are believed to have caused widespread electrical black-outs, some craft have dropped metallic parts, analysis shows a purity unknown on Earth. UFOs have been seen by the cosmonauts and are said to have disturbed American and Russian space-flights; many have plunged below the sea, hundreds have landed. Dr Jacques Vallée, the noted scientist and NASA consultant, lists 923 cases in a century of landings from 1868-1968;[201] Mr Charles Bowen with brilliant colleagues has edited a most detailed survey[21] of world-wide reports of landings of unconventional aerial objects and their alleged occupants. Comprehensive studies by researchers in America, France, Italy, Spain, Germany, Brazil, Japan, published in a vast literature of books and periodicals gives overwhelming photographic and well-attested documentary evidence from a multitude of observers, astronomers, scientists, doctors, airmen, seamen, motorists, housewives, children, people in all walks of life, whose solemn word on any other subjects would be promptly believed; their testimonies despite official ridicule surely prove beyond all doubt that alien aeroforms are surveilling our own Earth.

Scores of landings and alleged encounters with Extraterrestrials could be quoted with diverting detail, perhaps here it may suffice to mention only the most famous – or most notorious – enigma of all, rightly or wrongly symbolic of Spacemen in our twentieth-century.[221]

'A Man from another world stepped onto the planet Earth on November 20, 1952. My wife and I and our friends witnessed this happening, which took place 10.2 miles from Desert Center, California, on the highway toward Parker, Arizona. The full account is given in *Flying Saucers have Landed* by Leslie and Adamski.'[121]

This startling statement was made by George Hunt Williamson,[9] a noted anthropologist, former Chairman, Department of Anthropology, Great Western University, San Francisco, listed in 'Who's Who in America' and in 'American Men of Science', author of several influential books. Mrs Betty Williamson is a chemist and anthropologist, with degrees from the Universities of Eastern New Mexico and of Arizona. Both are thoroughly trained as scientific observers and researchers; they are Members of the American Anthropological Association and the American Association for the Advancement of Science. With Dr and Mrs George H. Williamson on this historic occasion, when George Adamski met Orthon from Venus, were Mr and Mrs Al. Bailey, Mrs Lucy McGinnis and Mrs Alice Wells, they were closely questioned by the Press on what they had seen, their stories agreed. While admitting that the unanimous evidence of such reputable witnesses would certainly be accepted in any law-court world-wide, sceptics state that they could not have seen a Spaceman, arguing that Spacemen do not land on Earth because no one has seen them, if anyone says he has seen a Spaceman, he must be wrong since Spacemen never land here, otherwise someone would have seen them, but no one has seen Spacemen, they do not land. So ran the elusive logic of the Condon Committee!

George Adamski born in Poland, April 17th, 1891, was brought to America a year later; a successful teacher and lecturer in cosmic philosophy, he began studying the heavens, from 1941 living on the slopes of Mt Palomar, site of the world's largest telescope; he had long wondered at the radiant Spaceships haunting the skies and prayed one would land.

> 'It was about 12.30 in the Noon hour on Thursday, 20 November 1952, that I first made a personal contact with a man from another world. He came to Earth in his Space-craft, a flying saucer. He called it a Scout Ship.'

With his friends Adamski had driven into the Californian desert hoping to see some Flying Saucers; shortly after 12 Noon they saw the fuselage of a very large ship without wings coloured orange with a black or dark insignia on the side. Hoping for a personal contact Adamski asked his friends to leave him in a chosen spot, then he set up his telescope and waited. Almost instantly Adamski saw a beautiful small craft drifting between two mountain-peaks, this he photographed before it disappeared. Shortly afterwards his attention was drawn to a man near a ravine about a quarter of a mile away, who motioned him to approach. A strange feeling of friendliness came upon Adamski, he looked round to reassure himself that both were in full sight of his companions. The Stranger looked like any other man, somewhat smaller, young with shoulder-long hair and surpassing beauty.

> 'Now, for the first time I fully realised that I was in the presence of a man from space – A HUMAN BEING FROM ANOTHER WORLD!'

By signs and telepathy the Spaceman revealed that he had come from Venus in the large craft or 'Mother-ship', then transferred to the small craft or Scout-ship, which Adamski had just photographed; as they 'conversed' on cosmic affairs this ship returned. 'It was a beautiful small craft, shaped more like a heavy glass bell than a saucer'; the ship was apparently made of a specially processed metal, a three-ball landing-gear was half-lowered. The top of the craft surmounted by a large ball was dome-shaped with a ring of gears or heavy coil built into and encircling the side wall at the base were round portholes, some transparent, others opaque. Adamski heard two occupants with voices like music; the Venusian entered the ship which glided over the crest of the mountains and disappeared into Space. Plaster-casts of the Venusian's footprints in the sand were made by Dr Williamson, who later alleged that the cosmic symbols therein referred to the lost continent of Mu which had been destroyed but would rise again. A long way for Orthon to come, to tell us something we already knew!

On 13 December 1952 the Spacecraft returned, Adamski took four much-debated photographs; three months later on 15 February 1953, he again met the Venusian, whom he called Orthon, and his friends, Firkon from Mars and Ramu from Saturn; they whisked him in their Scoutship to a great Mother-ship in Space where he discoursed with a Cosmic Master. On 21 April 1953 Adamski spoke with another Master in a Saturnian Spaceship from which he gazed down on the Moon then inhabited – so he said!

The experiences of Adamski incredible to our modern minds recall those encounters of Abraham and Moses with Jehovah, the trips of Enoch with Angels to the heavens. Again we wonder!

In 1959 George Adamski visited Europe. This present Writer was privileged to meet him in Newcastle-upon-Tyne and sadly disappointed by his refusal to answer my simple questions. Will no-one answer them?

On his world-tour Adamski was received by Queen Juliana and Prince Bernhard at Soestdijk Palace near the Hague, then received in audience at the Vatican by Pope John who presented him with a beautiful gold medallion. On April 23 1965 George Adamski died. In a moving valedictory Desmond Leslie wrote 'If he is reborn on another planet, he has promised to come back and contact us when possible.'[122] The day after Adamski died, about 5.30 pm Arthur Bryant, an elderly groundsman, was out walking toward Scoriton Down on the edge of Dartmoor, when he was startled by a saucer-like craft hovering in a nearby field; three figures alighted, two looked Aliens, the third seemed an ordinary Earth-youth about fourteen or fifteen with short dark-brown hair and dark brown eyes. In English with an American accent he said he was 'Yamski' and came from Venus, then made reference to 'Des Les' apparently suggesting Desmond Leslie.[26] A most intriguing tale! Did Adamski return from the dead? Some of his followers think so. Could George inspire a new cosmic religion?

Since George Adamski new Prophets have arisen in many countries claiming contacts with Extraterrestrials from planets known and unknown in our own Solar System, within the Milky Way and Galaxies beyond, even from etherian worlds in Inner Space. Some of these 'Contactees' may be paranoids, publicity-seekers, fortune-hunters, but an astonishing number are just ordinary people acutely embarrassed at being chosen by the Celestials, they tend to keep silent about their encounters fearing ridicule. Communications to Sensitives from discarnate Entities by telepathy, automatic-writing or radio mix spiritual wisdom with dire warnings of calamities to come, somewhat superfluous since Nostradamus and many seers already prophesy world-wide disasters later this century. An expansive literature alleges visitations by Aliens, Supermen, seductive Women, Giants, Dwarfs, Humanoids, Monsters in assorted Spacecraft motivated by anti-gravity, cosmic rays, spatial tension, psychic force or thought-power, approaching, even surpassing, the speed of light; some ships of etherean matter cannot be seen by common mortals only by psychics, so they say. Spacemen land and live among us allegedly directing Earth's evolution, the state of our world surely proves that their's is inspiration we can do without. Some Celestials reveal great knowledge, others talk nonsense; solitary Space-surgeons work healing miracles, many cosmic Gangsters kidnap people, even ships and aircraft, apparently looting our planet unknown to the Police. The Visitants are said to have retreats on mountain-tops, bases on the ocean-bed, cities inside the Earth itself. Man shares our world with an Alien Race, we have been invaded for centuries, soon the Celestials will take Earth for themselves. Fact merges into fiction, every fancy haunting the human mind, the most bizarre conception confounding belief finds fertile expression in the field of Spacemen. Scientists scorn such irrational ideas as aery romance but are bewildered to find some semblance of truth; the Church condemns these wonders unless they be found in holy books becoming religion.

The much criticised Condon Report published in January 1969 could not agree the non-existence of UFOs, a negative conclusion not without some small satisfaction. Dr J. Allen Hynek after careful review states

'In summary, then, my twenty-one years of monitoring of UFO reports has shown that reports of UFO observations remain after we delete the pronouncements of crackpots, visionaries, religious fanatics and so forth.'[172]

Dr James E. McDonald comments

'It is difficult for me to see any reasonable alternative to the hypothesis that something in the nature of extraterrestrial devices engaged in something in the nature of surveillance lies at the heart of the UFO problem.'[172]

Dr Carl Sagan discussing Extraterrestrials evaluates the problem saying

'As a concluding word let me say that I believe the search for extraterrestrial intelligence to be an exceedingly important one both for science and for society. It is difficult to think of a more important scientific question.'[172]

Radio-astronomers all over the world are listening for intelligent signals from the stars, principally on the 21 cms waveband of hydrogen atoms in free Space, which is likely to be known to Extraterrestrials. Peoples of stellar civilisations may have means of communications beyond our knowledge, they may have long since transcended Earth's radio.

Sir Fred Hoyle, the famous astronomer, gives a classic analysis.[102]

'You are all familiar with an ordinary telephone-directory. You want to speak to someone, you look up the number, and you dial the appropriate code. My speculation is that a similar situation exists, and has existed for billions of years in the Galaxy. My speculation is that an interchange of messages is going on, on a vast scale, all the time, and that we are as unaware of it as a pygmy in the African forests is unaware of the radio-messages that flash at the speed of light around the earth. My guess is there might be a million or more subscribers to the galactic directory. Our problem is to get our name into that directory.'

The French physicist, Jacques Bergier, suggests[12] that advanced civilisations may have surpassed electro-magnetic wavebands, laser or maser beams, and use fields of power or particles still undiscovered by our Science, such emissions may register directly on to the highly developed minds of Sensitives like Rudolf Steiner, the great Mystic, early this century.

Scientists must test each new discovery in strict experiment before accepting its validity, archaeologists try to confirm their finds from contemporary records. Scholars of genius provide a brilliant panorama of the Universe from current knowledge and resurrect Man's glorious past, all freely admit that the avalanche of new research soon makes their ideas obsolete. The Science and Arts of the twenty-first century will surely revolutionise present conceptions of Man on planet Earth.

Our world-wide survey of history may be challenged, interpretations greatly differ, all the data here presented is free for debate. Whatever our preconceived opinions, the final words must rest with the Ancients themselves. Our ancestors believed they were inspired by the Gods, the Spacemen.

What has been shall be again, the future lies in the past!

CHAPTER TWENTY-SIX
Tomorrow

The third young Moon followed her queenly sisters transmuting the leaden skies to silver, her radiance illumined the people of Xonta hastening to welcome a new wonder. Ranil, a psycho-scientist, with his wife and two daughters paused for a moment in their luminous salon before the Image of the Divine Androgyne symbolising the Creator, then reclined on divans for their frugal supper of cheese and fruit. The two teenagers talked of the Man from Outer Space whom the starship Zena had just brought from the remotest galaxy; they hoped he was not married, both were so bored with Xonta's supercilious youths; soon they would see the Celestial in that very room materialised by the telemat. Ignoring their chatter Ranil as proud inventor was explaining yet again to his bewildered wife that the physical universe was like the surface of a soap-bubble, this latest ship instead of skimming across the bubble had dived inside into etherean dimensions at a tangent emerging afterwards into a sector in the opposite hemisphere never surveyed before. She still could not understand his baffling explanation, fortunately Lana, their elder daughter, silenced her Father by switching on the telemat, a system of fluorescent panels in the walls.

In the centre of the mosaic floor materialised Torin, the Zena's Commander, his white robe with insignia of the Divine Androgyne showed him as a Master of the Cosmic Wisdom. Displaying an unfamiliar chart of the heavens, he explained how through hyper-space they had penetrated to a galaxy beyond even their most powerful telescopes. On its return the ship was about to dematerialise to the etherean plane when the scanners sighted a metallic object floating in Space, a magnetic beam attracted it into the Zena's hold. On examination the Commander was surprised to find the bodies of four men nearly as tall as himself though not so bronzed, three were dead, the fourth almost frozen. After treatment the Astronaut recovered and under telepathic interrogation revealed he was from an unknown planet called Earth, his fascinating thought-patterns would entertain the Xonteans.

Torin was joined by a young man in blue uniform with a breast-pocket badge showing stars and stripes, whose boyish grin charmed the impressionable Lana; accustomed though she was to the telemat, she never ceased to marvel at the perfect living images magically projected into every Viewer's home. The stranger seemed absurdly immature, almost barbaric compared with the cultured Xonteans yet his natural appeal endeared him at once to all women watching him. Lana half-arose to fling her arms around him, then sat down entranced as he talked to her. An instrument attuned to the Earthling's brain-rhythms translated his speech into nasal Xontean with strange idioms enchanting his listeners. The Commander welcomed him courteously as the first Ambassador to Xonta from a remote galaxy and hoped his enforced stay would prove pleasant, meanwhile they would be honoured if their Guest would enlighten them with a description of his own planet, Earth, about which they confessed ignorance. The Astronaut smiled cheerfully that he should thank the Xonteans for saving his life but surely he was dead, this must be Heaven. His name was Joe Smith, Colonel in the American Space Command Leader of the 1980 manned probe to Mars; their ship had met a storm of meteorites which fused all electrical circuits breaking contact with Earth. For weeks they had drifted off course in icy dark, one by one his companions died; he thought he had died too, especially when he awoke to behold the beauties of Xonta.

Joe explained that Earth was the third inner planet of the Sun, a star near the edge of the Milky Way; he was surprised the Xonteans had never heard of Earth; the experienced Commander admitted that this sector of the Universe was new to him, it could be reached only through hyper-space. Travel across etherean dimensions was theorised by some American scientists, said Joe, he had thought them crazy, now he knew better. He tactfully complimented the Xonteans on their good looks like Movie-Stars, which thrilled the watching Lana and her moon-struck sister. Torin remarked that ages ago the first Xonteans originated from an advanced galaxy; Joe said they were lucky, people on Earth just descended from monkeys and for millions of years lived in caves until the Egyptians started history about 5000 BC. Even the Commander laughed. Joe thought it an unlikely tale but the archaeologists ridiculed legends of great civilisations in the past with Spaceships and believed only what they dug up.

Joe's description of life and customs on Earth perplexed then convulsed the delighted Xonteans; such a diverting tale had not enchanted their cultured ears for generations. Politeness to the Stranger made the studio-audience restrain their laughter but the strange beliefs and political antics of those peoples on Earth were utterly beyond all sanity. Undaunted Joe expounded the current teachings of Science and Religion and the contending Social Systems of Earth threatening world-war; he said it was race between destruction by hydrogen-bombs or poisoning by pollution, everyone feared these evils but could do nothing to avert inevitable doom. Joe began with a grave countenance as though lecturing his Students at Space Command, then conscious of his new environment he suddenly realised the utter absurdity of conditions on tiny Earth an infinity away; thereafter Joe could no longer talk with conviction and lapsed into racy satire entrancing the amused Xonteans. He found the term BC particularly difficult to explain; he said it meant 'Before Christ', the Son of God, Who incarnated on Earth and died on a Cross. This perturbed Torin; he said that God was imagining the visible Universe with countless billions of stars, the many invisible Universes of different dimensions with parallel Universes of anti-matter. Why should God send His Son to Earth, a planet not even known to the Galactic Federation? The Xonteans knew all Creatures to be Sons of God. Since becoming an Astronaut and viewing Earth as a tiny star, Joe said he guessed all religions might be partly right and partly wrong; religion brought comfort to many people who tried to live good lives. Earth was plagued by wars past and wars to come, life was short and often cruel, the Xonteans were lucky to have such a wonderful world. No Man on Earth knew the real Truth about God and the Universe, people had to believe in something, a few smart thinkers ruled men's minds, what they did not know they made up, wars were stupid but Earthlings were slowly getting sense.

Torin smiled at that frank admission, this man from Earth had more wisdom than he imagined. He explained that a million years ago the Xonteans too waged wars until Science merged with Religion into a cosmic philosophy inspiring the planet to peace and beauty. Joe confessed that Earthlings did not know why they were born nor why they died, so how could they know why they lived? Perhaps on some future expedition the Commander might return him to Earth to tell men about this marvellous world across the Universe? With all his American charm Joe added that if some fair Xontean cared to teach an exiled Earthling the language of her lovely planet he might even marry and settle down there. Ranil's daughters cooed in delight, Lana waltzed out to claim her future husband.

This romance of tomorrow, not quite so improbable as it appears, suggests that Man's greatest embarrassment on confronting Extraterrestrials may be his own ignorance. We Earthlings glory in our ego-centricity, fostered by the false materialism which taints our contemporary culture; five great religions contend for Truth, Science creates to destroy, men plod on their cosmic pilgrimage without purpose, no world-figure can now reveal the meaning of the Universe. Despite the genius of so many Scholars in diverse fields of human endeavour no cosmic wisdom inspires our world, to people of other planets our earthly ethics may seem barbaric. To communicate with Extraterrestrials on their cultural level Man must expand to cosmic consciousness, attune his soul to all Creation; Man must know himself; first he must revise his views of his own past.

People on Earth were never alone, our evolution is long inspired by Spacemen throughout History.

BIBLIOGRAPHY

1 Alder, Vera Stanley. *The Finding of the Third Eye*. Rider & Co., London.
2 Alder, Vera Stanley. *The Initiation of the World*. Rider & Co., London.
3 Aldred, Cyril. *Akhenaton, Pharoah of Egypt*. Abacus, Sphere Books, London.
4 Andreas, Peter and Adams, Gordon. *Between Heaven and Earth*. Harrap, London.
5 Apollodorus. *History*. Loeb Classics, Heinemann.
6 Aristophanes. *Plays*. Everyman, Dent.
7 Arnold, Sir Edward. *The Light of Asia*. Routledge & Kegan Paul Ltd., London.
8 Arnold, Kenneth & Palmer, Ray. *The Coming of the Saucers*. Amherst Press, Wisconsin.
9 Aston, W.G. *Nihongi or Chronicles of Japan*. G. Allen & Unwin.
10 Beaumont, Comyns. *The Riddle of Prehistoric Britain*. Rider, London.
11 Bellamy, H.S. *Moon, Myths and Man*. London.
12 Bergier, Jacques. *Mes hypothèses sur Rudolf Steiner*. Planète 40. M'J 1968. Paris 8.
13 Bernard, Raymond. *Flying Saucers from the Earth's Interior*. P.O. Box 485, Joinville, Santa Caterine, Brazil.
14 Besant, Annie. *Man, Where, Whence and Whither*. Theosophical Society, London.
15 Bibby, Geoffrey. *Four Thousand Years Ago*. Collins, London.
16 Blavatsky, H.P. *Isis Unveiled*. Theosophical Publg. Co., Pasadena.
17 Blavatsky, H.P. *The Secret Doctrine*. The Theosophical Publg. Co., Pasadena.
18 Blondet, Maurizio. *E il Polo la culla dell 'Umanita?* Gli Arcani', Armenia Editore, Milano.
19 Boncompagni, Solas. *L'Occhio che discese dal Cielo*. 'Il Giornale dei Misteri' 14,m 1972, Firenze.
20 Boncompagni, Solas. *Sumeria, terra d'incognito*. 'G di M.' 27, giugno, 1973, Còrrado Tedeschi, Firenze.
21 Bowen, Charles. *The Humanoids*. Neville Spearman Ltd., London.
22 Brother Philip. *Secret of the Andes*. Neville Spearman Ltd., London.
23 Brunelli, Vittorio. *Gli Dei con un piede nella, Cina*. 'Clypeus' 34, maggio'Junio 1971. Torino, Italy.
24 Brunton, Paul. *The Hidden Teachings Beyond Yoga*. Rider & Co., London.
25 Bruton, Paul. *A Search in Secret Egypt*. Rider & Co., London.
26 Buckle Eilleen & Oliver, Norman. *The Scoriton Mystery*. Neville Spearman Ltd., London.
27 Budge, Sir A.E. Wallis. *Egyptian Religion*. Routledge & Kegan Paul, London.
28 Caesar, Julius. *De Bello Gallico*.
29 Calabri, Mara. *Divinita, Riti e Magie del Popolo Sumero*. 'Il Giornale dei Misteri', ott.1971. Firenze.
30 Cardinali, Quixe. *Dalle Galassie Ai Continenti Scomparsi*. Newton Compton Italiana, Rome.

31 Cardinali, Quixe. *11 Ritorno delle Civilta perdute*. Newton Compton Italiana, Rome, Italy.

32 Carnac, Pierre. *La Piramide e I Fori del Diavolo*. 'Il G. di M.' luglio, 1073, Firenze.

33 Cellini, Benvenuto. *La Vita di Benvenuto Cellini*. G. Barbera Editore, Firenze, 1920.

34 Ceram, C.W. *Gods, Graves and Scholars*. Gollancz, Sidgwick & Jackson, London.

35 Cerve, Wisher S. *Lemuria*. AMORC, San Jose, California.

36 Charles, Dr C.H. *The Book of Enoch*. S.P.C.K. London, 1962.

37 Charles, Dr R.H.C. *The Book of Jublilees*. S.P.C.K. London.

38 Charles, Dr R.H.C. *Fragments of the Book of Noah*. Oxford University Press.

39 Charroux, Robert. *The Mysterious Unknown*. Neville Spearman Ltd., London.

40 Cheetham, Erika. *The Prophecies of Nostradamus*. Neville Spearman Ltd., London.

41 Chionetti, Marta Luchino. *Corrado Licostene*. University of Turin.

42 I Chronicles III vv 3-7.

43 II Chronicles III vv 10-11.

44 Chronicon de Lanercost. *MCCI-MCCCXLVI*. Impressum Edinburgh, 1839.

45 Churchwood, James. *The Children of Mu*. Neville Spearman Limited, London.

46 Churchward, James. *The Lost Continent of Mu*. Neville Spearman Limited, London.

47 Cicero. *De Natura Deorum, Book 1, Ch 2*. Loeb Classics, Heinemann.

48 Clark, Jerome & Farish, Lucius. *The 1897 Story*. Flying Saucer Review, S'O 1968.

49 Coleman, Loran E and Hall, Mark A. *Some Bigfoot traditions of the North American Indians*. INFO Journal, Vol 2 No.3.

50 Cory, Wm. *Ancient Fragments*. Wm. Pickering, London, 1828.

51 Cotogni, Alberto. di. *Visioni nel Cielo*. 'Il Ciornale dei Misteri', No 37, April 1974, Corrado Tedeschi Editore, Firenze Italy.

52 Cramp, Leonard, G. *Pieces for Jig-Saw*. Somerton Press, Cowes, I.OW.

53 Creighton, Gordon. *A Russian Wall-Painting and Other Spaceman*. Flying Saucer Review, J'A 1965.

54 Daniel X.

55 David-Neel, Mdm Alexandra & the Lama Yongden. *The Superhuman Exploits of Gesar of Ling*. Rider, London.

56 David-Neel, Mdm Alexandra. *With Mystics and Magicians in Tibet*. Penguin, London, 1936.

57 Dio Cassius. *History*. Loeb Classics, Heinemann, London.

58 Diodorus Siculus. *Biblioteca Historica*. Oxford University Press, Oxford.

59 Dionysius. *Caelum. Hier. XIV*.

60 Dionysius of Halicarnassus. *Roman Antiquities*. Loeb Classics, Heinemann.

61 Donnelly, Ignatius. *Ragnarok*. Sampson Low, London, 1888.

62 Drake, W. Raymond. *Gods or Spaceman?* Amherst Press, Amherst, Wisconsin, 1964.
63 Drake W. Raymond. *Spaceman in Ancient East*. Neville Spearman, London, 1968.
64 Drake, W. Raymond. *Uomini, Dei o Esseri Spaziali*. Casa Editrice MEB, Turin, Italy.
65 Dutt, Romesh. *The Ramayana and the Mahabharata*. Dent, London.
66 Edwards, Frank. *Flying Saucers, Serious Business*. Mayflower, Dell, New York.
67 Edwards, Frank. *Stranger than Science*. Pan, London.
68 Euripides. *Plays*. Everyman, Dent.
69 Exodus III v 1-6.
70 Ezekiel I.
71 Fenoglio, Alberto. *Cronistoria su Oggetti Volanti del Passato*. Clypeus 111-2 1966, Torino.
72 Ferrari, Bianca. *Gli Etruschi sono una sciarada*. Clypeus, Anno IX No.3, giugno, 1972.
73 The Books of Charles Fort. Holt & Co., New York.
74 Fort, Charles. *The Book of the Damned*. Henry Holt & Co., New York.
75 Fort, Charles. *New Lands*. Holt & Co., New York.
76 Foster-Forbes, J. *Giants of Britain*. Thames Publications, London.
77 Fuller, John. *Interrupted Journey*. Dial Press, New York.
78 Gardner, Martin. *The Ambidextrous Universe*. Pelican, London.
79 Gaster, Theodor E. *The Scriptures of the Dead Sea Sect*. Secker & Warburg, London.
80 Genesis I.
81 Genesis VI.
82 Genesis XI.
83 Genesis XIX.
84 Geoffrey of Monmouth. *History of the Kings of Britain*.
85 Gianfranceschi, Luciano. *Vita e Spiritualita degli Etruschi*. Il G. di M, No.15, giugno, 1972, Firenze.
86 Ginzberg, Louis. *The Legends of the Jews*. Simon and Schuster, New York.
87 Goethe, Johann Wolfgang von. *Faust*. Der Verlag K. Knaur, Nachi, Berlin.
88 Graves, Robert and Patai, Raphael. *Hebrew Myths. The Book of Genesis*. Cassell, London.
89 Graves, Robert. *New Larousse Encylopaedia of Mythology*. Paul Hamlyn, London.
90 Grimm, Jacob. *Deutsche Mythologies (Trs. J.S. Stollybrass)*. Edinburgh University Press, Edinburgh.
91 Hansen, L. Taylor. *He Walked the Americas*. Neville Spearman Ltd., London.
92 Heard, Gerald. *The Riddle of the Flying Saucers*. Connoll & Nicholson, London.
93 HEbrews, XIII.
94 Hebwynd J.D. & Rytov, V.A. *The Living Universe*. Neville Spearman Ltd., London.

95　Herodotus. *History (Trans. E. Powell)*. Loeb Classics, Heinemann.
96　Hesiod. *Theogony*. Loeb Classics, Heinemann.
97　Heyerdahl, Thor. *Aku-Aku*. Allen & Unwin, London.
98　Hoke, Helen. *Dragons, Dragons, Dragons*. Watts, New York.
99　Holinshed. *Chronicles*. Everyman, Dent, London.
100　Holliday, F.W. *The Dragon and the Disc*. Sidgwick & Jackson, Ldondon.
101　Homet, Marcel. *Sons of the Sun*. Neville Spearman Ltd., London.
102　Hoyle, Fred. *Of Men anjd Galaxies*. Heinemann, London.
103　The INFO Journal. P.O. Box 367, Arlington, Virginia, 22210.
104　Job XII.
105　Josephus. *Antiquities of the Jews, Book IV, C Viii-48*.
106　Joshua X.
107　Judges VIII.
108　Judges XIII.
109　Keel, John A. *Our Haunted Planet*. Neville Spearman Ltd., London.
110　Keel, John A. *Operation Trojan Horse*. Souvenir Press, London.
111　King, George. *The Nine Freedoms*. The Aetherius Society, California.
112　I Kings VI.
113　I Kings VIII v 10-11.
114　Kirby, W.F. *Kalevala, The Land of Heroes*. Everyman, Dent, London.
115　Kolosimo, Peter. *Astronavi sulla Preistoria*. Sugar Editori, Milano.
116　Kopal, Zdenek. *Man and the Universe*. Hart Davis, London.
117　Kramer, Samuel Nosh. *Mythologies of the Ancient World*. Doubleday, New York.
118　Lacote, Felix. *Buddhaswamin Brihat Katha Shiokasanigraha*. Paris Imprimerie National, 1904.
119　Laforghiana No. 2. *Anno VII marzo-aprile*. Via Duchessa Jolanda 1, Turin, Italy.
120　Layne, Dr Meade. *The Flying Saucer Mystery*. Borderland Sciences Research Association Foundation Inc. P.O. Box 548, Vista, Calif.
121　Leslie, Desmond & Adamski, George. *Flying Saucers have Landed*. Neville Spearman Ltd., London.
122　Leslie, Desmond. *George Adamski*. Flying Saucer Review, J'A 1963.
123　Levi, Eliphas. *The History of Magic*. Rider & Co., London.
124　Lissner, Ivar. *The Living Past*. Penguin, London.
125　Lorenzen, Coral & Jim. *UFOs. The Whole Story*. Signet, New American Library, New York.
126　Lorenzen, Coral. *The Flying Saucer Hoax*. Wm. Frederick Press, New York.
127　Lucian. *A True Story* (Trans. A.M. Harmon). Loeb Classics, Heinemann, London.
128　Lumley, Henry de. *A Paleolithic Camp at Nice*. Scientific American, May 1969.
129　Mackenzie, Donald. *Myths of China and Japan*. Gresham, London.
130　Macol. *Il Mistero delle terre scomprse, Atlantide*. Il Giornale dei Misteri, Aprile 1971 Corrado Tedeschi, Milan, Italy.
131　Marco Polo. *Travels*. Dent, London.

132　Mark, XIII vv 24-27.
133　Marshall, J. *Mohenjo-daro and the Indus Civilisation.* Cambridge University Press, London 1931.
134　Matsumura, Yusuke J. *The Brothers, Vol 3, No. 1.* C.B.A. International, Yokohama.
135　Matsumura, Yusukue J. *Whole Aspect of the Sun Disk.* The Brothers, Vol. 3, No. 2. C.B.A., Yokohama.
136　Michel, Aime. *An Enigmatic Figure of the XVIIIth Century.* Flying Saucer Review, M'A 1972.
137　Michel, John. *The View over Atlantis.* Garnstone Press, London.
138　Migne. *Annales Laurissenses, Patrologiae.* Tom.CIV, Saeculum IX, Anno 840.
139　Milani, Mino. *Civilisation-Makers.* Tom Stacy, London.
140　Montfaucon de Villars. *Le Comte de Gabalis.* A.G. Nizat, Paris, 1963.
141　Moretti, Angelo. *La piu grande rivoluzione scientifica del secolo.* Il Giornale dei Misteri, Novembre 1972. Corrado Tedeschi, Firenze, Italy.
142　Murry, John Middleton. *Jonathan Swift.* Cape, London.
143　Notizario UFO 1 1970 J'F. Florence, Italy.
144　Numbers, XI v4.
145　Orlandi, Dino. *Il Cammino di chi sopravisse.* Il Giornale dei Misteri, No.25. Aprile 1973. Corrado Tedeschi, Florence, Italy.
146　Palmer, Ray. *Flying Saucers, June 1970.* Amherst, Wisconsin, U.S.A.
147　Paracelsus. *Auwahl aus seinen Schriften.* William Goldmann, Munchen.
148　Pauwels, L. & Bergier, J. *The Dawn of Magic.* Anthony Gibbs & Phillips, London 1963.
149　Pauwels, L. & Bergier, J. *The Eternal Man.* Souvenir Press, London.
150　Pernaud, Regine. *Joan of Arc.* Macdonald, London.
151　Pinotti, Roberto. *Visitatori dallo Spazio.* Armenia Editors, Milan, Italy.
152　Philippe, Robert. *Ulysse, est-il allé en Bretagne?* Planète, No.22, M'J 1965.
153　Phylos the Thibetan. *A Dweller on Two Planets.* Neville Spearman Ltd., London.
154　Phylos the Thibetan. *An Earth-Dweller's Return.* Neville Spearman Ltd., London.
155　'Planete' 15, M'A 1964. Editions Retz., 42 rue de Berri, Paris, 8.
156　Plato. *The Republic, Book VII* (Trans. Dr A.D. Lindsay), Everyman, Dent.
157　Plato. *Selected Passages* (Trans. R.W. Livingstone), Oxford University Press.
158　Plato. *Timaeus.*
159　Platts, L. *Boital Pachis.* W. Allan, London, 1871.
160　Plez. Ugo. *La Preistoria che vive.* Casa Editrice MEB, Turin, Italy.
161　Pliny. *Historia Naturalis.*
162　Plutarch. *Numa Pompilius* (Trans. B. Perrin). Loeb Classics, Heinemann.
163　Plutarch. *Romulus* (Trans. B. Perrin). Loeb Classics, Heinemann.
164　Plutarch. *Themistocles* (Trans. B. Perrin). Loeb Classics, Heinemann.
165　Plutarch. *Timoleon.*

166 Prescott, W.H. *The History and Conquest of Mexico*. Everyman, Dent, London.
167 Prescott, W.H. *History of the Conquest of Peru*. G. Allen & Unwin, London.
168 Pritchard, J.B. *Ancient Near Eastern Texts*. Princeton University Press, New York.
169 Ribera, Antonio. *El Gran Enigma de los Platillos Volantes*. Pomaire, Barcelona.
170 Ribera, Antonio. *Platillos Volantes en Ibero-America y Espana*. Editions Pomaire, Barcelona, 1966.
171 Rugoff, Milton. *Marco Polo's Adventures in China*. Cassell, London.
172 Sagan, Carl & Page, Thornton. *UFOs. A Scientific Debate*. Cornell University, Ithaca, USA.
173 Saggs, H.W.F. *Everyday Life in Babylonia and Assyria*. G.P. Putman & Sons, New York.
174 Saggs, H.F.W. *The Greatness that was Babylon*. Sidgwick & Jackson, London, 1962.
175 St. Augustine. *De praedestinatione sanctorum, 215.*
176 Il Samuel XVII v 23.
177 Sandrelli, Antonio. *Qualcosa viaggia piu in fretta della luce*. Clypeus, 22 April 1969, Turin, Italy.
178 Schiefner & Ralston. *Tibetan Tales from Indian Sources*. Routledge & Kegan Paul, London, 1906.
179 Schure, Edward. *Great Initiates*. Rider & Co., London.
180 Schure, Eduard. *From Sphinx to Christ*. Rider & Co., London.
181 Scott-Elliot, W. *The Story of Lost Atlantis and the Lost Lemuria*. The Theosophical Publishing Co., Pasadena, Calif.
182 Settimo, Gianni V. *Qualcuno chiama da Epsilon Bootes*. Gli Arcani, luglio, 1973 Armenia Editore, Milano.
183 Shepherd, Walter. *Outline History of Science*. Ward Lock, London.
184 Shklovski, J.S. & Sagan Carl. *Intelligent Life in the Universe*. Holden Day, New York.
185 Sophocles. *The Dramas*. (Trans. Sir George Young) Everyman, Dent, London.
186 Sordi, Italo. Fortezze di vetro nella Scozia'prehistoriza, Gli Arcani, 1 No 2. luglio 72. Armenia, Milano.
187 Sordi, Paul. *I Robot del Passato*. Gli Arcani, Anno 1. No.6, Armenia, Milano.
188 Spence, Lewis. *Myths and Legends of the North American Indians*. G. Harrap, London.
189 Spence, Lewis. Myths and Legends of Egypt, Harrap, London, 1915.
190 Spence, Lewis. *The Outlines of Mythology*. Premier, Fawcett World Library, New York.
191 Stendek, June 1970. C.E.I. Apartado 282, Barcelona.
192 Swedenborg, Emmanuel. *Heaven and its Wonders and Hell*. Swedenborg Society, London.
193 Swift, Jonathan. *Gulliver's Travels*.
194 Taddeo, Maurizio. *The Ancient Civilisation of India*. Barrie & Jenkins, London.

195 Tarade G. & Millou. *L'Enigma di Palenque.* Clypeus, Anno III 4-5.
196 Thomas, Paul. *Flying Saucers.* Neville Spearman Ltd., London.
197 Trench, Brinsley le Poer. *The Sky People.* Neville Spearman Ltd., London.
198 Trevor, James. *They Live in the Sky.* New Age, Los Angeles, 1958.
199 Underwood, Guy. *The Pattern of the Past.* Pitman, London.
200 Vallee, Jacques. *Anatomy of a Phenonemon.* Neville Spearman Ltd., London.
201 Vallee, Jacques. *Passport to Magonia.* Neville Spearman Ltd., London.
202 Varro. *De Lingua Latina.*
203 Vasari, Giorgio. *Lives of the Painters.* Temple Classics, London.
204 The Vedic Hymns. *Mandal V Hymns. 54.*
205 Velikovsky, Immanuel. *Ages in Chaos.* Sidgwick & Jackson, London.
206 Velikovsky, Immanuel. *Earth in Upheaval.* Sidgwick & Jackson, London.
207 Velikovsky, Immanuel. *Oedipus and Aklnaton.* Sidgwick & Jackson, London.
208 Velikovsky, Immanuel. *Worlds in Collision.* Sidgwick & Jackson, London.
209 Verrill, Hyatt & Verrill, Ruth. *America's Ancient Civilisations.* G.P. Putman & Son, New York.
210 Vesco, Renato. Considerazione preliminari sulla questione delle *presunte apparizioni preistoriche degli UFO.* Clypeus, Turin. 31 June 1970.
211 Villars, Montfaucon de. *Le Comte de Gabalis.* Nizat, Paris.
212 Von Hagen, Victor Wolfgang. *The Ancient Sun Kingdoms of the Americas.* Panther, London.
213 Wendt, Herbert. *Before the Deluge.* (Trans. R. & C. Winston). Gollancz, London.
214 Werner, E.T.C. *Myths and Legends of China.* Harrap, London.
215 Wheeler, Sir Mortimer. *The Indus Civilisation.* Cambridge University Press, London.
216 Wignall, Bernard. *The Okehampton Incident* Flying Saucer Review, N'D 1967.
217 Wilcox, Elizabeth. *Mu, Den sjunkna Kontinenten.* Parthenon, Halsinborg, Sweden.
218 Wilkins, Harold. *Flying Saucers on the Attack.* Ace Star Book, New York.
219 Wilkins, Harold T. *Flying Saucers Uncensored.* Arco, glvondon, 1956.
220 Williams, Jay. *Joan of Arc.* Cassell, London.
221 Williamson, G.H. *Other Tongues – Other Flesh.* Neville Spearman Ltd., London.
222 Williamson, G.H. *Road in the Sky.* Neville Spearman Ltd., London.
223 Williamson, G.H. *The Saucers Speak.* Neville Spearman Ltd., London.
224 Willis, Ron. *Ciucuilco, older than the Pyramids.* INFO Journal, Vol. III. No. 2.
225 Zaitsev, Vyacheslav. *Visitors from Outer Space.* Sputnik 1, Moscow.
226 Zungri, Giuseppe, *L'Enigma dei Cieli.* Casa Editrice MEB, Turin, Italy.

INDEX